OCCUPATION: RUIN, REPUDIATION, REVOLUTION

Plate 1 'I took bread and cheese and slipped out the door' (Kerouac 1970, 157). 2014

Occupation: ruin, repudiation, revolution

constructed space conceptualized

Edited by
Lynn Churchill and Dianne Smith
Curtin University, Western Australia

ASHGATE

© Lynn Churchill and Dianne Smith and the contributors 2015

All rights reserved. No part of this publication may be reproduced, stored in a retrieval system or transmitted in any form or by any means, electronic, mechanical, photocopying, recording or otherwise without the prior permission of the publisher.

Lynn Churchill and Dianne Smith have asserted their rights under the Copyright, Designs and Patents Act, 1988, to be identified as the editors of this work.

Published by
Ashgate Publishing Limited
Wey Court East
Union Road
Farnham
Surrey, GU9 7PT
England

Ashgate Publishing Company
110 Cherry Street
Suite 3-1
Burlington, VT 05401-3818
USA

www.ashgate.com

British Library Cataloguing in Publication Data
A catalogue record for this book is available from the British Library.

Library of Congress Cataloging-in-Publication Data
Occupation: ruin, repudiation, revolution: constructed space conceptualized / [edited] by Lynn Churchill and Dianne Smith.
    pages cm
    Includes bibliographical references and index.
    ISBN 978-1-4724-4063-1 (hardback : alk. paper) – ISBN 978-1-4724-4064-8 (ebook) – ISBN 978-1-4724-4065-5 (epub)
    1. Architecture – Human factors. 2. Place (Philosophy) in architecture. I. Churchill, Lynn, editor. II. Smith, Dianne (Dianne Joy), editor.

    NA2542.4.O32 2015
    720.1 – dc23
                                                                                    2014046298

ISBN: 9781472440631 (hbk)
ISBN: 9781472440648 (ebk – PDF)
ISBN: 9781472440655 (ebk – ePUB)

Printed in the United Kingdom by Henry Ling Limited, at the Dorset Press, Dorchester, DT1 1HD

Contents

List of Figures vii
List of Plates ix
Notes on Contributors xi
Foreword: Against the Interior, by Charles Rice xv
Acknowledgements xvii

| 1 | Introduction: What?
Lynn Churchill and Dianne Smith | 1 |

PART I RUIN

2	*Damnatio Memoriae*: Interiors and the Art of Forgetting Edward Hollis	15
3	Self-ruining and Situated Vagrancy: The Geography of Performance Benedict Anderson	31
4	'Crude Hints Towards an History of my House in L[incoln's] I[nn]Fields': Occupying Ruin Lynn Churchill	49

PART II REPUDIATION

| 5 | Tragedy and Assimilation: Occupying the Patterned Surface
Kirsty Volz | 67 |
| 6 | Ordinary Things, Domestic Space and Photography:
Takashi Yasumura's Interiors
Jane Simon | 83 |

| 7 | Seeing the Unseen: This is Not an Interior
Vanessa Galvin | 99 |

PART III REVOLUTION

8	Occupying Utopia: Collusion, Persuasion, Revolution *Lynn Churchill*	117
9	Hypersexual Occupations *Nicole Kalms*	137
10	With Feet Firmly Planted on Unstable Ground *Jesse O'Neill*	157
11	An Insane Perspective to the Occupation of Interiors *Dianne Smith*	171

Index   *189*

List of Figures

3.1 *National Memorial to the Murdered Jews of Europe*

3.2 Interior view of abandoned fabric factory, Minde, Portugal

3.3 Plan of anthems layout, *Plaza of Nations*

3.4 Perspective view of anthems layout, *Plaza of Nations*

3.5 Feldbahnloren Konigsplatz, Platz der Republik 1948, Landesarchiv Berlin/Gnilka, Ewald; F Rep. 290, Nr. 0172325

3.6 Teufelsberg Trümmerschutt 1952, Landesarchiv Berlin/Schwab, E., F Rep. 290, Nr. 0264853

5.1 Florence Broadhurst's pattern Cranes (26) in olive/green

5.2 Image from Australian artists Gotye's music video, 'Somebody that I Used to Know' (feat. Kimbra). From the album *Making Mirrors*. Video directed by Natasha Pincus. Body artwork by Emma Hack

6.1 'A Pair of Slippers' 1997, from the series *Domestic Scandals*

6.2 'A Father' 1998, from the series *Domestic Scandals*

6.3 'A Tape Recorder' 2002, from the series *Domestic Scandals*

6.4 'A Fan Heater' 1999, from the series *Domestic Scandals*

6.5 'Japanese Oranges' 2002, from the series *Domestic Scandals*

6.6 'Rolls of Toilet Paper and a Plastic Flower' 1998, from the series *Domestic Scandals*

7.1 KENZO-inspired apartment. Design by Olga Akulova

7.2 KENZO-inspired apartment. Design by Olga Akulova

9.1 The Newman House by Cassandra Fahey

9.2 General Pant Group's advertisement from 2010. Melbourne Central Shopping Centre, Melbourne, Australia

9.3 Kittens Car Wash 2014, Bentleigh East

9.4 Axonometric diagram, Kittens Car Wash, Bentleigh East

9.5 Solid Objectives *Pole Dance*, 2010

9.6 Axonometric diagram, *Pole Dance*, 2010

11.1 Ward entrance, Taunton State Hospital, Taunton, Massachusetts, from Payne (2009)

11.2 Patient toothbrushes, Hudson River State Hospital, Poughkeepsie, New York, from Payne (2009)

11.3 Patient ward, Buffalo State Hospital. Buffalo, New York, from Payne (2009)

List of Plates

Plate 1 'I took bread and cheese and slipped out the door' (Kerouac 1970, 157). 2014
This work is a composite image created by Loren Dyer from images made available under the Creative Commons Attribution – Share Alike 3.0 unported license. Original images are attributed to C. Goodwin ['Red range (2)', licensed under the Creative Commons Attribution – Share Alike 3.0 Unported license, http://commons.wikimedia.org]; Eadweard Muybridge (1830–1904) ['plate 61, *man in pelvis cloth running at full speed*'. 1887. Part of 'Animal locomotion: an electro-photographic investigation of consecutive phases of animal movements 1872–1885'. Public domain. http://digitallibrary.usc.edu]; and J.dncsn ['White lamp'. Licensed under the Creative Commons Attribution – Share Alike 3.0 Unported license. http://commons.wikimedia.org]

Plate 2 'Self portrait'. 2014
This work is a composite image created by Loren Dyer from images made available under the Creative Commons Attribution – Share Alike 3.0 unported license. Original images are attributed to Olcott Beaman (1837–1876), James Fennemore (1849–1941) and John K. Hillers (1843–1925) ['Grand Canyon. NARA – 517800'. Circa 1900. Public Domain. U.S. National Archives and Records Administration (ARC ID: 517734)]; Qz10 ['Suomalainen Mokki'. Public Domain. http://commons.wikimedia.org]; Daguerre, Louis(1787–1851) ['Boulevard du Temple'. 1838. Public Domain. http://commons.wikimedia.org]; Lindaglinda ['Beelitz'. Licensed under the Creative Commons Attribution 3.0 Unported license. http://commons.wikimedia.org]; and Roland zh ['2012 "tag der offenen werft" – zsg werft wollishofen 2012–03–24 15–35–50'. Licensed under the Creative Commons Attribution – Share Alike 3.0 Unported license. http://commons.wikimedia.org].

Plate 3 'Symbiosis'. 2014
This work is a composite image created by Loren Dyer from images made available under the Creative Commons Attribution – Share Alike 3.0 Unported license. Original images are attributed to 掬茶 ['Japanese Leather Paper Model "The Early Spring"' licensed under the Creative Commons Attribution – Share Alike 3.0 Unported license. http://commons.wikimedia.org]; Sarah Marie Jones ['Man Streaking After Skinnydipping' licensed under the Creative Commons Attribution – Share Alike 3.0 Unported license. http://commons.wikimedia.org]

Plate 4   'Palimpsest'. 2014
This work is a composite image created by Loren Dyer from images made available under the Creative Commons Attribution – Share Alike 3.0 Unported license. Original images are attributed to Rzuwig ['Perge Stadion 05'. Licensed under the Creative Commons Attribution – Share Alike 3.0 Unported license. http://commons.wikimedia.org]; NASA Earth Observatory; Jesse Allen ['Precision Farming In Minnesota – Natural Colour'. Public Domain. http://commons.wikimedia.org]; Stanislaus Walery (1863–1935) ['Art Deco Nude Gravure 14'. Circa 1920. Public Domain. http://commons.wikimedia.org] and L Dyer ['From the Hill'. 2008. Licensed under the Creative Commons Attribution – Share Alike 3.0 Unported license.]

Plate 5   'What is that … driving away … they recede … pixels? But we lean forward … ' (adapted from Kerouac 1970, 156). 2014
This work is a composite image created by Loren Dyer from images made available under the Creative Commons Attribution – Share Alike 3.0 Unported license. Original images are attributed to NASA Earth Observatory; Jesse Allen ['Precision Farming In Minnesota – Natural Colour'. Public Domain. http://commons.wikimedia.org]; Almare ['DECT Telephone Siemens SL565'. Licensed under the Creative Commons Attribution – Share Alike 2.5 generic license. http://commons.wikimedia]; Fantagu ['Modern Hunting Rifle'. Licensed under the Creative Commons Attribution – Share Alike 3.0 Unported license. http://commons.wikimedia.org], MSGT Michael Ammons. '1997 F-4 Heritage Flight Over Florida Edit 1'. Public domain. http://commons.wikimedia.org]; Rufus M. Porter (1792–1884) (editor) ['*Scientific American* – Series 1 – Volume 009 – Issue 10'. 1853. Public domain. http://www.nature.com/scientificamerican/archive/index_1909.html]; Alois Metz (1869–1921) ['Landschaft Mit Figuren'. 1910. Public domain. http://commons.wikimedia.org/]; Unknown author ['Navy Fighter Planes Parked On Work Adjacent To Building 75 At The Naval Air Station, Long Beach, California – NARA – 295426'. Public domain. US National Archives and Records Administration ARC ID: 295426 and unknown author ['Romerskt Sköldtak (Testudo), Nordisk Familjebok'. 1917. Public domain. Nordisk familjebok (1917), vol. 25, p. 1364].

Notes on Contributors

Benedict Anderson works in scenography, dance dramaturgy, architecture and film. Project venues include: ARCO Art Fair Madrid Spain, Fondation Cartier Paris and Lisbon Architecture Triennial. He has reviewed for Architecture Australia and publications include: 'Out of Space: the Rise of Vagrancy in Scenography' (*On Scenography* journal, 2013) and 'Breathe: Wearing Your Air' (co-author Nancy Diniz, *ACADIA* Journal, 2013). Positions include: Advisor, Bauhaus College Dessau, and Gäst Professor Institüt for Raumgestaltung University of Innsbruck. He is a partner in the Berlin based firm Thinkbuild Architecture (www.thinkbuild.com), Professor of Spatial Design and Director of the Centre for Contemporary Design Practices, University of Technology, Sydney; www.benedict-anderson.com.

Lynn Churchill's research, teaching and practice speculate on the human body's physical and psychical relationship with architecture in the context of twentieth and twenty-first century history, politics, economics and information technology. In 2013 she exhibited creative practice as research: *I think where I am not and I am where I do not think* (triptych), Moores Gallery, Fremantle, and in 2014 presented a paper by the same name at 2014 IDEA Symposium, Melbourne. Lynn is Head of Discipline, Interior Architecture, School of the Built Environment, Curtin University, and Director and Secretary of the Board of IDEA (Interior Design/Interior Architecture Educators Association).

Vanessa Galvin is a PhD Candidate in Architecture Interior Architecture at Curtin University, Australia. Her professional experience as a corporate interior designer has provided an essential and intimate knowledge of the specific practices and modes of thinking central to her research. This practical understanding enables her to challenge naturalized modes of thinking, saying and doing in order to conceive of interior space and its representational conventions in new ways. Her publications include 'Seeing the Unseen: Confronting the Real in Depictions of Lived Environments', in IDEA Conference Proceedings, Perth, 2012; and 'Picturing Ideal Space through Perfect Moments' in *International Journal of the Image* (2012).

Edward Hollis is Director of Research, School of Design, Edinburgh College of Art and University of Edinburgh, UK. Edward studied Architecture at Cambridge and Edinburgh Universities and for the subsequent six years he practised in Sri Lanka and then in Edinburgh. In 1999, he lectured in Interior Architecture at Napier University, Edinburgh. In 2004, he moved to Edinburgh College of Art, where he is now director of research in the school of Design. Hollis's research focusses on time, storytelling, and building. He published *The Secret Lives of Buildings* in 2009, and *The Memory Palace, A Book of Lost Interiors* in 2013.

Nicole Kalms lectures in the Department of Architecture at Monash University, Melbourne, Australia. Nicole's research interests are in the field of contemporary urbanism and feminism. In 2013 she was awarded the Women's Planning Network scholarship for her contribution to original research in planning policy and sexualized images in public space. Her recent research is published in the Architectural Humanities Research Association's new journal, *Architecture and Culture*. As the program coordinator of the Interior Architecture program at Monash University, Nicole leads a programme focussed on cross-disciplinary approaches to design and spatial theory. Nicole is currently completing a research project and book titled *Hypersexual Urbanism*.

Jesse O'Neill lectures in Design History, Culture and Theory at The Glasgow School of Art, Singapore. Jesse received his Doctorate of Philosophy from the University of New South Wales, Sydney, Australia. His research concentrates on colonial design, and he has previously, as Merewether Scholar at the State Library of New South Wales, written on the print culture and publishing trades of the early Australian settlements. In 2013 Jesse was appointed lecturer in the Forum for Critical Inquiry at the Glasgow School of Art. His current research and writing focuses on the history of design and the built environment in Singapore and the Straits Settlements.

Jane Simon lectures in Media Studies at Macquarie University, Sydney, Australia. Jane has published articles on amateur and experimental film, photography, artists' books and modes of writing about visual culture. She co-edits *Somatechnics* journal, and is currently working on a project which explores the domestic interior in contemporary art photography. Jane also specializes in photographic media and artists' books. Her artists' books are in international public collections including Manchester Metropolitan University's Special Collections Library and University of West England's Centre for Fine Print Research.

Dianne Smith is Associate Professor and Director of Research in the School of the Built Environment at Curtin University, Australia. Dianne's research focuses on discriminatory design, design for the cognitively impaired, the meaning of environments, the impact of colour on experience and our understanding of place, and design education. Recently she co-edited and co-authored *M2: Models and Methodologies for Community Engagement* (2014) and *Perspectives on Social Sustainability and Interior Architecture: Life from the Inside* (2014).

Kirsty Volz is the convenor of the interior design major within the Bachelor of Digital Media program at Griffith University, Australia. Kirsty has published research across the subject areas of interior design, scenography, drama, fine arts and architectural history. Kirsty is passionate about enriching the identity of interior design as a profession through practice, teaching, research and writing.

Foreword: Against the Interior

Charles Rice

Over the last decade, academic studies of the interior have increased substantially. No longer can the claim for the interior's marginal status (especially with respect to the domestic) be sustained. If anything, the interior has become central in historical and theoretical scholarship in design, architecture, and visual and material culture. This recent prominence has something to do with the interior's encompassing nature, with the idea that it can be detected as the binding agent between subjects, objects and situations, as more and more scholarship works through the cultural problematics of relation and immersion. If these are the two most prominent contexts for understanding contemporary experience (how do we find identity in relation; how is our sensorium extended through immersion?) then the interior acts as a reference for understanding how these questions are involved with a sense of encapsulation, of enclosure, that is, with a sense of location and locatability.

Understanding the interior as this reference is historically and philosophically useful. In modernity, the interior emerged to compensate for, but also to problematize, a sense of experience as connection, as longevity, as cultural grounding, a sense which had been all but obliterated through modernity's social and technological upheavals. In this history we can pinpoint a double moment of encapsulation staged at London's Great Exhibition of 1851. In Joseph Paxton's enormous glasshouse, the Crystal Palace, the world's goods were brought together in one place. The orderly conduct accompanying their visual consumption set the scene for a domesticated approach to commodities. Its counterpart was Henry Roberts' Model Houses for Four Families, which literally fabricated the form and conduct of the nuclear family. In these two structures of encapsulation, public and private could be organized and traversed, making the modern world in its metropolitan form governable.

Perhaps we are now too comfortable with what the interior has given to culture by way of our ability to fabricate experience within its confines, and to extend that fabrication through the construction of new (always interior) worlds.

The present collection of essays is, then, discomfiting. Rather than celebrating or extending the interior's recent prominence in scholarship, the essays take their point of departure from three key words which suggest a kind of dismantling of the interior's importance at the precise moment of its prominence. The condition of occupation, what might be thought to be a fundamental basis for understanding the interior's encapsulating quality, is met with ruin, repudiation and revolution, hardly very encouraging departure points. Or are they? These keywords suggest precisely what makes the interior so compelling as a context for research: its simultaneous ubiquity, as we have established, as well as its constant dissimulation. While we recognize its encapsulating presence, what is the interior in actuality? A kind of confrontation needs to be staged in order to get at this question.

How do you consciously push against the interior's ubiquity? By repudiating it. How do you break down its supposed unity, whether as artefact or conceptual condition? By accounting for it as ruin. How do you overcome the stasis that accompanies the interior's ubiquity? You mount a revolution.

What results from these questions is a refreshing sense of the elusive, especially at this point in scholarship on the interior, when there seems to be so much certainty about what it is. But more particularly, these keywords allow the essays to stage various strategic encounters with artefacts, designers, and concepts, even as the interior remains elusive. In the end, it is as a kind of rubric for such studies that the interior's value emerges, not as thing in itself, nor even as the dominant context for understanding relation and immersion, but as the always elusive target of work toward dismantling certainties.

Charles Rice is Professor of Architectural History and Theory, and Head of the School of Art and Design History at Kingston University London. He is author of *The Emergence of the Interior: Architecture, Modernity, Domesticity* (2007), and co-editor of *The Journal of Architecture*.

Acknowledgements

The editors would like to thank and acknowledge the following people for their generous and innovative approach to the book's proposition: to explore the concept of occupation, as positioned by the precepts ruin, repudiation and revolution:

- The contributing authors for their enthusiastic response to the intent of the book, and for their rigorous incisive approach to the precepts.
- Charles Rice, Professor and Head of School, School of Art and Design History, Faculty of Art, Design and Architecture, Kingston University, London for writing the Foreword.
- Christina Houen, Editor/Director of www.perfectwordsediting.com, for her project coordination, her dedicated editing and production work, her attention to detail and timely advice.
- Loren Dyer, PhD Candidate, Curtin University, for her montaging of images for the plates in the book.
- Allyson Crimp, Designer, of et-al.com.au for her image editing.

We thank Ashgate for their enthusiastic approach to publishing the book. Last and not least, we thank Curtin University for support enabling the research and production associated with the book project.

This book was seeded by ideas encapsulated in papers presented at the 2012 IDEA (Interior Design Interior Architecture Educators Association) Symposium: Interior: a State of Becoming, Perth Western Australia.

1

Introduction: What?

Lynn Churchill and Dianne Smith

> *What is that feeling when you're driving away from people and they recede on the plain till you see their specks dispersing? – it's the too-huge world vaulting us, and it's good-by. But we lean forward to the next crazy venture beneath the skies.*
>
> *We wheeled back through the sultry old light of Algiers, back on the ferry, back toward the mud-splashed, crabbed old ships across the river, back on Canal, and out; on a two lane highway to Baton Rouge in purple darkness; swung west there, crossed the Mississippi at a place called Port Allen. …*
>
> *With the radio on to a mystery program, and as I looked out the window and saw a sign that said USE COOPER'S PAINT and I said, 'Okay, I will'. we rolled across the hoodwink night of Louisiana plains – Lawtell, Eunice, Kinder, and De Quincy, western rickety towns becoming bayou-like as we reached the Sabine. In Old Opelousas I went into a grocery store to buy bread and cheese while Dean saw to gas and oil. It was just a shack; I could hear the family eating supper in the back. I waited a minute; they went on talking. I took bread and cheese and slipped out the door. We had barely enough money to make Frisco. Meanwhile Dean took a carton of cigarettes from the gas station and we were stocked for the voyage – gas, oil, cigarettes and food. Crooks don't know. He pointed the car straight down the road. (Kerouac 1970, 156–7)*

The intent of this book is to disturb the complexity of human occupation, to embrace a diverse range of vantage points – conceptual, theoretical and pragmatic – and to reveal something of the more intangible underlying realities. The hope is to broaden the discussion. What Jack Kerouac's prose evokes is the illusory and sensuous nature of human occupation, that at any particular moment, we occupy a montage of multiple points or places simultaneously. These places are generated by us and/or maybe already exist within each of us. Instantaneously, our thoughts and our emotions draw us from the immediate physical location to places beyond it temporarily and spatially; and the associated feelings may be integral to the point of origin or disconnected, and sometimes, disquieting. As Berleant (1992) described, we are at the centre of the world that we experience. Perhaps this explains why the experience of others in the same place and time will invariably differ from our own.

Kerouac's mid-twentieth century drug-infused account of his 1947 road trip across America contrasts dramatically to that of the contemporary world, where technologies have extended our ability to morph in different ways – that is, to extend and destabilize the boundary or periphery of our physical occupancy. As the following narrative potently depicts:

> I get driving directions and check for traffic using Google's real-time data. Don't take the 405 at this time of day. Clicking on the little orange person, I am taken out of my world of stereoscopic vision to one constituted by nine camera eyes and stitched together to form a panoramic digital bubble that lets me see streets, interiors, and even oceans 360 degrees horizontally and 290 degrees vertically, I start to see differently, as if I am flying above the world, zooming in and zooming out at will, in a multi-perspectival digital bubble. What does it mean that this panning and zooming has become (almost) natural, that it has become how I see and experience the world, or how I want to see and experience my world? (Presner, Shepard and Kawano 2014, 24)

What the more recent, less poetic driving in Los Angeles narrative describes is the experience of numerous simultaneous realities made possible by increasingly widespread access to information technologies. Thanks to our ubiquitous devices, many of us live our lives sliding between physical and virtual realities, exercising a multitude of exponential extensions to our physical limitations. Expanded by our devices, everyday occupation has become a constellation of experiences and connections: slippages between here and anywhere, unrestricted, non-linear.

For many of us who live the more privileged life, this dynamic matrix of realities is the new normal. However, what occurs in societies with less access to technologies? Does the woman washing her clothes at the well in the Indian village think of her past life or project into the future, whether it is about dinner for her family, sharing stories with friends while in the fields, or how she would like to be in Delhi or return to her youth? Here again, occupation is composed of the past, present and future – physically by the pump with washing in hand, but emotionally or intellectually elsewhere.

What of the young boy with severe brain injury resulting from being king-hit[1] outside the local hotel? Now, (with the help of his carer), his life takes place in a motorized, technologically advanced chair and a responsive 'smart-unit'. With a simple slight movement of the boy's head, the unit automatically opens and the lights, air conditioning, blinds and other internal devices respond to his coming home. What could be an extremely limited occupancy has been transformed by the unit's array of sophisticated technologies which serve to extend his body's limitations. We can interpret that the boy's dependence on technology is a complex integration with his sense of self.

We become the culmination of these experiences. When Wittgenstein describes the child in the box or under a draped sheet, for whom the 'cubby' has become a house – in this moment and this space, the house is real. Wittgenstein states: 'thereupon it is interpreted as a house in every detail … He quite forgets that it is a chest; for him it actually is a house … . Then would it not also be correct to say he sees it as a house?'(1967, 206). The physical world has transformed through imagination and experience to be a particular place which the child occupies.

These stories of the child, the boy, the woman, the driver and Kerouac amplify the state of occupancy within any tangible setting that may be challenged, overridden, or manipulated by realities not only from within or outside the body but also by the body's capacity to project across space and time. By observing examples from the extremities of human occupation, we come to understand how the everyday plays out.

The following chapters within *Occupation: ruin, repudiation, revolution* probe extreme and diverse constructions of human occupation. This introductory chapter situates the book's precepts and challenges the reader to consider occupation in terms of the relationship between the interior of the body, the body itself, and the exterior world. You are asked to consider whether you can occupy, comfortably or authentically, the implications of any or all of the vantage points raised? Here, we draw on the work of Merleau-Ponty to introduce occupation as experience, of Sigmund Freud to theorize the complex synergetic interplay between the internal and external worlds, and of Acconci, Orlan and Stelarc to locate one's body within the ambit of others across space, time and command.

Each vantage point teases the fixed views of occupation and sets the scene for the author's conceptualization of occupation, infused with notions of ruin, repudiation, and or revolution.

OCCUPATION AS EXPERIENCE

Phenomenology seeks to understand (and explain) how 'experience is lived and felt' (Tomkins 2013, 262). Merleau-Ponty (1962) proposes that we experience the everyday places, things and events in terms of what they mean for us personally (52). Our surroundings offer opportunities that mould our experiences – and therefore, who we are. Inanimate things are just that; however, depending on how a person occupies a space, these elements become things – a handle is a handle when the particular object is used in that way. 'For a person whose hands are paralyzed or amputated, though, or for the person who, having never encountered a doorknob before, does not know to twist it, this knob is not a handle, and the door may very well be experienced as intrusive … '. (Bredlau 2010, 418).

The details of occupation are largely unrecognized: we simply exist. The person and the environment that he/she senses are a continuum, as Merleau-Ponty (1962), Berleant (1992) and others have discussed. For example, Berleant states that we do not just aesthetically experience the world; we engage with it through a 'multisensorial phenomenal involvement with the environment, place or object, which is immediate … ' and which differs every time we engage with the situation (Berleant 1992, 28). It is of interest that until the experience is interrupted in some way, such that we become conscious of the insertion or invasion, and in association, our degree of vulnerability or power, it is just taken for granted. Ideas, illusions, objects, places, people or collectives can all potentially transform the taken-for-granted world into a site of negotiation and reflection. For example, ' … the touch of a stranger who barely brushes against me can be experienced as invasive while the deep embrace of a friend is respectful … '. (Bredlau 2010, 412).

The qualities of the experience of occupation are influenced by relationships between the person and everything that is other than him/herself in real time. However, it should also be noted that our immediate experience is seamlessly intertwined with our past and future worlds – we are what we bring to any moment.

> ... all aspects of temporality are rooted in the present .... We remember and imagine things from our current position, for we cannot be anywhere else than right here, right now. Even when we try to remember anger, or pain, or fear, we are still grounded in the here-and-now – we may use the expression 'go back in time' but, in Merleau-Ponty's phenomenology, it is more appropriate to say that we are bringing the past forward into the present. (Tomkins 2013, 262–3)

A person's life experience, although continually evolving, yields a sense of longevity that is greater than those associated with any one daily event (such as having breakfast today versus ways of living over the last year). We exist through a continuous self-referential process that is linked to our identity; that is, a person's a sense of identity is continually reconstructed through ongoing experiences. As Tomkins poses, experience relates to the ' ... question of who I am – of identity in the phenomenological sense of "what does it feel like to be me?"' (2013, 263).

Therefore, how occupation is experienced is intertwined with our being at any particular moment. However, the world we occupy is experienced as somewhat removed from us – a strategy which Bredlau states is necessary so our surroundings are not 'in our face' (2011, 412) and we can cope. She posits that we actively contribute to the experience:

> *Far from reflecting a lack of engagement, our usual experience of the world reflects our very active engagement with the world. The world keeps its distance because of our ability to give space the structure that makes this possible. The distance between us is the manifestation of a positive bond; the world shows us a courtesy that we demand. (Bredlau 2010, 412)*

What is implied is that the places we occupy offer the potential to entrap, damage, or support us. In the words of Bredlau:

> *The world is, after all, capable of mauling us. It has surfaces that can cut us, trip us up, impale us, and bruise us. The skills we develop help insure that a world that could well be wild and potentially quite damaging to us is, instead, so tame and supportive that we generally do not even think of it as capable of attack .... (Bredlau 2010, 418)*

Can the phenomenological aspects raised above relate to the book's themes? The taken-for-granted world (in phenomenological terms, the ready-at-hand) exists in a state that is pre-thought. This contributes to a changing self that lives within an evolving interpretation of place. Thus, one's life experience is in a state of ruining as past, present and future merge in an unconscious overwriting and transformative process. Objects and places can potentiate or afford acts that enable repudiation; and if disquieted, the experience may be constructed to enforce forms of revolution.

INTERNAL–EXTERNAL SLIPPAGE

Being elsewhere where our body is not has always been possible. Through human imagination, ancient myths, tribal storytelling, religion, classical theatre, psychotropic drugs and visual arts have always mindfully and deliberately inspired us to occupy somewhere where the body is not. As have illness, hunger, thirst, passion, ecstasy and exhaustion, although not necessarily wilfully.

To be human is to be both occupant and occupied in terms of space, time and sensation. Occupied by the past, present and future, our minds are not always able to control how the past re-visits us. This was the subject of Sigmund Freud's research.

Sigmund Freud, the psychoanalytic theorist, was interested in formative exchanges between the interior body and the external world; he posited that, as a consequence of exchanges between us and the context we occupy, we become who we are. For Freud, these exchanges generated his notional understanding of the human mind's topography, in which there was more than consciousness: the conscious mind (which is present at any time), preconscious mind (a place of retrievable memories and information) and the unconscious mind (the place of our archaic inheritance from which we are unable to wilfully access information) (1953, 697). Freud made explicit that we not only create and occupy the external world, but vice versa – we are occupied.

Speculating on what occupies our unconscious mind, Freud writes, 'in mental life nothing that has been formed can perish – that everything is somehow preserved and that in suitable circumstances … it can once more be brought to light' (1969, 6–7). Freud uses the analogy of the city of Rome to convey his concept of the enduring layers of the unconscious mind. A brief portion of his imaginings follows:

> On the Piazza of the Pantheon we should find not only the Pantheon of to-day, as it was bequeathed to us by Hadrian, but, on the same site, the original edifice erected by Agrippa; indeed, the same piece of ground would be supporting the church of Santa Maria sopra Minerva and the ancient temple over which it was built. (1969, 6–7)

According to Freud, a portion of our mind is occupied by our archaic inheritance (our ancestral knowledge) that has an enduring place within our mind, and yet we are unable to wilfully access this. We do encounter sensations and instincts from this place, but these encounters are unexpected, outside our control and perhaps outside our understanding. One common experience is the 'fight or flight' mechanism that may be triggered if we feel threatened. Sometimes we are unable to explain what triggered the mechanism.

WITHIN THE OTHER'S AMBIT

A series of works by performance artists Vito Acconci, Orlan and Stelarc, each of which are more or less acts of voyeurism, pursue extreme sensations of the condition, occupant: occupied. In each case, the artist is interested firstly in generating a ruinous event in which their body is occupied by the exterior world.

Secondly, by acts of repudiation, they change and gain command over space. Thirdly, they generate revolutions within the viewer's body by shifting the physical and psychological boundaries between the viewer's body and the artist's body.

Acconci's *Seedbed*, for example, comprised a pristine white gallery space with two speakers, and a false ramped timber floor under which the artist lay with his microphone connected to the speakers.

> Sounds emanating from the speakers revealed to the visitor as she walked around the gallery or attempted to peer into the floor, that she was affecting a sexual response from Acconci. While he masturbated under her feet, he used his microphone to tell of her complicity in his arousal. This was so for any visitor, they would all be implicated, accomplices to the event which dramatically demonstrated the body's vulnerability to penetration by the external world. (Churchill 2007, 156)

In this piece, Acconci demonstrated command over the space, and that he was able to penetrate the visitor's state of being and impregnate their physical and mental sense of self. By destroying these boundaries, Acconci made them hyper-present. Although notions of territory and boundary are repudiated by Acconci, moral questions are implicated. For example, has he violated her, the visitor? Does the performance space allow one to occupy another where the same incident in a suburban street would inflame recourse? What permission does the interior of a gallery give to do this – regardless of the artist's intent to provoke or question? Here notions of control, disempowerment and inescapable complicity are raised. How one is physically located influences occupancy – even for the other gallery goers. Unable to avoid becoming the voyeur, the experience altered the viewer.

Similarly invasive were the performances of Orlan's surgical procedures staged during the 1990s. Again involving the interior body, a space – the operating theatre – and the viewer as voyeur were forever altered. Orlan underwent procedures including liposuction and facial re-construction while conscious. Reading philosophy aloud, and dressed in haute couture (as were the medical team members – who became complicit), Orlan repudiated the space of the operating theatre. Each of these works was composed of the elements of human occupation: individual sensation, culture, teamwork, ideas, prosthetics, territory, boundaries, power, technologies and the vulnerability of human flesh and blood. Each performance was filmed with live feed in real time to viewers (voyeurs) in galleries elsewhere in the world (Orlan 2004). Later, bodily morsels left over from her surgery were framed and exhibited in galleries (Orlan, Wilson and McCorquodale 1996) where they reiterated Orlan's foray into the complexities of human occupation.

The work raises questions about societal definitions of personal boundaries. Contemporary technologies facilitate, if not escalate, these slippages, and may amplify the impacts. To exemplify, Stelarc's *Meat, Metal and Code* (Institute of Art and Ideas 2013) encompasses a number of his projects that make explicit our increasingly intimate relationship with technology. One such performance took place over four hours, during which the artist was in Luxemburg and the controllers at the Pompidou, Paris, at the Doors of Perception Conference, Amsterdam, and at the Media Lab, Helsinki. Notably, Stelarc could see the face of the person manipulating his body and the viewers could watch him being manipulated (Insitute of Art and Ideas 2013). The role of viewer as voyeur is raised once again.

Throughout Stelarc's performances, the raw human body is being written over through new allegiances – ruined; he repudiates what it is to occupy flesh and blood; the territory of both his own body and that of the viewer are re-invented and reconfigured to alter and mutually extend notions of occupant: occupied. References to the books' themes of *ruin, repudiation* and *revolution* are challenged through these extreme examples. Of interest is the micro view of self as a vessel or object to be violated, manipulated, viewed. This view brings into contrast the lenses through which the book's authors look at self in relation to urban settings, surfaces, images, and the like.

Overall, the first of the three positions articulated by Merleau-Ponty challenges us to understand occupation as the *lived experience* and the role of pre-thought and ready-to-handedness. It is not how things work or how they are named that is important but rather that the world is the world we *experience*. A Freudian view seeks to understand the influence of exchanges between the external world and the body in the formation of the topography of the mind. By understanding these influences we can change, transform or overthrow our current state of occupation. Acconci, Orlan and Stelarc force us to experience the edges of orchestrated occupation constructed by others, and into which we voluntarily or involuntarily become complicit.

Therefore, given the dynamics and complexities of human occupation, this book positions a broad interpretation of the concept of occupation.

RUIN, REPUDIATION AND REVOLUTION

The nuances of the everyday are not always apparent to the casual observer; yet, as the following chapters reveal, there is something to learn (or deny) from unusual or strange scenarios.

With each chapter, occupation is viewed through a different lens. This selection of works, in which extensive research is inspired by imagination and synthesis, begins to expand our everyday pre-conceptions of occupation.

The works initially arose as a series of propositions presented at the IDEA (Interior Design Interior Architecture Educators Association) Symposium 2012. *Interior: a State of Becoming 6–9 September 2012*, hosted and convened by Curtin University, Perth Western Australia, began to make explicit those aspects of human occupation that are perhaps a little obscure, intangible and less often discussed. Divided into three sections, this book luxuriates in the more strange considerations of occupation.

'Ruin' in this sense is an adaptation of Jacques Derrida's use of the notion of ruin in *Memoirs of the Blind – The Self-Portrait and other Ruins*, where he writes 'Ruin is that which happens to the image from the moment of the first gaze ... for one can just as well read the pictures of ruin as the figures of a portrait, indeed a self-portrait' (1993, 68).

What is inferred is that no idea, place or experience is as innocent as in the state of its creation or as the raw percept. Instead, human engagement taints the initial rawness to enable it to become something that it was not initially, but it inevitably has new significances and experiences that surround it. Embedded in the notion of ruin are processes, outcomes and impacts, each in itself susceptible to further evolution or decay. And as Derrida implies, it is the human who lays her or himself over the percept to create an extension of self.

In contrast, 'repudiation' evokes a continuum of human occupation that involves denial. Whether through acts of assimilation and disappearance or false representation and rejection, something is removed. Whether we occupy something or other, or whether we are being occupied by something or other, occupation inherently challenges our sense of belonging, ownership and acceptance. In this sense, repudiation is the act changing the 'something' so as to assert our selves and our presence.

'Revolution' is used to position occupation in terms of alteration, extending to overwriting history, and including acts that invent territory to shift physical and psychological boundaries and identities. Of course revolution is often inspired by desire for a better life, a dramatic change, a fresh start, or by desperation. Implicit in the acts, times, or places of revolution are power and status. This is most readily understood in nation against nation, one subgroup to another, but it can also be understood in terms of the complexities of one's own internal and sometimes conflicting dialogue: oneself against self, or of the dynamics between humans and nature. Acts that demonstrate possession are acts that command authority. Yet such authority can be extremely subtle as well as being explosive and destructive.

Firstly, our chapters interpret stories of ruin. With site being central to notions of occupation, Edward Hollis commences with the Roman Baths, from where he 'challenges the notion that change is always a process of becoming, for each of these stories is about how an interior is not created, or developed, but deliberately destroyed'. In Berlin, Benedict Anderson posits that 'performance, site and spectatorship become implicated when combined with the histories and conditions of site: each resulting in a self-ruining of the other'.

By delving into two museums, Sir John Soane's house as museum and Kodja Place, Lynn Churchill relates how these museums expose the concept of occupation in terms of ruin, repudiation and revolution: that it is not simply a question of the reliquary harbouring objects. Rather, it is one of philosophical alchemy: that as we construct the external world, we are working with our interior sense of self. In Jungian terms, these museums make explicit the myths by which we live. Motivated by reconciliation with the past and visions of the future, this chapter posits that these museums edit, re-frame and re-position particular relics to create spatial experiences that embody constructed myths.

The reader is then invited to explore how the interior, as a concept and as an experience, is transformed or represented to reveal alternative identities, in acts of repudiation. Kirsty Volz turns to patterned surface, while Jane Simon reveals the occupancy in thingness through imagery. The latter sets the scene for Vanessa Galvin's interrogation of the sanitized interior image and the unseen or unstated omissions implied in its glossy surface.

Volz asks what is it to work with the self as a two-dimensional representation in the outside world? Occupying the surface suggests a reflexive relationship with identity, that makes-over and re-shapes truths, lies and re-constructions.

Simon explains, 'the domestic is usually imagined through the lens of the intimate, the familial and the human subject. Rather than identifying domestic space through its human occupants, I reframe the focus to the occupation of domestic space by things', in order ' … to look at things outside of their use-value and to re-frame the quotidian outside of our normal modes of perception … '.

Galvin argues that the sanitized view 'results in a kind of professional decontamination of the image and presents a paradoxical relation between the banal actualities of occupation and the image's idealization. Ironically, this normalized understanding is upheld without question through our professional thoughts, words and practices'.

The final chapters challenge the readers to look at grand, revolutionary visions as the suppressors of human drives; at urban sexualization as a subjugatory positioning of the female; at the earth and floor as embodied memory and imagination; and lastly, at abandoned asylums as a juxtaposition of curiosity, fear, myth and experience. To create a particular hegemony has implications. For example, Churchill reflects that, as Sir Thomas More's sixteenth-century vision of Utopia

> *tracks the consequences of what may appear to be ideal, there is always a looming question (presumably planted by More): 'at what cost?'. What are the economics of the utopian vision of an ideal life, and who pays? In Utopia, the creation and maintenance of the ideal life depends on people being contained, and human drives being sublimated.*

In contemporary cities, Nicole Kalms argues that the evolution of urban visual dialogue involves 'sexualization, … hypersexualized billboard advertisements; hypersexualized bodies in urban space; and [that] architect-designed projects … [have] entered the hypersexual arena'.

At a micro level, social relations are implicated in occupation. Jesse O'Neill argues that the floor, whose symbolic power lies in its suggestion to make space anew, is imagination; and that earth, where the stakes are laid and bodies are buried, is memory, identity and ownership. 'Floor becomes a central device in allowing what can unfold upon it to re-imagine groups and spaces. It is connected to the social sphere, but creates a distinction; it is a destabilizing force that encourages radical transformation because it produces a new terrain wiped clean of old protocols'.

Meanwhile, abandoned spaces can be disquieting. Dianne Smith takes us to empty asylums, where the 'interior depicted speaks of occupation, not in terms of capturing life, but rather in terms of what preceded the vacating; and maybe, what we are afraid about deep down. Understandings are rooted in stories and myths … '. Asylums are overlain by the ruined hopes and desires of occupants and creators, and suggest the possibilities of repudiation or revolution that successive waves of reform have brought.

The ideas and theories explored by the authors of *Occupation: ruin, repudiation, revolution* compose a suite of stories that challenge the reader to reconsider how we occupy our world, directly or by being complicit with others. The diversity of viewpoints indicates a rapidly shifting and reforming context; a world where new information creates states of flux (emotionally, socially, economically, politically and environmentally). This book was catalyzed by the inspiration to rethink occupation in terms of such slippages and interconnections.

In this multi-faceted vision, the concept of 'here', meaning this place and this time, is in flux. 'Here' is not and never has been a confined stable construct morphing slowly across time and defined by fixed coordinates specifying a single position. The more privileged contemporary experience of here has become a faster, multi-layered space that we occupy: unrestricted by distance, filled with complex unconfirmed and often conflicting multiple viewpoints; for example, the many viewpoints generated during the on-again off-again cease fire in the Gaza strip of late July 2014. Our understanding of here, the place we occupy, is our human sensorium's synthesis of inputs from multiple sources. Understanding 'here' is fundamental to a lucid sense of self.

REFERENCES

Acconci, Vito. January 1972. *Seedbed*. Multimedia/performance. New York: Sonnabend Gallery.

Berleant, Arnold. 1992. *The Aesthetics of Environment*. Philadelphia, PA: Temple University Press.

Bredlau, Susan M. 2010. 'A Respectful World: Merleau-Ponty and the Experience of Depth'. *Human Studies* 33: 411–23.

Churchill, Lynn M. 2007. 'Architecture "Doing" Body: An Architectural Proposition Inspired by an Analysis of Francis Bacon's Paint "Doing" Body'. PhD diss., Curtin University of Technology.

Churchill, Lynn, and Dianne Smith, eds. 2012. *Interior: a State of Becoming: Book 1: Symposium Proceedings, State Library, Perth, WA, September 6–9, 2012*. Perth, WA: Curtin University.

Derrida, Jacques. 1993. *Memoirs of the Blind: The Self-Portrait and Other Ruins*. Translated by Pascale-Anne Brault and Michael Nass. Chicago: University of Chicago Press.

Freud, Sigmund. 1953. *The Major Works of Sigmund Freud*. Chicago: Encyclopaedia Britannica.

——. 1969. *Civilization and its Discontents*. Translated by Joan Riviere. London: Hogarth Press and the Institute of Psychoanalysis.

Institute of Art and Ideas. 2013. *Stelarc: Meat, Metal and Code*. 38 minutes 18 seconds. http://www.youtube.com/watch?v=prBMk72mwsg. Accessed 29 May 2014.

Kerouac, Jack. 1970. *On the Road*. London: Penguin.

Merleau-Ponty, Maurice. 1962. *Phenomenology of Perception*. London: Routledge.

Orlan. 2004. *Orlan: Carnal Art*. Paris: Editions Flammarion.

Orlan, Sarah Wilson and Duncan McCorquodale. 1996. *Orlan: Ceci est Mon Corps … Ceci est Mon Logiciel = This is My Body … This is My Software*. London: Black Dog.

Presner, Todd, David Shepard and Yoh Kawano. 2014. *HyperCities: Thick Mapping in the Digital Humanities*. Cambridge, MA: Harvard University Press.

Tomkins, Leah and Virginia Eatough. 2013. 'The Feel of Experience: Phenomenological Ideas for Organizational Research'. *Qualitative Research in Organizations and Management: An International Journal* 8 (3): 258–75.

Wittgenstein, Ludwig. 1967. *Philosophical Investigations*. Translated by Gertrude Elizabeth Margaret Anscombe. Oxford: Basil Blackwell.

NOTES

1. The term 'king hit' first arose in Australia as a result of a series of one hit punches resulting in death or serious brain injury. This term has since been replaced by 'coward-punch'.

PART I
RUIN

Plate 2   'Self portrait'. 2014

Damnatio Memoriae: Interiors and the Art of Forgetting

Edward Hollis

RUINOMANIA

> *Wondrous is this wall-stead, wasted by fate.*
> *Battlements broken, giant's work shattered.*
> *Roofs are in ruin, towers destroyed,*
> *broken the barred gate, rime on the plaster,*
> *walls gape, torn up, destroyed,*
> *consumed by age. Earth-grip holds*
> *the proud builders, departed, long lost,*
> *and the hard grasp of the grave, until a hundred generations*
> *of people have passed. Often this wall outlasted,*
> *hoary with lichen, red-stained, withstanding the storm,*
> *one reign after another; the high arch has now fallen.*
> *The wall-stone still stands, hacked by weapons,*
> *by grim-ground files.*
> *…*
> *Mood quickened mind, and the mason,*
> *skilled in round-building, bound the wall-base,*
> *wondrously with iron.*
> *Bright were the halls, many the baths,*
> *high the gables, great the joyful noise,*
> *many the mead-hall full of pleasures.*
> *Until fate the mighty overturned it all.*
> *Slaughter spread wide, pestilence arose,*
> *and death took all those brave men away.*
> *Their bulwarks were broken, their halls laid waste,*
> *the cities crumbled, those who would repair it*
> *laid in the earth. And so these halls are empty,*
> *and the curved arch sheds its tiles,*
> *torn from the roof. Decay has brought it down,*
> *broken it to rubble. Where once many a warrior,*
> *high of heart, gold-bright, gleaming in splendour,*
> *proud and wine-flushed, shone in armour,*
> *looked on a treasure of silver, on precious gems,*

> on riches of pearl …
> in that bright city of broad rule.
> Stone courts once stood there, and hot streams gushed forth,
> wide floods of water, surrounded by a wall,
> in its bright bosom, there where the baths were,
> hot in the middle.
> Hot streams ran over hoary stone
> into the ring.
> (Exeter poet, 'The Ruin' 2013)

Musing on ruins is nothing new: the anonymous 'Exeter poet', translated above by Siân Echard, meditated on the remains of Roman Bath in the ninth century, and a millennium later, the landscape theorist Richard Payne Knight was still praising their picturesque qualities in *The Landscape: a Didactic Poem*, written in 1795:

> *Blest is the man in whose sequester'd glade,*
> *Some ancient abbey's walls diffuse their shade;*
> *With mouldering windows pierc'd, and turrets crown'd*
> *And pinnacles with clinging ivy bound.* (Ballantyne 1997, 244)

And, as these two fragments of poetry illustrate, ruins have always been rearranged to tell specific stories to specific times – stories of sorrowing wonder to the Anglo-Saxon mead hall, and urbane frisson to the enlightenment drawing room.

Ruins occupy a particular place in mythologies of modernism, dedicated as it was at the beginning of the twentieth century by the Italian Futurists to the deliberate destruction of the past: 'Come on!' wrote Marinetti (1902, n.p.) in *The Founding and Manifesto of Futurism*, 'Set fire to the library shelves! Turn aside the canals to flood the museums! … . Oh, the joy of seeing the glorious old canvases bobbing adrift on those waters, discolored and shredded! … . Take up your pickaxes, your axes and hammers and wreck, wreck the venerable cities, pitilessly!'

And even the historian John Summerson (1949, 236) described the aesthetic appeal of ruins in terms that his contemporaries might also have applied to the modernist *plan libre*:

> … the building is free – everybody's building, nobody's building. The barrier between 'outside' and 'inside' has likewise been destroyed; space flows through the building … . The building has become comprehensible as a single whole – no longer an exterior plus one or more interiors but a single combination of planes in recession, full of mystery and surprise.

In contrast, post-modern architectural writers like Aldo Rossi (1982) or Colin Rowe and Fred Koetter (1978) used ruins as a metaphor for their vision of culture as the arena of competing, fragmented narratives, and of bricolage as its paradoxical master narrative. Describing seventeenth-century Rome, built on the foundations of an earlier, ruined city, Rowe holds up as a model a city made of a

> *collision of palaces, piazza, and villas, that inextricable fusion of imposition and accommodation, that highly successful and resilient traffic jam of intentions,*

and anthology of closed compositions and ad hoc stuff in between, which is simultaneously a dialectic of ideal types plus a dialectic of ideal types with empirical context … . (Rowe and Koetter 1978, 106)

In more recent times, in tune with a less optimistic *zeitgeist*, the pyschogeographies of Iain Sinclair (1997, 2006, 2009), Patrick Wright (1985, 1991), and Patrick Keillor (1997, 2010) have, in writing and film, imagined a post-imperial, post-industrial London as a ruin of its recent selves; and in the last decade, human geographers such as Tim Edensor (2005, 2013) and Caitlin DeSilvey (2006, 2013) have built on this interest in the post-industrial urban landscape to consider the ruin as the objective correlative of both Rowe and Koetter's (1978) post-modern bricolage and of the Futurist vision of anarchy. In 'Industrial Ruins: Space, Aesthetics, and Materiality', Edensor (2005, 4) writes:

Bereft of … codings of the normative – the arrangement of things in place, the performance of regulated actions, the display of goods lined up as commodities or for show – ruined space is ripe with transgressive and transcendent possibilities. Ruins offer spaces in which the interpretation and practice of the city becomes liberated from the everyday constraints which determine what should be done where … accordingly, they offer opportunities for challenging and deconstructing the imprint of power on the city.

Ruinomania has long been an obsession at least as protean as its subject, but a common strand from the ninth century to the twenty-first has been the idea of the ruin as the vehicle, or

… an allegory of memory … fragmentary, imperfect, partial and thoroughly incomplete. There is no clear sign that the meaning of the past is self-evident and easy to decode if you possess the necessary expertise. There is an excess of meaning in the remains: a plenitude of fragmented stories, elisions, fantasies, inexplicable objects and possible events which present a history that can begin and end anywhere, and refuses the master narratives of history … .
(Edensor 2005, 140)

Rowe and Koetter's (1978) post-modern city symbolizes the contested, relativistic nature of post-modern memory, while the modernist love of ruination was born out of the desire to forget. The picturesque ruin was a memorial to a past whose rougher edges have been polished into oblivion.

Long before them all, the Exeter poet mused on the ruins of buildings so incomprehensibly large that he called them 'giant's work'. Trying to imagine them in occupation, he could only impose his own social norms on those broken and alien forms. A chic spa for Mediterranean expatriates became, in his words a 'mead hall' for warriors that the Romans would surely never have recognized. On the one hand, the wondering verse of the Exeter poet is an act of memory.

On the other, all it can show is how much he cannot remember. In the verses of the Exeter poet, the 'wondrous wallstead, wasted by fate' has suffered the cruellest punishment that time can inflict: *damnatio memoriae*, or the damnation of memory.

DAMNATIO MEMORIAE

Damnatio memoriae is a punishment with ancient origins. In a ritual instituted by the second King of Rome, Numa, any Vestal Virgin who broke her vows of chastity would suffer *damnatio memoriae*. A room would be excavated for her within the stone mass of the city walls. It would be set with a bed, and provided with food like a little home; and when it was ready, the Vestal Virgin would be led there, and walled into the wall to die. Far worse, her name would be erased from the *fasti*, the archives that were carved in marble into the walls of the house of the Vestals (Plutarch 1926).

As Harriet Flower (2006) has argued in *The Art of Forgetting*, her study of the practice of *damnatio memoriae*, oblivion was the natural state of affairs in the Roman mind. Therefore the perpetuation of the reputations of the great and the good was a special act of *pietas* – of resistance to the progress of time. The building of monuments and the cutting of inscriptions in stone was an act of *pietas*, as was the patrician tradition of hanging ancestral portraits in the *tablinum* – the reception room – of the family home, to which Vitruvius devotes a whole passage of *De Architectura* (2008).

Damnatio memoriae was selectively and skilfully used in Roman public life. In 509 BC one of the first consuls of republican Rome, Publius Valerius Poplicola, was forced to demolish his own home on the Palatine Hill, because the people suspected him of wanting to re-establish the monarchy. In 58 BC, when the aristocratic oligarch Cicero was proscribed, his house was pulled down and a temple of Liberty built in its place (Hales 2003, 40–49).

Conversely, in 49 BC a house on the Palatine that had been confiscated from the republican senator Hortensius became the core of a new one built for Augustus, the Emperor who had condemned him. Not only did the punishment enable Augustus to deprive Hortensius of his chief economic asset and to humiliate him socially: it also enabled him, by residing in a relatively modest house, to appropriate, for his own ends, Hortensius' reputation for republican probity (Hales 2003, 24).

That we know these stories is one of the paradoxes of the practice of *damnatio memoriae*, for no-one can have expected that those who suffered the punishment would actually pass into oblivion. This paradox is at its most evident in the most common form of the practice, the defacing of inscriptions, in which the act of erasure is not invisible, but leaves a trace of its own, as well as, all too often still visibly, the outline of the very thing that the sanction was intended to erase. Flower (2006, xiii) comments:

> *In speaking of wax tablets, which were widely used by the Romans and which were supposed to contain a perfect record ... no change could be made without the editing process itself being revealed by the wax.*
>
> *In short, a tablet's wax serves to reveal change, not to facilitate it ... the visible indications of obliteration, the sense of the absent in the present, carried the greatest significance.*

Places and things pass away, but their passing is not always a tragedy of omission. The practice of *damnatio memoriae* has been discussed here in an ancient

Roman context; but it has been practised in many times and places. This chapter will use three stories to explore what the practice can reveal about not just loss and memory but also, as we shall see, those things which are lost and remembered.

FIRST STORY: NERO'S GOLDEN HOUSE

The Exeter poet wasn't the first or the last person to find Roman ruins strange and monstrous, and 600 years after he wrote his poem, on 14 January 1506, a marble monster was dug up from the ground in a vineyard in Rome.[1] It was huge: muscular, nude, and so tightly coiled in the embrace of a serpent that it was almost impossible to tell where the man stopped and the snake began.

The Laocöon was taken away; but even after it was gone, people still turned up to root around, for they were convinced that if the vines had turned up one monster, they must hide others. The painters Raphael and Giovanni da Udine came to find the remains of the palace of Titus, in which Pliny[2] had written, and the Laocöon had been kept in ancient times.[3]

They descended into the caves under the vineyard, and hanging from ropes, clutching torches, they found a domed interior whose walls had been painted with images of impossible architectures, with beasts and men intertwined, furniture that grew leaves, fish that belched feathers, and goats with the faces of sphinxes. *Grotteschi*, they called them, grotesques, because they were painted onto the walls of grottoes.[4]

Wonderful and wonderfully preserved this interior might have been; but it didn't belong to any Palace of Titus. Rather, it was buried under one. These rooms had been used as cellars, as servants' quarters, hypocausts (spaces to house underfloor heating), and storerooms, but they clearly hadn't been designed for these lowly functions, and the patterning of their brick and concrete revealed them to belong to some other older, structure.[5]

The identity of that interior was, as Raphael and da Udine already knew, contained in one of the ancient Roman poet Martial's epigrams:

> *Here where the heavenly colossus has a close view of the stars*
> *And high structures rise on the lofty road*
> *There once shone the hated hall of the cruel king*
> *And one house took up the whole of Rome*
> *Here where rises the huge mass of the awesome amphitheatre*
> *In sight of all was Nero's pool.*
> *Here where we admire the baths built so quickly for our benefit*
> *A proud park deprived the poor of their houses.*
> *Where the Claudian temple spreads its wide shade*
> *Stood the last part of the palace*
> *Rome is returned to herself under your rule, Caesar*
> *The delights of their master have become those of the people.*[6]

The Emperor Nero was the 'cruel king', his was the 'one house' that 'took up the whole of Rome'. His was the colossus that was removed to make way for the 'awesome amphitheatre' of the Colosseum, and his the park that deprived the poor of their houses. The burial of his 'hated hall' under new structures was a sign that 'Rome is returned to herself' and that 'the delights of their master have become those of the people'.

And the very origins of 'the hated hall' lay in an alleged crime. In *The Twelve Caesars*, Suetonius[7] wrote that it had been built after a terrible fire, if not caused, then abetted, by the Emperor himself.

> Pretending to be disgusted by the drab old buildings and narrow, winding streets of Rome, he brazenly set fire to the city ... . Nero watched the conflagration from the Tower of Maecenas, enraptured by what he called the 'beauty of the flames'; then put on his tragedian's costume and sang the sack of Ilium from beginning to end.

Nero certainly took advantage of the destruction, and appropriated the land cleared by the fire, upon which he built himself a home so marvellous that it was called *Domus Aurea*: the 'golden house'. There was a park, lake, a colossus, and the interior, containing a dining room lined, in the words of Suetonius[8] with 'ceilings of fretted ivory, the panels of which could slide back and let a rain of flowers, or of perfume from hidden sprinklers, shower upon his guests. The main dining room was circular and its roof revolved, day and night, in time with the sky'.

Tacitus[9] levelled a much more serious charge against the Golden House than extravagance:

> Its wonders were not so much customary and commonplace luxuries like gold and jewels but lawns and lakes and faked rusticity – woods here, open spaces and views there. With their cunning, impudent artificialities, Severus and Celer [the architects] did not baulk at effects that nature herself had ruled out as impossible.

For the emperor had turned the city into the countryside. He dined in a dining room that revolved like the heavens. He turned himself, a man, into a colossus. It is ironic that when he moved into the Golden House, Nero is reputed to have said: 'Now I can at last live like a human being!'[10] In fact, the house was designed to liberate him from the shackles of humanity.

It did, but not, perhaps, as it should have done. Amid the splendour of his gilded halls, or perhaps in some artfully rusticated spot in the gardens, Nero, according to Tacitus,[11] 'devised a kind of game, in which, covered with the skin of some wild animal, he was let loose from a cage and attacked the private parts of men and women, who were bound to stakes, and when he had sated his mad lust, were dispatched'.

He killed himself within four years of moving in – if he hadn't, his subjects would have done it for him. Nero's successors decided that the best thing to do with the monstrous Golden House was damn up its rooms from light and air. They buried the domed interior under public buildings;[12] and they commissioned Martial to write his poem – the literary equivalent of the burial.

ABSENCE AND PRESENCE

This is a story we know from the histories of Suetonius (1979) and Tacitus (2012); but that very fact contains an irony, for both of them were more or less contemporaries with Martial; and their accounts of the Golden House were accounts of a building that they could never have seen. Their Golden House was no less rhetorical than his epigrams.

In his *Twelve Caesars*, Suetonius regularly used the houses of the emperors to characterize their faults and virtues. The republican probity of the first emperor, Augustus, for example, was expressed in the modesty of his house, which Suetonius (1979, 95) described as: 'remarkable neither for size nor for elegance, the courts being supported by squat columns of peperino stone, and the living rooms innocent of marble or tessellated floors'. Augustus's house had also been buried for a century by the time that Suetonius was writing, and like the *Domus Aurea*, there is no evidence that Suetonius ever saw it (though he was shown some of the furniture that it contained).

Tacitus's charge against the house was more subtle, but equally rhetorical, for he charged both the *Domus Aurea* and its builder with crimes against nature: the 'impudent artificialities' of Severus and Celer the architects, in which the city was turned into the countryside, the use of effects 'which nature herself had ruled out as impossible', and the eyes of creatures painted on the walls which would follow people around the room (Tacitus 2012, XV: 42, 1).

The *Domus Aurea* was both, therefore, Nero's alleged crime, and, in posterity, his punishment. As Flower (2006, 230) comments: 'ultimately there are two "Golden Houses" for the generations living after Nero, the actual one, which is being steadily revealed by further excavation in Rome, and the image of the Golden House in literature'.

The form of only one of these houses is known: the one imagined in literature. The other one – if ever there was such a house – was buried so thoroughly under later construction that its extent remains unknown. There is certainly no agreement as to the whereabouts of the wonderful dining room – some identify it with the grottoes discovered by Raphael and Da Udine, others with another site on the Palatine Hills, and others still with a long lost temporary wooden structure. Others claim the room never existed, except in the writings of Suetonius (Boethius 1960, 119).

Like the 'wondrous wallstead' gazed upon by the Exeter poet in the ninth century, it is a mystery, but unlike it, the *Domus Aurea* was not 'wasted by fate' – it was deliberately destroyed.

SECOND STORY: THE TRIAL OF CHARLES I

Damnatio memoriae is a punishment that long survived the collapse of the Roman Empire, and has also taken other forms less explicitly straightforward than the burying of buildings.

When, a millennium and a half after the suicide of Nero, in 1649, Charles I was put on trial for his life in Westminster Hall, he famously demanded: 'I would know by what power I am brought hither',[13] for the trial was a constitutional perversion: the king had been put on trial by a court of justice that was, by tradition, constituted to act on his behalf. The world had, in the words of the title of Christopher Hill's classic work on the English Revolution,[14] been turned upside down.

The King did not need to be told this, for it was evident in the way in which the furniture had been arranged.

In happier times, the King usually sat at the King's Bench, a throne and a long table, at the south end of the hall. It had been the place where his medieval forbears had once sat to feast in front of their knights and thegns,[15] and to dispense justice in the sight of the people.

But the King could not be there all the time, and by 1178 an edict had been passed licensing judges appointed by the King to dispense this justice on his behalf while he was away. While the King had been present, the bench had been made of oak, but when he ceased to use the hall regularly for eating in, it was remade in marble; the presence of the chair was recorded in court rolls in 1215, and the table in 1245.[16]

Over time, the court that sat at the King's Bench appropriated the name, and as their business became more complex, so the marble seat and table began to disappear under other pieces of furniture: partitions to divide the court from the rest of the hall; a dais for the judges to sit upon, a bar to which plaintiff and defendants could be called, and a table for the clerks to take court records.[17]

But, under this paraphernalia, the King's Bench remained, and when the King or his Queen returned to the hall, the wooden *meubles* (the moveable furniture) would be removed, and the *immeuble* (fixed) marble beneath would be exposed. Drawings of the coronations of Anne Boleyn and Elizabeth I survive that show them sitting on the chair, at the table, at the head of the hall, as their ancestors had done before them.[18]

So it should have been in 1649, when the King returned to his hall in Westminster. But at his trial, the King was not led to his usual seat. Rather, he was led to one facing it, in the position of the accused. The King's Bench had been buried under a new wooden dais, upon which sat three rows of wooden benches, filled with the commoners who had been drafted in to sit in judgment upon him.[19] No single one of them dared condemn the king; and so they answered the monarch's question as to their authority with the number of the common people they claimed to represent:

> The Commons of England, assembled in Parliament, … according to that fundamental power that is vested, and trust reposed in them by the People (other means failing through your default) have resolved to bring you to trial and judgement, and have therefore constituted this high court of justice before which you are now brought.[20]

After King Charles had been condemned to die, the dais was removed, the marble King's Bench smashed, and its broken pieces buried under the floor of the Hall. It was not restored, even at the Restoration, and although the Kings and Queens of England have sat in the same place, the marble chair in which they once sat has disappeared.[21]

The architecture of medieval palaces was generic; and it usually fell to the furniture temporarily arranged within them to articulate the intricacies of household politics: it is significant that medieval depictions of palaces, of parliaments, courts, and banquets almost never include architecture. The *damnatio memoriae* of Charles I was affected less by the burial of his bench than by the movement of his seat in relation to it. He was damned by a rearrangement of furniture.

DAMNING INTERIORS

As the story of the trial of Charles I demonstrates, the *damnatio memoriae* of interiors does not always involve the defacing of durable objects like buildings. All too often, interiors are neither durable, nor objects. Susie Attiwill (2004, 4) comments:

> The use of the term 'interior design' is deliberate and not interchangeable with interior architecture. A distinction is made here to indicate that the design of interiors is not to be limited to inside built form. This is vital to the ability to apprehend emerging forces. Fixed architectural enclosures are no longer the dominant shaping and mediating element for interior and exterior relations, for example – the change in the work environment. An office was once defined by a building – an office building. Now a building may have different functions at different times, sometimes an office, other times a home. An office then becomes a temporal and spatial occurrence involving a reorganising of relations – for example, from domestic to office environment.

And this condition poses particular problems for the historian – quite simply, what is the history of the interior a history of?

In 'La Filosofia D'Arredamento', Mario Praz (1964, 20) writes of the interior that it is 'the resonance chamber where its [the soul's] strings render their authentic vibration' and that resonation was, he was sure, something that occurred in time. Although his book was published in English as *An Illustrated History of Interior Decoration* he was forced to admit that it was largely a history of illustrations of interior decoration, since almost all the interiors that were illustrated in it had long disappeared. Of these illustrations (often Biedermeier watercolours), Praz (1964, 38) noted that they ' … so accurately preserve the taste of that age that you would almost say the doors and windows depicted in them have never been opened since then, and that we breathed the spirit still enclosed there like … the scent of perfume that lingers in an ancient phial'.

They existed in image only, suspended in time; and when by some historical miracle, interiors from the past did survive, they were, as Praz wrote (1964, 34), dead in comparison: 'Where things are listed in a catalogue, given numbers, fixed to walls, or protected by velvet ropes so that no ill-disposed visitor may rob or deface – there, in common opinion – all is death and graveyard'.

For Praz, then, disappearance was the natural state of the interior, leaving behind ruins likely to be no more than a sheet of paper in a portfolio, delicately stained with watercolours that themselves fade as the page is opened to the sunlight. 'Why' he wondered (1964, 36), 'among the apartments I once visited, do I recall the most sequestered and funereal? Is it perhaps because they seem most in key with the ruin that has menaced or engulfed them?'

Quite unlike the marble monuments of the ancient Romans, interiors are, as Attiwill (2004, 6) points out, temporal and spatial occurrences, whose lifespan is short, and whose destiny is, usually, oblivion. Unlike buildings, interiors are made to pass, and to be forgotten. What ruins, therefore, can they leave behind, other than fading watercolours, and pieces of furniture, lost in other, later rooms? What evidence can the historian use to imagine the interiors of the past?

Damnatio memoriae, in which the passage into oblivion, rather than being an inadvertent sin of omission, is made visible, significant, and deliberate, may therefore present a useful answer to this question, since it invokes, for Flowers (2006, xiii) 'that sense of the absent in the present' that is part of every room.

There is a further methodological issue. Interiors happen in space and time, and the concept of the interior is also similarly temporally (and spatially) bounded. As Charles Rice (2006, 3) has pointed out, the concept of the interior I have described above – particularly that imagined by Praz – is a nineteenth century, Western, bourgeois, domestic phenomenon:

> *That is not to say that furniture and its arrangement, or indeed domestic habits and mores, did not exist before this time. Rather, the interior conceptualised a particular emerging and developing consciousness of and comportment to the material realities of domesticity, realities which were actively formed in this emergence ... the interior as a bourgeois manifestation is key to consider here.*

In this light, the examples of *damnatio memoriae* considered in this chapter might require some explanation, since they are neither nineteenth century nor bourgeois, and only faintly domestic. This is a deliberate anachronism designed to illuminate different perspectives on how 'occupied spaces' (to avoid the loaded use of the word 'interior') were imagined at different times, and, potentially how they might be imagined now, long after the nineteenth-century bourgeoisie have passed away.

Damnatio memoriae was, in origin, only ever meted out to citizens who, being active in the state, might have an expectation of being remembered. To put it brutally, everyone else was consigned to oblivion anyway. The rooms examined here are all, similarly, political in the 'high' sense of the word.

On the one hand this may be ascribed to the idleness of the author: rooms in palaces are self-conscious creations that have had crowds of witnesses to remember them, armies of servants to maintain them, and schools of archivists to record their contents.

On the other hand, rooms in palaces remind us that interiors (in the broader sense) need not be restricted to private residences. Mario Praz imagined the interior as the resonance chamber of the soul, and being a critic of Romantic literature, he assumed that soul would be individual. But interiors can be found in airships, superclubs, film sets, shops, museums, hotel lobbies, restaurants, hospital wards, public toilets and nuclear bunkers, as well as studies, boudoirs and sitting rooms. Like a medieval great hall, interiors can be the imagined dwellings of whole societies, rather than of a narrow middle class.

This chapter thinks beyond the historic category of 'interior' to imagine how interiors can be public, political spaces of participation and democracy. *Damnatio memoriae* is still practised today. The looting of the palaces of Colonel Gaddafi or Saddam Hussein are a form of the practice, as is, in a different mode, the expectation that every new First Lady will redecorate the White House upon her husband's election. Although interiors are nothing like the marble monuments of Roman public life, even when they seem to be private, they are an affair of state, and always have been.

THIRD STORY: THE LAST BOUDOIR OF MARIE ANTOINETTE

During her trial, the boudoirs of Marie Antoinette exercised a horrible fascination over the people of France. They were not only evidence of her extravagance and vanity, but also, the evidence presented at her trial argued, the scene of her most egregious perversions: in their mirrors, it was claimed, she watched herself do it with men, servants, women, and her own children.

> *In a fine alcove artfully gilded,*
> *Not too dark and not too light,*
> *On a soft sofa, covered in velvet,*
> *The August Beauty bestows her charms*
> *[and] the Prince presents the Goddess his cock ... .* [22]

And just as the room itself was used to condemn its occupant to death, so it, too, was punished.

No sooner had the queen vacated her apartments at Versailles than their treasures were severed from the person for whom they had been made. The queen knew it would happen, and one of her first acts after being carried off to Paris was to send her decorators, Daguerre and Lignereux, to the palace to make a secret inventory of the rooms before anyone touched them. It is the last record of those rooms as a home.[23]

Within the year, their contents, which had all been made to exclusive commission, were declared the property of the state, and craftsmen were sent to remove the royal *fleurs de lys* from all the furniture. Ironically, the work was carried out mostly by the people who had put them there in the first place: only Riesener, Marie Antoinette's favourite *ébéniste* was skilful enough to remove the delicate veneers without damage; and it served the purpose of his evolutionary re-education too.[24]

Once ideologically cleansed, everything was put up for sale on the open market. Tax breaks were offered to foreign buyers to ensure that as many pieces as possible went abroad, where it was all too easy to find buyers anxious to own relics of the glamour of the *ancien régime*.[25]

And once the rooms had been emptied they were turned to different public uses. Versailles was co-opted as a military hospital for a while, then as an art school, and then, after the Restoration, a museum to the glories of all the people of France.[26]

But no-one – not even Napoleon at his most megalomaniac, or the restored monarchy at its most vengeful – ever dreamed of reappropriating the rooms for living in. It would have been political suicide. Instead, every re-use was predicated on making public what had once been private – in giving to the many what had once belonged to the few.

In 1796, three years after the execution of Marie Antoinette, a certain Doctor Weber went to visit Versailles, and he described salons and bedrooms that had been 'ransacked (the beautifully crafted bronze locks on the door and the windows having been stolen), glass shattered, tables smashed, and canvasses ripped … ' but, he continued 'they [the revolutionary mob] had left the shutters, so cleverly lined with mirrors that it was impossible to tell whether the windows were open or closed'(quoted in Desjardins 1885, 358–9, author's translation).[27]

The *damnatio memoriae* of the boudoir of Marie Antoinette was complete: firstly, its privacy had been violated: the locks that kept it hidden from the public gaze were broken and removed, and the Petit Trianon, the house that contained it, was thrown open to visitors. Secondly, its luxurious furnishings had been vandalized. Thirdly, however, the evidence of the alleged crime – the mirrored panelling that lined the room, and bore witness to the notorious vanity of the Queen – had been retained, for all to see.

Its ability to reflect its occupant broken, its contents divorced from the person for whom it had been made, its privacy violated, the last boudoir of Marie Antoinette became a room, just like any other. The *damnatio memoriae* designed for it was the opposite of that meted out to Nero's Golden House. While that palace suffered burial, the boudoir suffered the reverse: its enclosure violated, it was thrown open, and ceased, in that moment, to be an interior.

CONCLUSION

Interiors are composites: the meeting places of many things; and applied to the interior, acts of *damnatio memoriae* involve the disruption of the order of the meetings between diverse objects, rather than the simple defacement of one.

Nero's Golden House was buried under a tide of concrete, preserved for the opprobrium of posterity. The trial of Charles I involved the rearrangement of the rules of a meeting by changes in spatial arrangement. The *damnatio memoriae* of Marie Antoinette involved the dissolution of the personal connection between the interior and the occupant for whom it had been made.

In each case, the punishment was made to fit the crime, and therefore reveals shared assumptions about what an interior is, and how it relates to the people who inhabit it. 'Now, at last I can live like a man', Nero said when he moved into the *Domus Aurea* (Suetonius 1979, 229), and Tacitus, Suetonius and Martial agreed with him; in Roman culture, the man and the house were one and the same. For both Charles I and the commissioners who placed him on trial there, Westminster Hall was the spatial manifestation of the state: a great arena in which everyone knew, or was meant to know, their place. The question he asked: 'I would know by what authority I have been brought *hither*' [author's emphasis] could only have been asked by one who had been led to the wrong chair. Marie Antoinette said of her private boudoir: 'When I am here, I'm not the queen. I'm a woman', (Beaussant 1996, 212) and the revolutionaries concurred: the room was the reflection of the flawed soul of the queen herself.

In all cases, an interior is imagined as a set of relationships: between people, but also with décor, objects, furniture and architecture; and as such it is always contingent. Nero was still building his house when he committed suicide. Marie Antoinette regularly redecorated her boudoirs, and the point of the furniture in Westminster Hall was that, unlike the architecture, it could be moved to cater for different occasions. Interiors are, at root, temporary arrangements. It was only their *damnatio memoriae* that preserved them for posterity, and ensured that the interiors explored here are remembered with far greater vividness than all the other halls, cabinets and boudoirs that, like most of the rooms we live in, are lost through attrition and default.

The sale of Marie Antoinette's furniture, and the opening of her boudoir to the public gaze, turned her and her hidden interiors into one of most compelling tourist attractions in French history. The Empress Eugénie turned the Trianon into a museum made in her memory. At the Wallace collection in London, the fine pieces of furniture that once populated the apartments of Marie Antoinette are accompanied by an even rarer treasure: a copy of the bill poster advertising their sale.

The shocking effect of the seating plan at the trial of Charles I could only be felt by those who already understood the codes that it inverted. After it was finished, and the table was broken, it was buried, rather than thrown into the river, or disposed of altogether. Now resurrected, it has not been restored to its former place, although the monarchy for which it was made survives in altered form.

And the burial of Nero's *Domus Aurea* was, despite itself, an act of preservation. The colours of these *Grotteschi* that Raphael and Giovanni da Udine found in Nero's Golden House were still just as bright in 1560 as they had been for Nero, for, as Vasari (1878, Vol. 5, 19) later wrote, they 'had not been open or exposed to the air, which is wont in time, through the changes of the seasons, to consume all things'.

All interiors are in a state of perpetual motion. The changes in the palatial interiors described here are driven by political shocks and jolts. The changes they undergo are deliberate, public, and very well documented. But the same process is happening all the time to every interior. Rooms are redecorated, the furniture moved around, and the junk cleared away. Such processes remind us that the interior is not just becoming. It is also in a perpetual state of entropy. Change is always an act of violence, of revolution, of violation upon what exists – of forgetting.

But memory is integral to forgetting. 'Hot streams run over hoary stone' wrote the Exeter poet (2013) – the evanescent steam carving paths through Roman rock, pulling down the very building that had been built to contain it, and to turn into an interior in which

> … hot streams gushed forth,
> wide floods of water, surrounded by a wall,
> in its bright bosom, there where the baths were,
> hot in the middle.
> Even the engine of destruction describes the very thing it was created to destroy.

REFERENCES

Attiwill, Susie. 2004. 'Towards an Interior History', *IDEA* 2004: 1–8. http://idea-edu.com/journal/2004-idea-journal/. Accesssed April 2013.

Ballantyne, Andrew. 1997. *Architecture, Landscape, and Liberty*. Cambridge: Cambridge University Press.

Beaussant, Philippe. 1996. *Plaisirs de Versailles Theatre et Musique*. Paris: Fayard.

Boethius, Axel. 1960. *The Golden House of Nero: Some Aspects of Roman Architecture*. Ann Arbor: University of Michigan Press.

Collins, Mark, Phillip Emery, Christopher Phillpotts, Mark Samuel and Christopher Thomas. 2012. 'The King's High Table at the Palace of Westminster'. *The Antiquaries Journal* 92: 197–243.

Concise Oxford Dictionary. 7th Edition. 1982. Oxford: Clarendon Press

DeSilvey, Caitlin. 2006. 'Observed Decay: Telling Stories with Mutable Things'. *Journal of Material Culture* 11 (3): 318–38.

DeSilvey, Caitlin and Tim Edensor. 2013. 'Reckoning with Ruins'. *Progress in Human Geography* 37 (4): 465–85.

Desjardins, Gustave A. 1885. *Le Petit Trianon Histoire et Description*. Versailles: L. Bernard.

Edensor, Tim. 2005. *Industrial Ruins: Space, Aesthetics and Materiality*. Oxford, New York: Berg.

Exeter poet. 2013. 'The Ruin'. Translated by Siân Echard. Accessed 1 December, http://faculty.arts.ubc.ca/sechard/oeruin.htm. Translation copyright Siân Echard, 2013.

Flower, Harriet. 2006. *The Art of Forgetting: Disgrace and Oblivion in Roman Political Culture*. Chapel Hill, NC: University of North Carolina Press.

Grant, Michael. 1970. *Nero Emperor in Revolt*. New York: American Heritage.

Griffin, Miriam T. 1984. *Nero: The End of a Dynasty*. London: Batsford.

Hales, Shelley. 2003. *The Roman House and Social Identity*. Cambridge: Cambridge University Press.

Hill, Christopher. 1991. *The World Turned Upside Down: Radical Ideas During the English Revolution*. London: Penguin.

Hughes, Peter. 1996. *The Wallace Collection: Catalogue of Furniture*. Vol. II. London: Trustees of the Wallace Collection.

Jallut, Marguerite. 1969. 'Les Collections de Marie-Antoinette'. *Arts* 20 (20): 209–20.

Keiller, Patrick. 1997. *Robinson in Space*. Film. London: British Broadcasting Corporation (BBC), Koninck Studios.

——. 2010. *Robinson in Ruins*. Film. London: British Film Institute.

Marinetti, Filippo. T. 2013. *The Founding and Manifesto of Futurism*. Accessed 1 December, http://www.unknown.nu/futurism/manifesto.html.

Muddiman, Joseph George. 1928. *The Trial of King Charles the First (Notable British Trials)*. London: Butterworth.

Nolhacs, Pierre de. [1937] 2002. *Le Resurrection de Versailles, Souvenirs d'un Conservateur 1887–1920*. Versailles: Perrin.

Payne Knight, Richard. 1997. 'The Landscape: A Didactic Poem'. In *Architecture, Landscape, and Liberty*, by Andrew Ballantyne, 244. Cambridge: Cambridge University Press.

Pliny the Elder. 2013. 'Pliny the Elder, The Natural History', translated by John Bostock and H.T. Riley. Accessed February, http://www.perseus.tufts.edu/hopper/text?doc=Plin.+Nat.+toc.

Plutarch. 1926. *'Life of Numa' Lives, with an English Translation by Bernadotte Perrin*. London: Heinemann Loeb Classical Library.

Praz, Mario. 1964. *An Illustrated History of Interior Decoration from Pompeii to Art Nouveau*. Translated by William Weaver. London: Thames and Hudson.

Rice, Charles. 2007. *The Emergence of the Interior: Architecture, Modernity, Domesticity*. Abingdon: Routledge.

Rossi, Aldo. 1982. *The Architecture of the City*. Translated by Diane Ghirardo and Joan Ockman. Cambridge, MA: MIT Press.

Rowe, Colin and Fred Koetter. 1978. *Collage City*. Cambridge, MA: MIT Press.

Sinclair, Iain. 1997. *Lights out for the Territory: 9 Excursions in the Secret History of London*. London: Granta Books.

——. 2009. *Hackney, That Rose-Red Empire: A Confidential Report*. London: Granta.

Sinclair, Iain, ed. 2006. *London: City of Disappearances*. London: Granta.

Suetonius, Gaius Tranquillus. 1979. *The Twelve Caesars*. Translated by Robert Graves. London: Penguin Classics.

——. 2007. *The Twelve Caesars*. Rev. edn, translated by Robert Graves. London: Penguin Classics.

Summerson, John. 1949. *Heavenly Mansions and Other Essays in Architecture*. London: Cresset Press.

Tacitus, Cornelius. 2012. 'Annals'. Translated by Alfred J. Church, William J. Brodribb and Sara Bryant. Perseus Digital Library. Accessed 22 February, http://www.perseus.tufts.edu/hopper/text?doc=Perseus%3Atext%3A999.02.0078%3Abook%3D16%3Achapter%3D18.

Thomas, C. 2001. *The Wicked Queen: The Origins of the Myth of Marie-Antoinette*. London: Zone Books.

Vasari, Giorgio. 1878. *Lives of the Painters, Sculptors and Architects*. Translated by Jonathan Foster. London: George Bell and Sons.

Vitruvius. 2008. *Ten Books on Architecture, Illustrated Edition*. Translated by Morris Hicky Morgan. London: Echo Library.

Warden, Gregory. 1981. 'The Domus Aurea Reconsidered'. *Journal of the Society of Architectural Historians* 40 (4): 271–8.

Wright, Patrick. 1985. *On Living in an Old Country: The National Past in Contemporary Britain*. Oxford: Oxford University Press.

——. 1991. *A Journey through Ruins: The Last Days of London*. Oxford: Oxford University Press.

Volpe, Rita and Antonella Parisi. 2010. 'Laocoon: The Last Enigma'. Translated by Bernard Frischer. *Digital Sculpture Project*, http://www.digitalsculpture.org/laocoon/volpe_parisi/. Accessed April 2013. (This article originally appeared under the title 'Laocoonte. L'ultimo Engima', in *Archeo* 299, January 2010, pp. 26–39.)

NOTES

1. Volpe and Parisi 2010.
2. Pliny 2013 XXXVI, 4.
3. Vasari 1878, Vol. 5, 19.
4. Vasari 1878, Vol. 5 19.
5. Boethius 1960, 113.
6. Quoted in Griffin 1984, 138.
7. Suetonius 1979, 236.
8. Suetonius 1979, 229.
9. Quoted in Grant 1970, 170.
10. Suetonius 1979, 229.
11. Tacitus 2012, 16:18.
12. Boethius 1960, 113.
13. Muddiman 1928, 81.
14. Hill 1991.
15. Thegns: Old English for 'Lords': see *Concise Oxford Dictionary* 1982, 1109.
16. Collins et al. 2012, 207.
17. Collins et al. 2012, 216.
18. Collins et al. 2012, 213–14.
19. Muddiman 1928, 77.
20. Muddiman 1928, 77.
21. Collins et al. 2012, 229.
22. Quoted in Thomas 2001, 186.
23. Jallut 1969, 211.
24. Hughes 1996.
25. Hughes 1996.
26. Nolhacs 1937.
27. Translated from: 'Les salles et chambres étaient devasteés (on avait enlevé jusqu'au serrures des portes et fenêtres, superbe travail en bronze) les glaces cassées, les consoles brisées, les dessus de portes peints, arrachés … .on avait laissé les boiseries travaillées avec le plus grand art et les fenêtres en glace dont la transparence était si trompeuse qu'on ne pouvait pas remarquer de différence entre des fenêtres ouverts ou fermées … .des débris de différente espèces de jeux, des chars brisés, des fragments de figures fantastiques d'animaux ayant servie à des traineaux … .'. (Desjardins 1885, 358–9)

3

Self-ruining and Situated Vagrancy: The Geography of Performance

Benedict Anderson

VAGRANCY ACTS

Peeling back the hoarding, I enter the Jewish Museum, still under construction, in the Berlin district of Kreuzberg. It is early 2001, and sounds of construction workers echo as I move through the darkened interiors of the building. The fear of being caught trespassing by workers I can't see, but whose conversations I can hear, is coupled with the possibility of getting lost inside the building. An acute awareness of the need to self-direct my body through the semi-dark spaces, mixed with trepidation, has brought my body into conflict: tense muscles, finely tuned hearing and focused sight. Treading lightly and constantly on the move, I manage my intrusion through disappearance, creating my 'invisible' self.

To feel secure and to give myself orientation, I set about spatially noting various reference points to mark my passage: bags of concrete, chalk construction markings and electrical cables. However, as I move through the building, the angularity of each room, staircase and wall compound the disorientation I am feeling. With my camera I set about trying to capture the spaces that interest me: surfaces and textures, light qualities and construction details. To frame an image, I have to forego previous (formal) ideas of setting up a shot that will reveal, with each image I take, a type of 'ruining' of the space I am attempting to photograph (Derrida 1993, 65). Nothing appears to capture what I am seeing as I play back the images on the small digital screen.

Designed by Daniel Libeskind, the Jewish Museum inscribes Jewish/German history through the architecture of disruption. The disruption comes via the unearthing of Jewish history 'to write the ground' as the foundation of the building on which Berlin's future identity is to be formed. The building conveys the struggle of re-presenting history by becoming the subject of that history: scarred, oppressive and emancipated. Empathetically, the unfinished building I experienced distilled the dilemma of what to show of the terror that engulfed the Third Reich's 'final solution' – the *shoah*: what is left that is not burnt or buried?[1]

My reason for this act of trespassing was to try and understand various themes I was grappling with at the time, namely: German and Jewish history in counterpoint to my study of Richard Wagner's seminal opera *Der Ring des Nibelungen* (Ring Cycle). I was trying to fathom Wagner's concept of *Der Deutche Geist* (German Spirit) and the resurgence in the staging of his operas post-East/West German unification.[2] I thought by breaking into the building, I might understand the relationship between annihilation and redemption as employed by Wagner throughout the Ring Cycle. Using the photographs I had taken inside the Jewish Museum, and after altering the orientation of each image, I reconstructed my spatial narrative through motion graphics, resulting in a site-specific visual performance; a 'prototype scenography' for the staging of Wagner's Ring Cycle (Anderson and Künstler 2002).

I don't know how much time I spent inside the building, nor do I remember how I stepped back out and closed the hoarding behind me. Marked by this unlawful occupation, the effects on my body from the heightened awareness, intrusion and fear would later evolve into my concept of 'situated vagrancy', that is, the emergence of spatial opportunities of location in site-specific performance. Historically, the account of vagrancy is limited. According to the *The Shorter Oxford Dictionary*, vagrancy is 'The action or fact of wandering or digressing in mind, opinion, thought, etc. … Idle wandering with no settled habitation, occupation, or obvious means of support' (*The Shorter Oxford Dictionary* 1992, 2447). Given this description, through temporary settlement, vagrancy indicates spatial opportunity and at the same time spatial risk in the form of 'illegal occupation' of ground, which is neither public nor your own. Yet, the 'literature on vagrancy, though at first glance voluminous, is in fact quite remarkably limited in the range of perspectives it offers – far too many accounts are in the Victorian tradition of descending into an abyss' (Cook 1979, vii). Accounts of vagrancy as 'descending into the abyss' form part of the failure to recognize spatial complexity as integral to the situation of vagrancy, especially when considered in my field of site-specific performance. Unlike an abyss, my concept of situated vagrancy works in territories of space and place, capturing the appearance of bodies, spectators and performers experiencing each other, constantly redefining space towards scenographic encounters.

The experience of situated vagrancy, disorientation and fear that I felt inside Libeskind's Jewish Museum was later to resurface in another space constructed for remembrance in Peter Eisenman's *National Memorial to the Murdered Jews of Europe* ('the Memorial').[3] Covering 1.9 hectares (4.7 acres), the Memorial comprises 2,711 *Stalae* (gravestone-like concrete blocks) arranged in a systematic grid in an undulating topography. At their lowest, around the periphery of the Memorial, the *Stalae* increase in height towards the middle as does the depth of the topography. The unease of each of the *Stalae*'s lean, the porosity of the space between their mass 'over' my body, immersing my body, reproduced the interior experience I felt in Libeskind's unfinished Jewish Museum.

As I walk in broad daylight, unlike the half-darkness I experienced in the Jewish Museum, the *Stalae* exert a spatial disorientation, through an avoidance of space, yet trigger spatial conflict. The *Stalae* bring into action a dramaturgy of occurrences, accidents and vagrancies between my body and other unseen bodies.

In Eisenman's *Text as Zero*, notably influenced by Baudrillard's concept of simulacra, he suggests that '[i]n an age of simulation perhaps the one remaining example of a vanishing authenticity is violence, the destruction of the "frame", the de-framing of reference' (1993, 42). Engaging this notion, Eisenman's Memorial sets in motion a constant stream of disappearances and reappearances of bodies within the *Stalae*. Children run and play, while adults also perform their versions of 'lost and found', both seemingly implying 'misuse' or even a 'ruining' of remembrance. Yet, it is the liveliness of both adults and children that actuates the Memorial, realizing an active collective memory. Appearing and disappearing within the *Stalae*, coupled with the constant attention needed to avoid others, constitutes the ocular and interactive encounters that dominate the experience of the Memorial.

Enveloped within the Memorial, visitors work themselves into an understanding of the Holocaust, performing a tangible yet partial reflection. In this sense, the Memorial constructs a self-portrait to the enormity of the subject; its materialization, understanding and experiencing. Derrida locates the self-portrait through the concept of self-ruining: 'In the beginning there is ruin. Ruin is that which happens to the image from the moment of the first gaze … For one can just as well read the pictures of ruin as the figures of a portrait, indeed, a self-portrait' (1993, 68). The message conveyed by the Memorial is an ongoing self-portraiture of depth, despair and reflection. In this manner, Eisenman's Memorial constructs a ruining from time past to time present. In aesthetical terms, this ruining is the unstable lean of the *Stalae*, the undulation of the site, and in memorial terms, it is the remembrance of German/Jewish history through 'performative' encounters: 'It is like a ruin that does not come *after* the work but remains produced, *already from the origin*, by the advent and structure of the work' (Derrida 1993, 65, original emphasis).

Eisenman's Memorial is experienced through physical motion: run, play, lost, found; enacting the Memorial. The undulating topography coupled with the angularity of the *Stalae* destabilizes and submerges the body, trapping it through a progressive disorientation of space that is reinforced by the loss of the horizon. Being 'lost' in the Memorial is compounded by the inevitability that there is nowhere to hide. Consistent with the notion of situated vagrancy, the Memorial displaces the visitor by creating an environment of constant risk and unease. Through the *Stalae*'s mass and repetition, the Memorial's success lies in its ability to enact visitors as embodied witnesses to the horrors of the Nazi's 'final solution'. Eisenman's Memorial inscribes history not by retelling it but through scripted notations of disorientation as a way of enacting remembrance.

Out of site, both the Jewish Museum and the Memorial bring space and history into contention. Each writes German and Jewish histories through an interior and exterior dialectic as catalyst to creating meaning out of history. Material, form and program interact with history, echoing the enormity and impossibility of portraying that history – the Holocaust. The Jewish Museum and the Memorial immerse the public through separation – peeling people away from each other yet simultaneously uniting them through solitude and reflection. The public is granted the freedom of the wanderer, but like the vagrant of no abode, there is a need to be constantly in a state of awareness and on the move. Each is a struggle out of space for the representation and re-presentation of history.

3.1 *National Memorial to the Murdered Jews of Europe*
Source: Anderson 2014.

Each ensnares history and the body within acts of situated vagrancy and self-ruining in coming to terms with the subject. The Jewish Museum and the Memorial realize 'memorial' through the performative conditions of site and subject that nevertheless remain materially problematic to express.

SPATIAL OPPORTUNITIES

My practice in site-specific performance is concerned with the conditions of site: history, ruins, abandonment and instability of ground. Tied to the concept of situated vagrancy and Derrida's (1993) concept of self-ruining in self-portraiture, my work reappraises the relationships between site and history, performance and spectatorship through an expanded spatial practice of linking scenography with dramaturgy. Projects undertaken in abandoned spaces and sites of ruin have led me to understand that performance conditions site as much as site conditions performance: '[w]hence the love of ruins. And the fact that the scopic pulsion, voyeurism itself, is always on the lookout for the originary ruin' (1993, 68). Conjuring origin and imaginary, Derrida's 'originary' formulates the attraction to ruins: historical, romantic, decay, self or otherwise. The 'scopic pulsion', that is the irresistible urge to look, manifests the voyeuristic approach we bestow on self within ruins. No longer separable, performance, site and spectatorship become implicated, each a ruining of the other. Situated vagrancy co-mingles within this ruining, reflecting site, performer and spectator, to create a collective scenography for site-specific performance.

Highlighting a series of projects from my own practice, including *Patrwn* in Minde, Portugal (2010) and two current projects *Anthem Geographies* (2012) and *Performing Archaeology* (2014), the remainder of this chapter explores the concept of self-ruining and situated vagrancy through spatial opportunities. Each project develops a theory of how the site of performance complicates the space around it, expanding the notion of the interior to incorporate external conditions of site. What draws these projects together is their relationship to geography, site, history and ruining. Each will be considered in terms of what happens when the material conditions of site, performance and spectator engage with the body, evolving the concepts of self-ruining and situated vagrancy.

Patrwn: Scenography of Ruins

An unrealized yet relevant attempt to work within ruins came through an invitation to develop a series of performances in a number of disused and decaying fabric factories in the town of Minde, located 100km north of Lisbon. Once the thriving centre of Portuguese fabric production until its decline in the early 1990s, many of Minde's factories closed when cheaper manufacturing became available in China. Now dotted with decaying factory buildings, the opportunity arose through an initiative by Tiago Guedes, the artistic director of the town's yearly arts festival, to reappraise Minde's industrial heritage through visual art and performance. To be produced and funded by Welsh and Portuguese arts institutions, *Patrwn* (Welsh for pattern)

3.2 Interior view of abandoned fabric factory, Minde, Portugal
Source: Anderson 2010.

reflects the fabric-making industry and its co-production. The idea behind *Patrwn* was to transform these former spaces of industry into spaces for art events.

Working with long-term collaborator Marc Rees, we conceived an ambitious plan to thread performance and visual art across three factories located one kilometre apart. The decaying condition of two of the buildings meant working out navigational routes governed by calculated risk and public safety. The intention to embody situated vagrancy and self-ruining necessitated the ability to foreground each site's material conditions to define the aesthetical nature of the work. The dramaturgy and choreographic direction of the performances and their spectatorship demanded more than just situating the attraction of the sublime in environments of decay and ruin; it required a rethinking of the notion of the sublime to define our point of departure. Jean-François Lyotard remarks that the sublime can be defined by the limit of difference: '[t]he sublime is not a pleasure, it is a pleasure of pain: we fail to present the absolute, and that is a displeasure, but we know that we have to present it, that the faculty of feeling or imagining is called on to bring about the sensible (the image)' (1991, 126).

Lyotard's notion of the sublime returns us to Derrida's foregrounding of ruin as the impetus of capturing oneself in self-portraiture. Interpreting the returned mirrored gaze in the act of self-portraiture gives rise to the displeasure of self-perception. To capture is to self-ruin the image of what one is seeing:

> In the beginning, at the origin, there was ruin. At the origin comes ruin; ruin comes to the origin, it is what first comes and happens to the origin, in the

> beginning. With no promise of restoration. This dimension of the ruinous
> simulacrum has never threatened – quite the contrary – the emergence of a work.
> (Derrida 1993, 65)

In spatial terms, Derrida's concept of self-portraiture as self-ruining (Rembrandt's self-portraits are an example) and Lyotard's notion of the sublime enacted through displeasure raise a third spatial concept: the indeterminacy of site and boundary between performer and spectator. Jose V. Ciprut positions indeterminacy by describing its counterpoint: 'Determinism is the philosophical conception and claim that every physical event and every instance of human cognition, volition, and action is causally determined by a continual, uninterrupted sequence of prior events. It confines chance, jettisons mystery, limits the inexplicable, and restricts doubt of total randomness' (2008, 1).

Developing the potential indeterminacy of site in relation to performance and spectatorship brought a return of the hesitant anticipation I experienced as I moved through the Jewish Museum: 'Anticipation guards against precipitation, it makes advances, puts the moves on space in order to be the first to take, in order to be forward in the movement of taking hold, making contact, or apprehending' (Derrida 1993, 4).

Patrwn was conceived through situated vagrancy coupled with an attention to indeterminacy of site and territories of the performance. Performances would be based on the performer's ability to negotiate the unstable structures and surfaces of ruin and decay, as much as the audience's ability to occupy the same spaces for their viewing. Importantly, industrial waste was still very evident inside the factories, resulting in a miasma of toxic odours and seepage from inks, dyes and fabric bleaching. Constantly on the move, performers and audience would anticipate each other, choreographically and dramaturgically 'writing' themselves into the spaces of the performance on the one hand and their erasure on the other. The resulting 'room writing' within each site would determine the performance and its spectatorship, evolving to 'writing the performance' formed out-of-site. Transferring this notion of 'writing the performance' establishes a duality in the authoring of performance without consciously knowing.

> But when, in addition, I write without seeing … in the night or with my eyes
> glued elsewhere, a schema already comes to life in my memory. At once virtual,
> potential, and dynamic, this graphic crosses all the borders separating the senses,
> its being-in-potential at once visual and auditory, motile and tactile. Later, its
> form will come to light like a developed photograph. But for now, at this very
> moment when I write, I see literally nothing of these letters. (Derrida 1993, 4)

Conceived through blindness, Derrida's 'writing without seeing' goes some way to pinpoint my own practice of how I 'read' site as performance without consciously projecting propositions for site-performance-audience relationships. What comes into play are 'sense visions' for reading both the spatial dynamics of site for performance and its spectatorship, something I previously experienced in Eisenman's Memorial. Martin Jay argues that 'vision hostage to desire is not necessarily always better than casting a cold eye, a sight from the situated context of a body in the world may not always see things that are visible' (1998, 19). Jay's 'vision hostage to desire' can be linked to Derrida's 'self-ruining', for the aesthetics of reflection are at the core of what we see rather than what appears, whereas 'casting a cold eye' whilst implicating judgment, is derived from recognition and acceptance. Sensing and visioning performance in spaces unknown can be aligned to Derrida's concept of 'blind writing' and Ciprut's indeterminacy (2008), wherein: '[a]s rare and theatrical as these experiences may be – I called them "accidental" – they nonetheless impose themselves as an exemplary *mise en scène*… by feeling out an area that he must recognize without yet cognizing it' (Derrida 1993, 4). Foregrounding and occupying the factories' unstable environments and combining Derrida's accidental *mise en scène* brought together new opportunities for spatial negotiation of site-specific performance and spectatorship.

The scenography of ruins is the sublime attraction to the potential of site and ruin in the making of performance, wherein 'the performative fiction that engages the spectator in the signature of the work is given to be seen only *through* the blindness that it produces as its truth' (Derrida 1993, 65, original emphasis). Such 'truth' can be found in the conditions of site, decay and abandonment where 'performative fiction' is cast by site rather than cast on site. Both situated vagrancy and self-ruining serve to script the scenography of ruins by opening up new territories between site, performance and audience. No longer is the performance and audience marked through spaces of separation as realized in the architecture of the theatre; rather, performers and audience engage with the indeterminacy of site and the practice of spatial occupation. Like Minde's economic decline, funding for *Patrwn* has temporally fallen to its own economic ruin, reflecting the current indeterminate status of cultural production in Portugal. *Patrwn* remains a proposition of ideologies for an as yet un-scored scenography of ruins.

Plaza of Nations: Performing Geography

Situated vagrancy and self-ruining can be further highlighted through a current project exploring boundary, geography and national identity. Conceived by Yekatherina Bobrova and myself, the project *Plaza of Nations* marks a disturbance to the jurisdiction of space in the symbols that speak the laws pertaining to national identity. National anthems, it can be argued, behave in the same way national flags do. National anthems serve as a country's mouthpiece in words and music, as national flags emblematically serve through composition, colour and design. Metaphorically, both symbolize the interior identity of a nation designed for an exterior resonance within the world. Flags flutter in the wind to reveal their design, while anthems require a score for musicians to play and words for the public to sing. Flags and anthems come together in public performances such as national day celebrations, state funerals (soldiers, presidents, the highly honoured) and sporting events such as the Olympic Games. Anthems and flags are not only the visible symbols of a nation's identity but also conjure the space of that country, that is, its borders, relations with neighbours and 'place' in the world.

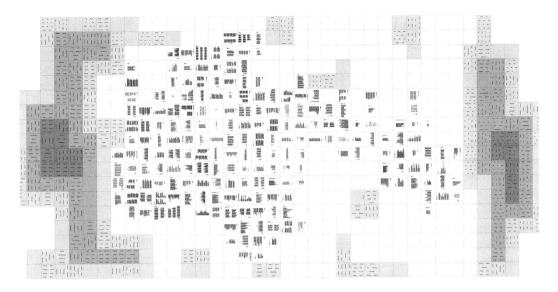

3.3 Plan of anthems layout, *Plaza of Nations*
Source: Image courtesy of Yekatherina Bobrova 2013.

Figuratively sited in the Jubilee Gardens, in the location of the London Eye (a towering Ferris wheel offering a view of the London skyline on the banks of the River Thames), the site for the *Plaza of Nations* draws on the diversity of local and international visitors attracted daily to this tourist magnet. The concept of *Plaza of Nations* is to create a plaza of national anthems as a spatial geographical landscape that merges cultural and political divisions separating nation states. Miwon Kwon suggests that the intersection between site and concept is born from a discursive relationship: 'Consequently, although the site of action or intervention (physical) and the site of effects/reception (discursive) are conceived to be continuous, they are nonetheless pulled apart' (2002, 29). As continents are 'pulled apart', and in the process countries are defined either by natural geographies such as continents, rivers, mountains and seas, or by human-made borders dividing one country from the other, the *Plaza of Nations* seeks to re-form these separations into a single and interconnected site. As such, the plaza is a 'walk-on world', shaped without borders, yet inscribed with the lyrics of all the national anthems.

The layout of the plaza is determined by the positioning of each country in relation to its global position, '[w]hich is to say, the site is now structured (inter) textually rather than spatially, and its model is not a map but an itinerary, a fragmentary sequence of events and actions *through* spaces' (Kwon 2002, 29). To determine each nation's position, the world map is flattened and placed over a plateau measuring 38 × 18 metres. Arranged in a grid formation referencing latitude and longitude increments, each nation is represented equally by a 1 × 1 metre sandstone block. Dedicated as the 'site of inscription', each national anthem is inscribed into the sandstone block in the presiding official language of the country along with any other official languages, as well as English. All of the current 192 internationally-recognized sovereign states are represented in the *Plaza of Nations*. In addition, the 10 states with limited international recognition, often blocked by the non-recognition of another state, are equally represented, for example: Nagorno-Karabakh by Azerbaijan, Taiwan by China and state of

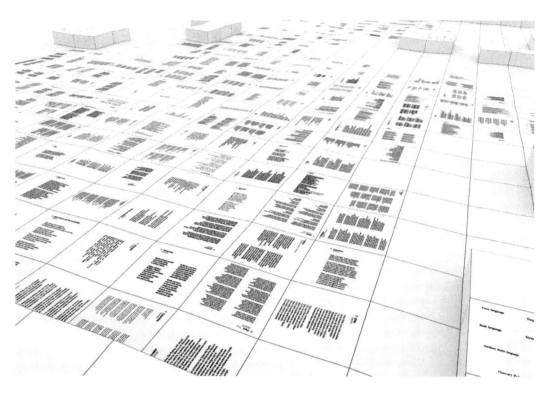

3.4 Perspective view of anthems layout, *Plaza of Nations*
Source: Image courtesy of Yekatherina Bobrova 2013.

Palestine by Israel. The geography of the plaza is also formulated by recognizing the diverse and interwoven history that languages have played throughout time. 'Unearthing' the relatively recent extinction of many languages, including those of indigenous peoples, the plaza aims to be an inclusive representation of the past and present global diversity. To acknowledge endangered and extinct indigenous languages, each is marked by their inscription into the sandstone blocks framing the plaza's boundary.

To differentiate between nations, each anthem is distinguishable by its own font, amounting to the use of 202 fonts. The sandstone blocks are joined at a 1:20 gradient creating an undulating topography forming a 'foundation stone' reflecting a 'world geography' and mirroring the United Nations Charter.[4] Interspersed seating surrounds and emerges from within the plaza, allowing for the public to sit and hear recorded anthems through an audio system embedded in the seating. Conversely, at a steady walking pace, visitors can follow each country's national anthem as it oscillates around the plaza.

The plaza invites the public to walk on and over nations and their anthems. Each walk enacts the act of situated vagrancy; a stepping onto the moral, social and political ideologies, as well as the sovereignty enshrined in each anthem. As nationalistic fervour has drawn the world into divisions through military, colonial, religious and economic appropriations of space, the public work themselves in and out of these divisions through vagrant occupations of this recollected and relocated world. Territorially, sovereignty becomes revolutionized through the ruining and repudiation of borders between each country. Performatively, the plaza activates the public to cross borders and to step on the politics of identity separating nations.

As wanderers crossing invisible borders, the public becomes implicated in and out of the spaces of nationhood through the indeterminism of situated vagrancy. Itinerate crossings over and on nations construct a geography of performance through a self-organizing body-politic for a self-choreographing public performance. To stand and read Israel's anthem means standing on the Palestinian anthem and vice versa. Over time, the public becomes incriminated in the erasure of the anthems by wearing down the sandstone blocks as they read the anthems, evolving the plaza into a geographical record of past national separation.

In the *Plaza of Nations*, situated vagrancy becomes an indelible public act for self-ruining of one's own and other nation states by removing the boundaries of national identity. However, in *Patrwn*, situated vagrancy was conceived through the conditions of decay and ruin within the fabric factories, enacting the notion of self-ruining in both performance and spectatorship. Through situated vagrancy, *Plaza of Nations* incites performance and spectatorship by beginning with a decisive acknowledgement of national identity and specificity of place in the world, yet ends with their ruining. Finally, the *Plaza of Nations* performs geography by rewriting the ground through the erasure of territorial division. This re-writing in turn constructs the social space in which the public becomes implicated in removing the dogma of sovereignty, jurisdiction, space and occupation to recast the ideology of what constitutes nation and state, ground and territory.

Teufelsberg: Performing Archaeology

I have a collection of archive images showing women, men, boys and girls, vast holes, trucks, trains and rubble. The images detail the clearing of rubble from the bombed-out buildings resulting from the air war on Berlin between 1942 and 1945 during the Second World War (1939–45). The emptying of Berlin's mounds of rubble via a system of small trains and rail tracks that traversed the city's temporal topographies would reappear in the rise of seven *Trümmerberge* (rubble hills) constructed in Berlin's metropolitan regions. In addition to the seven *Trümmerberge*, the eighth and largest hill is *Teufelsberg* (Devil's Mountain), constructed in the outer western Berlin district of Wilmersdorf. To peer into my photographic archive is to view people captured in the physical labour of clearing rubble from Berlin's streets, leading to the rise of the rubble hills; working with ruins.

Where there were no trains, women and men would push the carriages of rubble to waiting trucks in order to be carted away. Besides the trucks and rail carriages, the clearing of rubble was a vast task carried out by hand and by tools of the hand. This hard manual labour of the *Trümmerfrauen* (rubble women) and the men, boys and girls, singularly changed the overall geography of Berlin, making possible the disappearance of the destroyed city and its reappearance as walk-up public parks. Yet within this labour, on closer inspection of the images, the clearing away of rubble show a people working with resilience as a way to cope and reply to the destruction of their city. According to James Craig and Matt Ozga-Lawn, this 'suggests a certain kind of immunity to trauma, a shrugging-off of the chaos of events – a bouncing back' (2012, 9).

3.5 Feldbahnloren Konigsplatz, Platz der Republik 1948, Landesarchiv Berlin/Gnilka, Ewald; F Rep. 290, Nr. 0172325
Source: Image courtesy of Landesarchiv Berlin.

Conceived through situated vagrancy and self-ruining, my project is to concentrate on the construction of *Teufelsberg* and mount an archaeological excavation to unearth the remnants of the lost city of Berlin and build a memorial to the *Trümmerfrauen*. According to Andrew Benjamin, 'The remnant enables the co-presence of destruction and creation. Creation occurs by recognizing or holding onto the remnant. This is a form of destruction precisely because any intervention in a site is a destructive act' (2012, 76).

Benjamin's 'recognizing or holding onto the remnant' is both apparent and historically pertinent with Berlin's history of destruction and reconstruction. Nazi Germany's First Architect Albert Speer developed this vast urban plan hand in hand with his famous treatise titled *Theory of Ruin Value* (1970). Speer and Hitler's building schemes for Berlin, constructed in the lasting material of stone, were conceived to pass into ruins as remnants of the 1,000 year *Reich*. This passage from grandeur to ruin was supposed to produce a simulation that would include Berlin as the third cornerstone, after Athens and Rome, in the Classical ordering of modern civilization.

By the end of the war in 1945, Speer's 1,000-year theory of ruin had reached its zenith in just three years (1943–45) through the Allies' policy of total destruction in its aerial bombing campaign of 131 German towns and cities. Berlin's post-war reconstruction saw Speer's plan realized not through grand architectural ruins to rival Athens and Rome but as new urban geographies constructed out of ruins. Berlin's entry into the triangle of Classicalism came in the form of a shared topography with Athens and Rome in the construction of Berlin's seven hills,

3.6 Teufelsberg Trümmerschutt 1952, Landesarchiv Berlin/Schwab, E., F Rep. 290, Nr. 0264853
Source: Image courtesy of Landesarchiv Berlin.

the *Trümmerberge*, and the additional *Teufelsberg*. This reordering of Speer's scheme supplants the poetics of nature that inserted itself into Berlin. No longer a flat city, it is now a walk-up city, a city of views, topographies and geographical links. Collectively, *Teufelsberg* and the *Trümmerberge* perform 'annihilation geography' out of the ruins of Berlin.

Despite its association with ruins, death and destruction, there is something profound about walking up *Teufelsberg*. Firstly, it is a big hill; in fact it comprises three hills. Secondly, it is human-made with the highest point rising 115 metres; and thirdly, it is entirely constructed from the remnants of war, yet it is a veritable playground. In summer, you can run and fly a kite, stroll through the forest, picnic and swim in the *Teufelssee* (Devil's Lake). In winter, you can go tobogganing in the snow. My first experience of walking up *Teufelsberg* was knowing that I was literally walking on and metaphorically occupying former people's houses, tens of metres below me. As I walked, my temporal occupation of the surface of *Teufelsberg* brought history into contention, and brought back the same type of feeling I experienced in the Jewish Museum and the Memorial.

Returning to my archive collection, one picture shows a female driver, a *Trümmerfrauen* sitting on the bonnet of a truck with a wide smile, a man in a long coat shaking her hand. Below, and attached to the truck's grille, is a sign that has 10,000,000 m³ written on it, and the year is 1952. The figure stands for the amount of rubble in millions of cubic metres that had been carted from the streets of Berlin. Other pictures I have show 21,000,000 and finally 25,000,000. The *Trümmerfrauen's* achievements are a cause for celebration in ridding the rubble from Berlin's choked streets –

a vast undertaking given the city's complete annihilation. From the early 1950s to the mid-1960s, the images move from black and white to the typical brownish tones of photos from instamatic cameras of the 1970s. The photographs I have accumulated are my ready-made archive that charts the history of *Teufelsberg* from its planning in 1947 to its completion in 1968.

The building of *Teufelsberg* repositioned Speer's theory of ruin to a new plan – a plan of physical emancipation – evident in the self-portraits of the archive images. The psychological transference from the horrors of destruction in the ruining of the city of Berlin to the hand of labour, and the exhaustion of the work in shifting the ground of that city, establishes new and alarmingly dislocated associations to devastation and ruin. W.G. Sebald (2004) charts the collective impartiality permeating every level of German civilian life and literature that awoke in the aftermath of the Second World War. He attributes a collective German forgetfulness to a 'self-anaesthesia' 'shown by a community that seemed to have emerged from a war of annihilation without any signs of psychological impairment' (2004, 11).

Sebald's 'self-anaesthesia' draws on images of the annihilation of German towns and cities during the Second World War:

> [T]he question of whether and how it could be justified was never the subject of open debate in Germany after 1945, no doubt mainly because a nation which had murdered and worked to death millions of people in its camps could hardly call on the victorious powers to explain the military and political logic that dictated the destruction of German cities. (2004, 13)

This, Sebald informs us, accounts for the lack of any substantial historical documentation from a German perspective of their horror and loss in the war. Sebald tells us that where there were accounts, they 'did not alter the fact that the images of this horrifying chapter of our history have never really crossed the threshold of the national consciousness' (2004, 13). Sebald's 'self-anaesthesia' finds its place in the spatial anaesthesia contained in *Teufelsberg* in the form of the buried and forgotten city and in the memories of Berliners. For example, the forest of trees, shrubs and flowers now covering the rubble of former homes and lives of Berlin pre-1945 adds to the post-1945 forgetting of Berlin's destruction. Smout Allen argues that human-controlled landscape 'has taken on an artificial patination. Alien materials interrupt the processes of growth and decay. New and evolving features created by man are, to an extent, absorbed by the fluid and yielding nature of our surroundings' (2007, 6). Given that the trees and shrubs planted in *Teufelsberg* are real, I can't help but think of their 'plastic' and 'alien' connection to the history of Berlin's destruction contributing somehow to its forgetting. This forgetting can be further illuminated by Sebald's reference to the Danish reporter Stig Dagerman, who, on a train in Hamburg in 1945, distinguished himself as a foreigner, for 'no one looked out of the windows, and he was identified as a foreigner "because he looked out"' (2004, 30). Out of *Teufelsberg* rises the self-portrait of forgetting: geography for looking away rather than looking in.

Spatially thinking through this last example highlights the relationships between situated vagrancy and self-ruining through an archaeology of performance. To do this serves two purposes: the first allows for a constant change in the reading of the site; the second allows *Teufelsberg* to remain indifferent to Berlin's lost urbanity now covered by the park. In this way, site, occupation and ruin become implicated through Berlin's disappearance and sublime recasting as a phantom city. *Teufelsberg* reconstructs Berlin's self-portrait of destruction and ruining to its present sedate environment as a walk-up park in which one can view the *Neu Berlin* (New Berlin) falling away in the distance. The photographs of the collective labour of the *Trümmerfrauen*, girls, boys and men, hour by hour, day by day, year by year, in the construction of *Teufelsberg* illustrate Derrida's concept of self-portraiture of a people within ruins, physically and immemorially.

The future of my project has been spatially thought but not yet spatially conceived. My conception of performing archaeology is to re-image *Teufelsberg* through the concept of the self-portrait. To conceive a self-portrait for *Teufelsberg* through archaeology is to excavate from the buried city of Berlin to reveal the realities of the *Trümmerfrauen*; the labour of their hands and the hardships they endured. The proposed memorial comes not through the creation of a figurative form but through a gestural archaeology of extracted cores of rubble. By 'unearthing' the surface of *Teufelsberg*, by drilling and extracting its rubble more than 60 years after its building, the project will reform Sebald's concept of 'self-anaesthesia' through self-portraiture. The project is designed as a series of standing monograms of core rubble directed to the memory of the *Trümmerfrauen* of Berlin. In varying heights and widths, the monogrammed self-portrait of ruins will consist of 21 standing columns accounting for each year of *Teufelsberg's* construction (1947–68). The memorial for *Teufelsberg* re-enacts history as performance archaeology: to the remembrance of the *Trümmerfrauen* and as a way of accounting for the buried city of Berlin.

CONCLUSION

Reflecting on my experiences in the Jewish Museum and Memorial brought an awareness of an emergent self-portrait within ruins. Employing the concepts of situated vagrancy and self-ruining as instrumental in my thinking and approach to *Patwrn*, *Plaza of Nations* and *Teufelsberg*, I have come to understand that performance, site and spectatorship become implicated: each a self-ruining of the other. In this way, situated vagrancy and self-ruining foreground a simulacrum of the self-portrait and site; performer and spectator as one. Through vagrant occupations and constant motion, performer and spectator co-mingle within ruining, reflecting site and history to create a collective scenographic performance. Common to each project, site, history and spectatorship are activated through material compositions as active participants that choreographically and dramaturgically 'write the performance' of the work. *Patwrn*, *Plaza of Nations* and *Teufelsberg* are therefore not only connected to concepts of situated vagrancy and self-ruining but also as site-specific performances staged within complex material spaces that contest the materialization of history by embodying that history. Through their relationship to material, ground and the under-surface, each project establishes its geography by 'writing the ground' with an attention to history.

The Greek origin of geography tells us that *geo* is earth and *graphien* is to write. Reading geography requires comprehending the writing of the ground, whereas archaeology unearths ground to write histories of the land. Topography, on the other hand, records and measures ground, informing cartography to write the terrain. These feature in all three projects. *Patwrn: Scenography of Ruins* draws on the specificity of site to write a dialectic of ruins between performer and audience, underwriting the ground. *Plaza of Nations: Performing Geography* writes the site as a performative ruining of geography, boundaries and national symbols. *Teufelsberg: Performing Archaeology* on the other hand, unearths land to extract ruins so as to build remembrance to the *Trummerfrauen* of Berlin. Out-of-site, *Patwrn*, *Plaza of Nations* and *Teufelsberg* perform a turning over of site to unearth a scenography, geography and archaeology of ruins. Each site is a struggle out of space and out of history, evolving self-ruining and situated vagrancy.

REFERENCES

Anderson, Benedict. 2012. 'Out of Space: The Rise of Vagrancy in Scenography'. *Performance Research* 18 (3): 109–18.

Anderson, Benedict and Lars Künstler. 2002. *In Angle/Im Winkel*. Digital animation. 5.15 mins.

Ciprut, Jose V., ed. 2008. *Indeterminacy: The Mapped, the Navigable and the Uncharted*. Cambridge: MIT Press.

Cook, Tim, ed. 1979. *Vagrancy: Some New Perspectives*. London: Academic Press.

Craig, James A. and Matt Ozga-Lawn. 2012. *Pamphlet Architecture 32: Resilience*. New York: Princeton Architectural Press.

Derrida, Jacques. 1993. *Memoirs of the Blind: The Self-Portrait and Other Ruins*. Translated by Pascale-Ann Brault and Michael Naas. Chicago: University of Chicago Press.

Eisenman, Peter. 1993. 'Text as Zero: Or: The Destruction of Narrative'. In *Re-working Eisenman*, by Peter Eisenman, 42. London: Academy Publications.

Jay, Martin. 1988. 'Scopic Regimes of Modernity'. In *Vision and Visuality*, edited by Hal Foster, 3–23. Seattle: Bay Press.

Kwon, Miwon. 2002. *One Place After Another: Site-Specific Art and Locational Identity*. Cambridge: MIT Press.

Lyotard, Jean Francois. 1991. *The Inhuman: Reflections on Time*. Translated by Geoffrey Bennington and Rachel Bowlby. Stanford: Stanford University Press.

Sebald, W.G. 2004. *On The Natural History of Destruction*. London: Penguin.

Smout, Allen. 2007. *Augmented Landscapes: Pamphlet Architecture 28*. New York: Princeton Architectural Press.

Speer, Albert. 1970. *Inside the Third Reich: Memoirs by Albert Speer*. Translated by Richard Winston and Clara Winston. London: Weidenfeld and Nicolson.Stead, Naomi. 2003. 'The Value of Ruins: Allegories of Destruction in Benjamin and Speer'. *Form/Work: An Interdisciplinary of the Built Environment* 6: 51–64.

The Shorter Oxford Dictionary. 1992 edn. Oxford: Clarendon Press.

NOTES

1. *Shoah* is Hebrew for Holocaust – the murder of 6,000,000 European Jews between 1942 and 1945 by the Nazi regime during the Second World War.

2. West and East Germany were formally unified in 1990 after the fall of the Berlin Wall in 1989.

3. The original competition for Germany's National Holocaust Memorial has a long history. After Eisenman (with then collaborator Richard Serra) won the competition, the design was for many years debated in the German *Bundestag* (Parliament). There was concern for its aesthetical form and for its capacity to embody the 'right aesthetics' expected for Germany's National Holocaust Memorial. This debate kept the project in a perpetual state of limbo until finally a decision was announced accepting the design with changes.

4. For example Article 2: 'The Organization is based on the principle of the sovereign equality of all its Members'. Source: http://www.un.org/en/documents/charter/chapter1.shtml.

4

'Crude Hints Towards an History of my House in L[incoln's] I[nn]Fields':[1] Occupying Ruin

Lynn Churchill

INTRODUCTION

> *The Museum is the colossal mirror in which man finally contemplates himself, in short, in all his aspects, finds himself literally admirable and abandons himself to the ecstasy expressed in all the art journals. (Bataille 1995, 64)*

In his critique of architecture, Georges Bataille denounced modern architecture as complicit in the politics and economics of human experience. He condemned the architectural typology 'museum' for its role in editing and controlling how we see and understand ourselves in relation to our spatial and temporal experience of the immediate context and the world beyond. Specifically, Bataille was interested in 'the links formed provisionally between visitors and visited' (1996, 23), drawing our attention to visitors being affected by the provocation of the physically and temporally displaced object, and the way in which the object from elsewhere elicits 'devoted' contemplation. He explains:

> *when a native of the Ivory Coast places polished stone axes of the Neolithic period in a container filled with water, bathes in the container, and sacrifices chickens to what he believes to be* thunderstones *(fallen from heaven in a thunderclap), he is doing no more than prefiguring the attitude of enthusiasm and profound communion with objects which characterises the visitor to a modern museum. (1995, 64, original emphasis)*

It is with a similar perspective that this chapter considers two seemingly disparate museums: Sir John Soane's nineteenth-century London house crammed with books, paintings, fake archaeological relics, architectural drawings and models and the ephemera of daily life such as lottery tickets; and the Kodja Place Visitor and Interpretive Centre (2007), filled with reflections on the past and fuelled by the community's collective hopes for the future. Isolated, culturally diverse and fractured, the Kojonup community came together in the 1990s to confront past deeds, and to re-tell their (at times) disturbing story through the museum as medium.

Somewhat in contrast, Soane's motivation to curate his own house as museum appears to have evolved and intensified over a lifetime of occupying his creation.

Perhaps typically, in both instances the two museums stemmed from the human desire to articulate the future by reconstructing the past. As entities, these museums have drawn from the past, editing, re-framing and re-positioning matter, identity, temporality and loci for the purposes of making their own myths explicit.

Therefore, this inquiry is not driven by curiosity about their collections. Rather, it is motivated by the spirit of interrogating 'occupation'; the repositioning of often mysterious remnants from elsewhere in time and place. My aim is to create a context in which to consider the shifting of relics and human identity. Moving on beyond Bataille's cynicism, the intention here is to consider the construction and organization of the exterior world as a means to re-present and make explicit our inner self's (individual and collective) form and lineage, our shape, place and connections across time.

Therefore, it is not simply a question of the reliquary displaying objects within. Rather, it is one of the philosophy of alchemy – that we create an understanding of who and where we are through our orchestration of the material world. In contemplation of re-framing and re-positioning matter and meaning in relation to human occupation, I turn to Carl Jung and the seminal question: 'what is your myth – the myth in which you do live?' (2010, 171). As I will discuss further, Jung's methodological approach was alchemy, a process of constructing the exterior world as a means to affecting his interior world – he 'had very soon seen that analytical psychology coincided in a most curious way with alchemy' (205). Hence the provocation on which this chapter speculates is: whatever our myth, our struggle with occupation of the interior and exterior worlds is orchestrated through the construction of matter, and the process of constructing the exterior world is one of ruin, repudiation and revolution – things most of us will come to know.

AN HISTORY OF MY HOUSE

Walking through Soane's house in February 2013, almost two centuries after his death, my experience was as though moving through one of the artist Giovanni Battista Piranesi's etchings, four of which were presented to the young Soane by the artist himself when the two met in 1778 (Wilton-Ely 2013, 12). Trained in architecture and stage design, Piranesi's experimental topographical engravings are both architectural and dramatic. His radical use of light, shadow and imaginative composition were controversial, as is evidenced by Sir William Chambers' critique in 1777:

> That men, unacquainted with the remains of Ancient Buildings, should indulge in licentious and whimsical combinations is not a matter of surprise, but that a man who had passed all his life in the bosom of Classical Art, and in the contemplation of majestic ruins of Ancient Rome, observing their sublime effects and grand combinations, a man who had given innumerable examples how truly

> he felt the value of the noble Simplicity of those buildings, that such a man, with such examples before his eyes, should have mistaken Confusion for Intricacy, and undefined lines and forms for Classical variety, is scarcely to be believed; yet such a man is Piranesi. (Quoted in Wilton-Ely 2013, 92)

Soane was soon caught between the seminal impact of Piranesi's visions and the views of his mentor, Chambers. Nonetheless, and somewhat strangely, Soane later re-presented Chambers' critique in 1806 to his own students at the Royal Academy where he had become a professor (Wilton-Ely 2013, 92). Meanwhile, back at home Soane was beginning to work on his museum. What Soane had begun to compose was a seemingly random three-dimensional cacophony of discordant objects resembling one of Piranesi's fantasies.

Like Piranesi, Soane developed mastery over natural light, and so as daylight passes over the house's openings, the light falls for a time on one object after another as though directing the viewer's contemplation. So it seems Piranesi may have catalysed Soane's first imaginings of his house-as-museum, and then inspired the decades of curatorial process that had begun in 1792 when Soanes purchased and rebuilt number 12, Lincoln's Inn Fields.

Conceived with intent as a ruin of the future, Soane's house was bequeathed to the British nation via an Act of Parliament (Knox 2009, 34)[2] enforced on his death in 1837, with the proviso that the entity he had created remain as he left it: crammed with Soane's closely curated selection of books, commissioned artworks, replica objects including false teeth, and the ephemera of daily life such as cheque book stumps and dinner invitation cards. In a document he wrote, printed and circulated in 1835–36, Soane explained:

> The natural desire to leaving these works of Art subject as little as possible to the chance of their being removed from the positions relatively assigned to them; having been arranged as studies for my own mind, and being intended similarly to benefit the Artists of future generations. (Quoted in Palmer 2009, 78)[3]

The Picture Room is one of the many rooms in Soane's house that is now open to the public. The more than 100 pictures hang from moveable planes that effectively reveal and disappear the works as the large hinged panels open and close. Amongst these are significant works such as William Hogarth's satirical *An Election* (1754) and a number of ink and wash drawings by Piranesi, ten of which are detailed drawings depicting three ancient Greek temples rediscovered in 1746 ('Piranesi's Paestum: Master Drawings Uncovered' 2013) in Paestum in southern Italy. Typical of Piranesi's evocative, imaginative and surreal compositions, these drawings capture the ruins of three massive Doric temples from approximately 500 BC in moody, poetic light.

By 1812 Soane had expanded into number 13, where he incorporated the gallery, and then later he expanded again into number 14. Amassed over a lifetime, Soane's eclectic collection was mindfully positioned in relation to his finely tuned orchestration of light and space. In the absence of artificial light and left to the mercy of the vagaries of daylight, the collection and the spaces he created appear capricious, altering dramatically with diurnal and seasonal rhythms. Resembling Piranesi's drawings, the house filled with broken objects that are often fakes, appearing mysteriously from somewhere else, is compellingly beautiful. In symbiosis, the composition fills the mind with questions. What would it be to live amongst this collection? What was he doing?

In addition to paintings by Hogarth, Turner and others, amongst this impressive private collection, there are thousands of architectural drawings by architects Christopher Wren, William Chambers and George Dance; the sarcophagus of King Seti I from the Valley of the Kings; and 150 architectural models including one of the 1820 excavations at Pompeii (Knox 2012). Soane's house as museum is, as I will discuss, a complex and ambiguous portrait of a man obsessed with compiling evidence to control his 'reception by posterity' (Palmer 2009, 67).

THE EXCAVATION

The source of Soane's passion for the enigma of the ruin can be traced to Chambers' introduction of Soane to King George III, who awarded the young architect a travelling scholarship to Italy, where he spent two years from 1778 visiting the archaeological sites of Naples and Paestum, and sketching Classical and Renaissance buildings (Thornton and Dorey 1992).

Two significant works emerged from his tour as influential: initially, Sir William Hamilton's three-volume *Campi Phlegraei* (quoted in Thornton and Dorey 1992, 17–19), the first two volumes of which were published in Naples in 1779 and the third in 1799 following the volcanic eruption of Mount Vesuvius. Then 33 years later, in 1812, Soane's own manuscript, a fiction entitled 'Crude Hints Towards an History of My House' was written from the point of view of an imagined future in which a fictional narrator contemplated the ruin of Soane's house and speculated on its creator and his creation.

Throughout this manuscript, Soane flirts with imaginings and exciting sensations of visitors in the future stumbling upon disassociated fragments re-presenting secrets and mysteries of his own life. Could this ruin be the place of worship, his narrator muses, or a temple, a place of catacombs and crypts? But what of the 'strange and mixed assemblage of ancient works or rather copies of (cast from) them, for many are not stone or marble … some have supposed it might have been for the advancement of Architectural knowledge' (Soane 1812, 69).[4] He became compelled to construct his material world to represent his life beyond the limitations of mortality – as mythology.

In 1992, perhaps as Soane had fantasized, Peter Thornton wrote about one of Soane's final acts days before his death in 1837 aged 83, in which he positioned a winged figure of Victory on a tall pedestal in the Breakfast Room before a large watercolour of his wife's tomb: '[Soane] saw the juxtaposition of these works of art as victory over Death' (Thornton and Dorey 1992, 94).

Soane's conceit was the value and intrigue he imagined his house would offer future generations. That this mythical construct would endure. His narrator continues:

> *What an admirable lesson is this work to shew the vanity of all human expectations – the man who founded this place piously imagined that from the fruits of his pious industry, and the rewards of his persistence [and] application he had laid the foundation of a family of artists. (Soane 1812, 72)*

However, as Helen Dorey points out in her introductory notes to Soane's manuscript:

> *the spirit of light-hearted imaginative speculation … soon descends into something much darker and more personal. The figure of the 'founder' or 'creator' of the ruins under discussion gradually comes to the fore and the text becomes a tortured and bitter lament for the failure of his dynastic ambitions and an account of perceived vendettas against him. The frenetic handwriting [of the original manuscript] indicates an almost manic outpouring written in great agony of mind and according to the annotations, in just three weeks. (Soane 1812, 54)*[5]

Soane's narrator descends into imagining that:

> *at last he had raised a nest of wasps about him sufficient to sting the strongest man to death – Revenge levelled [fabricated] tales of dishonour at him, which no innocence of heart or integrity of conduct could set right and to wind up the tragedy cruelty and cowardice, twin ruffians set on by malice in the dark combined together to strike at his infirmities and mistakes:- then persecutions and other misfortunes of a more direct and domestic nature preyed on his mind … melancholy, brooding constantly over an accumulation of evils brought him into a state little short of mental derangement. (Soane 1812, 72)*

So it is through this manuscript that we are able to understand something of Soane's 'inner pressure' and how his obsessive work to construct the material world for the purposes of re-iterating his position (in architecture and domestic life) was in fact at the same time work towards coming to terms with the more esoteric reality of his sense of self, his introjection and projection. What Soane's fiction makes explicit is who he understood himself to be and how he understood that the external world perceived and acknowledged this. Read in conjunction with the constructed reality of his museum, Soane's manuscript may be recognized, in Jungian terms, as an articulation of his own 'myth'.

In reality, while Soane began life relatively humbly as the son of a builder, he became a very successful figure within the British architectural profession. In his very early years as an emerging architect he was awarded Silver and Gold medals and a travelling scholarship that enabled him to spend three years in Rome and southern Italy. By 1806 he was appointed Professor of Architecture at the Royal Academy; he was knighted in 1831, and his substantial body of work, that included the interiors of the Prime Minister's residence at number 10 Downing Street, was recognized in 1835 when the architects of England awarded him the Gold Medal (Wilton-Ely 2013, 9).

However, while Soane attracted significant commissions throughout his career, including numerous Government buildings, the Law Courts at Westminster and appointment as the Architect to the Bank of England, his work, perhaps inevitably given its substance, was at times subjected to disparagement, which he found difficult to accept. He became known for his sensitivity to criticism. Perhaps it was as a consequence of this that Soane spent many years closely editing the documentation of his life – his correspondence, and his reflections on and explanations of moves made and judgements challenged (Palmer 2009).[6] So he re-positioned an account of his intimate and public life to re-present himself into the future – after death.

This cacophony of domestic and professional documents may have befuddled even Soane himself. The agglomeration appears not only to leave messages but also to create gaps and raise questions. As witnessed by his assistant George Wightwick, clarity and completion seemed to elude Soane. George Wightwick, whom Soane had engaged in the mid-1820s to assist in the writing of Soane's rebuttal of humiliating criticism of his design of the New Law Courts in Westminster, described Soane as a difficult personality, frustrated by himself, 'sporadic [in his] attempts to make his meaning clear' and complained that 'day after day a somewhat differently worded preamble was [their] chief occupation' (quoted in Palmer 2009, 68). When working with Soane, Wightwick found it difficult to proceed beyond the beginning.

Elsewhere, however, Soane managed to order personal correspondence, much of which concerns his embittered family relations with his two sons John and George and their dependants (Palmer 2009, 71). The patriarch invested heavily in the processes of editing and detailed indexing of manuscripts comprising summarized letters, diaries and memoranda evidencing familial tribulations, including ill-advised marriages, inheritances, disputes over the education of his grandchildren and his son George's imprisonment over serious debts, after which George broadcast damaging public criticism of his father's architecture (71).

On several occasions during his final years, the octogenarian noted in his diaries an awareness of his proximity to death: 'At home all day, very wet and dreary alone sorting and destroying papers! Put thy house in order for thou shall surely Die' (quoted in Palmer 2009, 76). Two months prior to his death, in one of his final curatorial moves that perhaps was made to ensure an enduring interest in what this chapter posits was Soane's creation of his own myth in perpetuity, he established three sealed repositories located separately in the house. In accordance with his strict instructions, these were opened sequentially on 22 November 1866, 1886 and 1896.

In 1866, when the then museum curator opened the first repository – which was actually a series of drawers and a cupboard – he discovered 'many worthless articles, some books, newspapers, circulars, letters … . Some false teeth. 3 lottery tickets' (Palmer 2009, 77).[7] In 1886 the next museum curator opened the next sealed repository – which was Soane's dressing room – to discover a similarly ordinary mixture of drawings, hair, gloves and other material none of which could 'could be considered secret', or frankly, worthy of the mystery. So it is unlikely to have been a surprise when in 1896, the curator opened the final and most strange receptacle – the bath in Soane's bathroom – to discover nothing of particular note.

One can only speculate what Soane was thinking when he created these repositories. Sadly, but of course, naturally, clarity and precision were never to be.

Soane's house leaves one with strong feelings of ambivalence: a contest between contempt for his human weaknesses including vanity and paranoia; and fascination for his vision brought to life by his enduring commitment to the construction of his myth. Ultimately, his material excesses are deeply alluring, especially in that so many are actually fake (Thornton and Dorey 1992). It is the human condition that is so alluring – our vulnerability, stupidity, endeavour – and that we find ourselves in the acts of others. Then, like Piranesi's drawings, there is the incredible beauty of Soane's house. Such opulence and indulgence in the construction of one individual's myth lies in contrast to the myth of Kodja Place.

KODJA PLACE

Centuries later, in remote regional south west Australia, the Kodja Place museum was to a large extent born from a desire to reconcile a cruel, dark past. The project began in the late 1990s when hundreds of Kojonup people who shared a readiness to atone for contemporary repercussions of past deeds were drawn together, prepared to confront their myth. They came to work on a project, to tell their stories. Seeded by feelings of mistrust in detached 'experts', the community decided to tell their differing perspectives on their sometimes embarrassing and painful story from a series of first-person points of view. Despite people having differences, everyone wanted the same thing, which was to tell the story together (Sexton 2008).[8] Consequently, ideas and quotations gathered from hundreds of people now comprise the telling of the story from many points of view in a way that delivers a direct hit on the visitor – because the words are personal, there is an immediacy in the visitor's experience.[9] Visiting the exhibition is like walking through the home of a large family, reading the different family members' diaries.

The story begins with the indescribable physical and emotional hardships that were faced by the often young and predominantly British and European migrants who left their homes to travel to this harsh bushland, proclaimed in 1897 as 'a Land of Promise' (Insight Communication and Design and Sally-Anne Hasluck n.d).[10] From the mid-nineteenth century the settlers were seeking prospects by opening up new farmland.

What the exhibition of photographs and stories portrays is that the settlers struggled with the harsh, heavily wooded virgin land that was completely unsuitable not only for grazing livestock or growing food, but also unsuitable for using horses or bullocks to pull machinery or transport materials. In the beginning, the men and women did everything. One of many photographs (c. 1990) now exhibited in the Kodja Museum portrays an elderly man with a quotation that reads: 'Bloody hell, I spent the first 40 years of my working life knocking down trees and now you want me to plant them again'.

The stories tell the viewer that most of the settlers had migrated from vastly different climates and terrains, often leaving behind a rich cultural life. But in Australia, it was the real threat of lives being lost or ruined by the many occurrences of bush fires, drought and floods that necessarily united and forged the New Australian community. Slowly, as the newcomers battled the harsh conditions to clear small portions of land where they were able to begin to plant a few vegetables and graze a few animals, the possibility to build new lives became a reality.

Beneath photographs of fires, ruined houses and lives burnt there is a drawer that museum visitors are invited to open. Inside are small filing card holders. Each card, in no particular order, has someone's brief yet potent narrative about a fire, an event, or some other consequence. Elsewhere, farming relics such as early, crude and inadequate axes and shovels are displayed, evoking the immense physical and mental fortitude required to break this new ground.

As viewers, we feel their first encounter with the new ground must have been a terrible shock. After originally landing in a settlement further south along the western Australian coast, known as Albany, British settlers and surveyors then moved north through thick bush looking for water. They survived because when Noongar people came across the settlers, they led them to the nearby spring for water and 'shar[ed] knowledge of the local flora and fauna' ('One Story many Voices', n.d., n.p.). Soon after, a garrison of soldiers followed the settlers, and by 1845, 'a stone Military Barracks was built alongside the Konjonup Spring' and 'farms began to be established' (Ibid.)

We begin to understand that domesticating the land had created an unimaginable transformation: trees were felled, fences built and dams were sunk. In the beginning, the bush was so dense that the settlers were forced to undertake the impossibly slow and difficult early stages of clearing without the assistance of horses. Timber in the south west of Australia is renowned for its hardness and so clearing was slow and difficult work. As soon as some land was cleared, a few cattle and other animals were grazed and vegetables were planted in unfamiliar soils, in an unfamiliar climate with inadequate tools.

There are personal accounts telling us that later and throughout the twentieth century, individuals who had invested their entire lives in building families, communities and very modest farming livelihoods in this new land would be overwhelmed by fire and flood. Brave, hopeful young people had come here to this rugged, isolated country where they knew no-one, only to be struck by the anarchistic nature of the Australian land – a force of nature, impossible to tame and difficult to come to terms with. Their willpower made their dreams of prospect and the building of their new lives possible.

By contrast, and almost as the subtext of the exhibition, the viewer glimpses the Noongar people's experiences of the rapid, imposed entropy of their ancient culture (Hasluck and Insight Communication and Design 2000, 14, 17, 19). Their relationship to country, their knowledge and lore developed over thousands and thousands of years was disrupted. The rules had completely changed, sovereignty had shifted. Everything was so very different. How could they have understood? Consequently they suffered.

The viewer finds something of the Noongar experience through a series of faded documents deep in the Kodja Place museum. A number of these trace Edward Smith's decades' long struggle not only to acquire land but to have the same freedoms as white people granted him and his family. Dated 1924, a Western Australian Government Department of Lands and Surveys officer writes to the Protector of Aborigines, Perth, asking if he has any objections to Smith, a 'half caste' purchasing land in Kojonup.[11] In a letter dated 1938, Smith writes to Sydney Stubbs, Government House Perth, describing his life as a dedicated farmer and a father who had educated his children. Smith is requesting 'All I want is free agency to go anywhere I wish as white man'. A letter to The Honorary Minister from the Commissioner of Native Affairs, dated 2 March 1939 states: 'while I am aware that the father, Edward Smith is a respectable man, I cannot say the same for his family, and it would be extremely dangerous to grant the father the privilege he desires'.

A letter from A/South West inspector to DCNA,[12] dated 14 November 1948, states:

> I took the opportunity when at Kojonup to inspect the camping conditions of Ted Smith. He has requested you at various times to allow family to be released from Carrolup Native Settlement, to live with him and his wife at Jingalup. His accommodation consists of three tents and two huts, one of which is used for eating. The surroundings are quite clean and Smith himself seems to be above the average native.

A document on display at the Museum entitled 'Western Australian Document of Citizenship' (pursuant to Section 2 of the Native Title Act 1905, 1954) recognizes Edward Smith as being 'one fourth or less Australian native blood and is not discerned to be Native for the purposes of the Native Welfare Act'.

These documents offer glimpses into a heart-wrenching story of ongoing invasion, denial of freedom and identity and the continuing judgment of people who were ruined by the invasion. It is hard to see how the New Australians' courageous risk-taking, incredibly hard work and ongoing struggle towards a better future can reasonably be compared to the ruinous invasion suffered by the Noongars.

So by the 1990s, it was the collective's hope for the future to unearth and tell their story, entitled 'One Story, Many Voices'. The slow and conciliatory process involving the community in collecting and documenting the story took place over a period of four years, with many community members participating. Central to the telling of the story was the local indigenous people's knowledge of time, 'country' and culture. But as Craig McVee acknowledged, the first step 'involved relationship-building between Noongars and *Wadjelas* [white people], so we could develop the project together' (McVee, Robertson and Young 2003, 2).

Negotiating the fraught terrain of reconciliation was the task the Kojonup community committed to, and they did so by working to construct the material world, to select textual evidence, symbols and objects and then re-position and re-present them in relation to each other for their own contemplation and also for outsiders to witness and reflect back to them. They were gathering the matter of their own myth.

When the viewer walks through the construction that is Kodja Place, what becomes obvious is that material and light have been sequenced and interwoven so as to convey the coincidence of disparate lives over the past two centuries. While the museum weaves the stories together spatially, it is the stories that present evidence of the separation and marginalization of the Noongars. For instance, the

Noongar women were not permitted to 'try on' clothing prior to purchase and so consequently, they were often left wearing ill-fitting clothing. Their humiliation is palpable.

So it is that 'museology is a field inherently fraught with misrepresentation and power imbalance, as lives lived and events passed are re-presented and re-interpreted elsewhere in time, place and culture' (Churchill, Smith and Lommerse 2012, 5). In part, the significance of Kodja Place stems from the community's intention to address this imbalance, having the 'primary goal ... to achieve displays that the Noongar community would be happy with' (McVee, Robertson and Young 2003, 4). For Noongar people it is very important that individuals do not speak for others.

While it was very important that Noongar traditional knowledge was respected, it was also vital that the representation of Noongar people not be restricted to one of a traditional hunter-gatherer lifestyle, but rather that they be recognized for the breadth of their contemporary realities in Australian life. For elders, it was important to show the lingering impact on the society and individuals of the Noongars' long battles to survive their displacement and loss of culture even though not everyone could or wanted to understand (Mitchell 2008).

Perhaps the most evocative encounter at Kodja Place happens outside the main building in the Rose Maze garden, where the fictional accounts of three representative women are interwoven. That the archetypal form of the maze, a derivative of the labyrinth, was chosen seems ideal. 'The labyrinth of the Minotaur at Knossos in Crete has a rich and bloody mythology', and the labyrinths built into the 'floors of early Italian churches were said to represent the entangling nature of sin' (Kronborg 2006). The maze, a form later adapted by European Royalty as a hedged pleasure-ground symbolic of 'courtship, penetration, conception and birth', was created at Kodja Place using roses, 'emblematic of grace and tenderness' (Ibid.).

Throughout Kodja's maze (partially funded by the State Government's Centenary of Women's Suffrage project) the wanderer discovers fragments here and there of the fictional women – Maria who migrated from Italy, Elizabeth who came from Britain, and finally, the young Noongar woman, Yoondi. The timeline of events is articulated by a number of pergolas symbolizing the 'Stolen Generation Enclosure', the 'Deaths in Custody Pergola', and the 'Hayshed Pergola'. Representative of the actual historical context, episodes along the paths between the pergolas tell of births, marriages, harvests, longings for home, longings for mother, the gift of family life, and the cruelty of racism, internment, war and premature death.

It is therefore interesting that the Kojonup Community created a fiction that served the construction of their stories in a number of ways. Through the fictional lives of Yoondi, Elizabeth and Maria, the community was able to embody the sources and breadth of their dark past; they were able to represent and reposition the essential story with a view to future understandings; and they were able to present their case to posterity for judgment. This, their essential story is the 'myth by which they live' of Sir John Soane.

Like the experience of moving through the gallery spaces inside the museum, wandering through the Rose Maze is a transformative experience, a simple space deeply embedded with meaning. It is impossible to emerge from these experiences of constructed space and selected objects without a greater awareness of each other. It is impossible to not be more switched on to human temporal lineage, past events and future consequences. What emerges from this fraught attempt at reconciliation is the extraordinariness of being ordinary.

What seems most important is that the community enabled many voices to tell the one story, that they are able to know their story from many points of view, that the story has materialized before themselves, and for others to witness, and that they have the opportunity to come to terms with the marks they and their forbears have made in the world and those the world has made on them.

Knowing other people's lives more closely – their opportunities and/or the injustices – is a tricky endeavour fraught with the potential to judge, misread or underestimate, particularly where there has been a shift in sovereignty. Yet, through the Kodja Place project, the Kojonup community committed to reconciliation with generosity, bravery, intelligence, civility and humour.

ALCHEMY AND MYTH

For me, thinking about the collection and re-presentation of life's objects and stories in the cases of Soane and the Kojonup community in the context of Carl Jung's theorizing of alchemy and myth making adds another layer of understanding of these significant projects. Jung was a complex man whose quest to come to terms with the inner and outer lives of the human sensorium led him to ask himself, 'what is your myth – the myth in which you do live?' (2010, 171). He lamented what he saw as a disconnection from our myths about life and death, brought about by the domination of rationalism and doctrinarism that pretends to have all the answers. He wrote: 'To the intellect, all my mythologising is futile speculation. To the emotions, however, it is a healing and valid activity; it gives existence a glamour which we would not like to do without' (300–301). Further, he recognized the role myths play in compensating for our relationship to death, eternity and the frailties of lives lived. Our human articulation of our myth creates temporal links, enabling us into the future and towards death (Ibid.)

> *My life is the story of the self-actualization of the unconscious. Everything in the unconscious seeks outward manifestation … . What we are to our inward vision, and what man appears to be sub specie aeternitatis [viewed in relation to the eternal; in a universal perspective], can only be expressed by way of myth. Myth is more individual and expresses life more precisely than does science. Science works with concepts of averages which are far too general to do justice to the subjective variety of an individual life. (2010, 3)*

There came a time for Jung when he realized he did not live by the Christian myth and that actually, he did not know what his myth was. It was during this time when Jung had been experiencing 'constant inner pressure' which he self-diagnosed as 'some psychic disturbance in [him]self'(2010, 173) that he had a dream he was walking along a 'lane with a long row of tombs … with stone slabs on which the dead lay … in their antique clothes, with hands clasped … in a curious fashion mummified' (172). Dressed as though they had lived in the seventeenth and eighteenth centuries, each of the mummies came to life as Jung approached them.

For Jung, this was the moment of revelation that ultimately led to his discovery of alchemy, and the idea that through the processes of working with life's concrete realities, the physical matter of existence, it is possible to reveal deep inner temporal connections to both the past and the future (both of which, for Jung, live within.) The proposition is that through concrete actions, it is possible to recognize the evolving inner self – that it is possible to work on the inner self (individual and collective) via manipulation of the concrete reality of the outer world.

After the mummy dream, Jung began to reflect on how the past 'belong[s] to our living being' (173), so, remembering his boyhood passion for playing with building blocks, he decided to return, in adult life, to construction. He recalled:

> *I began accumulating suitable stones, gathering them partly from the lake shore and partly from the water. And as I started building: cottages, a castle, a whole village. ... I thought about the significance of what I was doing, and asked myself, 'Now, really, what are you about? You are building a small town, and doing it as if it were a rite!' I had no answer to my own question, only the inner certainty that I was on the way to discovering my own myth. For the building game was only a beginning. It released a stream of fantasies which I carefully wrote down. (2010, 172)*

Following this incident, and over a period of some years, Jung delved into philosophical alchemy, finding that constructing material realities became a vital source of support and a counterpoise to 'that strange inner world' (2010, 174–5) of his professional life as a psychiatrist. He consolidated his interest in philosophical alchemy through readings that included Goethe, Foust and Nietzsche. Jung wrote: 'Grounded in the natural philosophy of the Middle Ages, alchemy formed the bridge on the one hand into the past, to Gnosticism, and on the other into the future, to the modern psychology of the unconscious' (2010, 201).

The development of Jung's understanding of alchemy enabled him to recognize alchemical symbols, which became a major component in his work. This is illustrated by his recollection of a recurrent dream in which he recognized the presence of his own house. There was always another strangely unfamiliar building attached to his house even though this building had been there a long time. This conundrum left Jung wondering why he did not know the neighbouring building. What he did realize at the time was that the unfamiliar building represented part of his own personality.

Eventually, one of these recurrent dreams revealed the building had a library with 'a number of books embellished with [fascinating] copper engravings … and illustrations containing curious symbols', (2010, 202) which captivated Jung, even though at the time, he did not recognize them. Later, his own library came to closely resemble that of his dream, and when he learnt to decipher alchemical symbols, alchemy became central to his work on the collective unconscious.[13] He wrote:

> *Our souls as well as our bodies are composed of individual elements which were already present in the ranks of our ancestors. The 'newness' in the individual*

> *psyche is an endlessly varied recombination of age-old components. Body and soul therefore have an intensely historical character and find no proper place in what is new, in things that have just come into being. That is to say our ancestral components are only partly at home in such things. We are very far from having finished completely with the Middle Ages, classical antiquity, and primitivity, as our modern psyches pretend … . Inner peace and contentment depend in large measure upon whether or not the historical family which is inherent in the individual can be harmonised with the ephemeral conditions of the present. (2010, 236–7)*

Jung's description of his awakening to philosophical alchemy sheds light on our relationship to the things we collect and arrange and the spaces we construct and occupy. He also reminds us of what we already know, that the more esoteric temporal connections and longings we sense are actually embodied in things, buildings, nature and also within our own bodies. It is in the context of the myths we construct through the processes of philosophical alchemy – our relationship with matter – that this chapter considers the two museums: Soane's House and Kodja Place.

The story of Kojonup would not be new to most Australians – we carry it with us. What the museum does is re-present a myth in a way that catalyses something to happen. It is a phenomenological experience that taps the viewer's senses. From the entrance, the long narrow gallery, with its substantial amount of material that slows the pace of the visitor down, that takes time to experience, to contemplate the matter, exemplifies this. Here there is depth in the positioning of objects that subtly moves the visitor laterally, counter-intuitive to the natural pace and prospect of linear space that usually is intent on the destination rather than the journey.

In other words, in this space the visitor physically moves in unexpected ways. As in nature, the material displayed has many layers between foreground and background. The more the visitor looks in, the more she will discover. This moment of encountering depth between objects in space is analogous to the Jungian proposition that we carry within us not only the present, but also to the past and the future. In that moment of presence, provoked by the object from another time and place, lies the prospect of harmonizing components of the past and the future that we carry within us. Our encounter with the physical realities of these objects is an opportunity for us to make some internal adjustments towards aligning our inner temporal connections, thereby gently or perhaps dramatically re-configuring our own myth.

There are further opportunities beyond the long narrow gallery where there is a large centric space. Here the design of the space choreographs the visitor to physically circumnavigate artefacts, or to focus on the undulating floor with its embedded signs. Some spaces are dark and tight; others are large and filled with natural light. Colour and texture articulate the constantly changing surfaces that contain space so that space itself is the myth. It is through the human experience of the matter that the myth is reiterated.

Similarly, in the Jungian sense, Soane appears to have worked to represent himself to himself. It is as though through working with the physical matter of his life, Soane was anxiously grappling with the turbulence of life, with a view to mortality, lineage and memoriam, all of which were thwarted by his difficult relationship with his two sons. Much matter and time was invested in Soane's search into the past, his editing of the present and his projection into the future on a quest for his myth.

CONCLUSION

And so it is a combination of the lingering 'constant inner pressure' of misdeeds, misunderstandings and misrepresentations experienced respectively by Soane, Jung and the Kojonup community that ultimately led them to work with re-versioned re-constructed material realities in their attempts to make their interior sensations explicit, not only to themselves, but also to the outside world. In each case, these concrete projects stemmed from deep sensitivities for articulating their myths – the past, present and future.

The question of the myths by which we live remains the recurring theme of the two museums that embody the human struggle to define and position our myths. It is the provocation this chapter speculates on: that whatever our myth, our struggle with occupation of the interior and exterior worlds is a process of ruin, repudiation and revolution. It is a process of deconstruction, alteration and renewal. And what seems most important is that we come to know our myths, that we are able to articulate them to ourselves and to others, that we come to terms with the marks we make in the world.

POSTSCRIPT

By strange coincidence, both Soane and the Kojonup Community created fictions that served the construction of their myths in a number of ways. Firstly, the fictions embodied the source of the 'inner pressure'; secondly, they represented and repositioned the fundamental myth with a view to future understandings; and finally, each presented a case for judgment by posterity. This chapter is not about scientific truth. Rather, inspired by Jung it is concerned with ways in which we second objects and space to re-present our myths into the future. The unlikely composition of the Sir John Soane Museum and Kodja Place provokes speculation, if not judgment, on the value of displaced objects in orchestrated re-presentation.

REFERENCES

Bataille, Georges. 1995. 'Museum'. In *Encyclopaedia Acephalica Comprising the Critical Dictionary & Related Texts*, edited by Georges Bataille, Robert Lebel and Isabelle Waldberg, 71. London: Atlas Press.

———. 1996. 'Museum'. In *Rethinking Architecture: a Reader in Cultural Theory*, edited by Neil Leach, 23. New York: Routledge.

Churchill, Lynn, Dianne Smith, and Marina Lommerse. 2012. 'Empowering Through Design: A Case of Becoming'. In *Interior: a State of Becoming: Book 1: Symposium Proceedings, State Library, Perth, WA, September 6–9*, edited by Lynn Churchill and Dianne Smith, 5. Perth, WA: Curtin University.

Hasluck, Sally-Anne, and Insight Communication and Design. 2000. *Kojonup Interpretation Concept Plan for the Federation Visitor Centre including Aboriginal Cultural Centre*. Claremont, WA: Freshwater Bay Press.

Insight Communication and Design and Sally-Anne Hasluck. No date (circa 1990s). Report on *Kojonup Federation Park Heritage Centre: 'The Kodja Place'*. N.p.

Jung, Carl Gustav. 1953. *Psychology and Alchemy*. London: Routledge & Kegan Paul.

———. 1967. *Alchemical Studies*. London: Routledge & Kegan Paul.

———. 2010. *Memories, Dreams, Reflections*. [USA]: Oxford City Press.

Knox, Tim. 2009. *Sir John Soane's Museum*. London: Merrell Publishers.

———. 2012. *Opening Up the Soane: Letter from the Museum Director in London*. http://www.soanefoundation.com/opening.html. Accessed 2 February 2013.

Kronborg, Jamie. 2006. 'The Australian Rose Maze the Kodja Place'. Tourism pamphlet distributed by Kodja Place and collected in February 2013 by the author. West Leederville, Perth: WIP Print.

Ludbrook, Juliet, Helene Barr Charlesworth and Kojonup (WA Shire) Council. 2002. *The Kojonup Australian Rose Maze: The Kodja Place, Kojonup Western Australia*. Kojonup, WA: Shire of Kojonup.

McVee, Craig, Margaret Robertson and Penny Young. 2003. 'The Kodja Place: One Story Many Voices'. Paper presented at the *Museums Australia National Conference: The Other Side*, Perth, WA, May 25. http://kodjaplace.com.au/files/Paper_to_2003-National_Museum_conference.pdf. Accessed 23 March 2013.

Mitchell, Natasha. 2008. *The Kodja Place: Reconciliation in Action*. Life Matters. Radio program. Guest speaker Craig McVee. Sydney: ABC Radio National, 12 September.

'One Story Many voices'. N.d. Pamphlet, The Kodja Place, Kojonup, WA.

Palmer, Susan. 2009. 'Sir John Soane: Rewriting a Life'. *Libraries & the Cultural Record* 44 (1): 65–81.

'Piranesi's Paestum: Master Drawings Uncovered'. 2013. *Enfilade*, 25 February. http://enfilade18thc.com/2013/02/25/exhibition-piranesis-paestum-master-drawings-uncovered/. Accessed 2 February 2013.

Sexton, Robert. 2008. 'The Kodja Place: Reconciliation in Action'. Radio National Life Matters broadcast 12 September 2008, 9.05 am. Accessed March 2013, http://www.abc.net.au/radionational/programs/lifematters/the-kodja-place-reconciliation-in-action/3183862.

Soane, John. 1812. 'Crude Hints Towards an History of my House in L[incoln's] I[nn] Fields'. MS annotated by Helen Dorey. London: Sir John Soane Museum, Lincoln's Inn Fields.

Thornton, Peter, and Helen Dorey. 1992. *A Miscellany of Objects from Sir John Soane's Museum: Consisting of Paintings, Architectural Drawings and Other Curiosities From the Collection of Sir John Soane*. London: Laurence King.

Wilton-Ely, John. 2013. *Piranesi, Paestum & Soane*. Munich: Prestel.

NOTES

1. 'Crude Hints Towards an History of my House in L[incoln's] I[nn] Fields' is the title of John Soane's 1812 manuscript, a fantasy, in which his house is re-discovered sometime in the future as a ruin offering glimpses of past occupation and possession.

2. In 1833, the recently knighted Sir John Soane obtained an Act of Parliament entitled 'An Act for settling and preserving Sir John Soane's Museum, Library, and Works of Art, in Lincoln's inn Fields, in the county of Middlesex, for the benefit of the public, and for the establishing of sufficient Endowment for the due maintenance of the same'. See Knox 2009, 34.

3. Susan Palmer, in 'Sir John Soane: Re-writing a Life', p. 78, quotes from Soane's document entitled 'Description of the House and Museum on the North Side of Lincoln's Inns Fields. The Residence of Sir John Soane'.

4. Soane's manuscript is incomplete, with much of it remaining as unedited notes.

5. Dorey, an historian who has undertaken several roles at the Soane museum including curator, has provided introductory notes to Soane's difficult to decipher hand-written manuscript.

6. Susan Palmer explores examples of Soane's compulsion with 'obsessive and laboured compiling of evidence using his own archives and his tendency towards revision – [that illustrate] both attempts at self-defence and at controlling his reception by posterity' (Palmer 2009, 67).

7. Palmer, who quotes here from the 1866 Museum Curator's report, notes also that 22 November 1815 was the date of Soane's wife's death.

8. Robert Sexton, Shire President at the time, citing a Noongar community member's plea.

9. The author, who had sleepless nights following a visit to Kodja Place, has for some time been talking with others about their experiences.

10. This report was prepared and presented as a framework for developing and guiding workshops with the Kojonup Aboriginal Community, the Kojonup Tourist Bureau and the Kojonup Historical Society.

11. This letter and subsequent letters quoted in this paragraph are on display at the The Kodja Place Visitor Centre, Kojonup, WA.

12. Author deduces that abbreviation in photocopy of original letter in museum stands for Department of Commissioner for Native Affairs, but this is not spelled out.

13. Several of Jung's major works discuss philosophical alchemy. These include *Psychology and Alchemy* (1953) and *Alchemical Studies* (1967).

PART II
Repudiation

Plate 3   'Symbiosis'. 2014

5

Tragedy and Assimilation: Occupying the Patterned Surface

Kirsty Volz

INTRODUCTION

The Woods Bagot 2007 refurbishment of the Qantas and British Airways Bangkok Business lounge in Survarnabhumi Airport features wall finishes designed by wallpaper designer Florence Broadhurst (1899–1977) and Thai silk trader Jim Thompson (1906–1967). This particularly distinctive selection of works by the two designers is highlighted on the airport's website (Suvarnabhumi Airport 2006), where our attention is drawn to the striking similarities and defining differences of these patterned wall surfaces, positioned, as they are, side by side. Thompson and Broadhurst would appear to be worlds apart, but here in the airport their work brings them together. Thompson, the son of a wealthy cotton family in America, worked as an architect before joining the army. He moved to Bangkok to start the Thai Silk Company in 1948. Broadhurst was born on a farm in Mt Perry, Queensland. She began her career as a performance artist in an Australian troupe in Shanghai, moving on to pursue a career in fashion design, catering to the middle and upper classes in London. Upon her return to Australia in 1959, Broadhurst started a print design company. Both Broadhurst and Thompson pursued multiple careers and died under mysterious circumstances. Broadhurst was murdered in 1977 at her Sydney print warehouse, which remains an unsolved crime. Thompson disappeared in the Malaysian highlands in 1967 and his body has never been found.

The uncanny parallels between these two pattern designers form the basis for this chapter, which seeks to expand on the existing literature on wallpaper and patterned wall surfaces. A search of existing literature in relation to patterned surfaces revealed frequent discussion of how the wall's surface engrosses or colonizes subjects that inhabit the space it decorates. There is also a focus in the literature on the female body and its absorption by the patterned wall. This chapter shifts the discussion away from focusing on one gender and proposes that the subject can purposefully occupy the patterned surface for personal and social gain. By investigating designs produced by both Thompson and Broadhurst, this chapter posits that the ability to hide within the patterned surface is what enticed the designers to create such notable patterns towards the end of their lives. The revealing nature of the stark white wall, compared with the screen provided by the pattern wherein the subject can hide, is elaborated by painter and advocate for polychromatic architecture, Fernand Léger (1973). Léger writes that 'the modern architect has gone too far in his magnificent attempts to cleanse through emptiness', and that the resultant white walls of modernity create 'an impalpability of air, of slick, brilliant new surfaces where nothing can be hidden any longer … even shadows don't dare to enter' (1973, 51). In this chapter I argue that to counter the exposure produced by the white wall, both Thompson and Broadhurst – separately of course – designed patterned surfaces that could harbour their controversial personal histories.

To support my thesis that the patterned surface provides a place of refuge for the subject to occupy, I investigate both filmic and visual art, where the subject is both literally and metaphorically assimilated with the surface. The selected filmic and visual art works both reference Florence Broadhurst's patterns. The film is an Australian work, *Candy,* directed by Neil Armfield and released in 2006, in which Broadhurst's wallpapers can be seen in the central character's house. The visual art works are Emma Hack's body illustrations, where she paints models' bodies into the patterns of Broadhurst's wallpapers. These works provide an extra layer of analysis to broaden and interrogate existing discussions on the assimilation of the female body within the patterned surface. I draw attention to examples of male bodies painted into surfaces and how the act of camouflaging with a wall's surface can be an act of empowerment and not necessarily an act of compliance and retreat.

This chapter unfolds in four parts. The first part identifies representations of assimilation between the patterned surface and subject in film and visual art. The second presents biographical research on Florence Broadhurst and Jim Thompson, proposing that in their separate ways they were drawn to design patterns because they each needed to occupy the inherent concealing properties. The third section returns to film and visual art to further analyse this occupation of the patterned surface. The last part focuses on the fictional character Candy from the Australian film of the same name, and the work of Australian body illustrator Emma Hack and her simulated assimilation of the body into surface.

BODIES OCCUPYING THE PATTERNED SURFACE

The phenomenon of '*faire tapisserie*' is loosely translated in English as a 'wall flower' but is best described as the optical illusion of flattening the body into the surface of a patterned (floral, in particular) wall surface. In the field of interior design this has been explored by a number of authors through the paintings of late nineteenth- to early twentieth-century artist Edouard Vuillard. His paintings detailed lavish interiors with richly patterned surfaces in which female subjects would seemingly disappear within the pattern, as described by Freyja Hartzell:

> *These broad expanses of densely flowered wallpaper constitute the painting's largest areas of flat patterning; this buzzing meadow threatens to engulf the*

picture plane altogether, drawing the eye to further patterns humming in the carpets, cushions and draperies. Rather than accommodating its occupant, this aggressive interior absorbs them. Vuillard replaces domestic draperies with flat unyielding renditions to their formerly pliant selves. The allure of the textile as a surrogate skin is ironically negated by his depictions of covers and linings in which the layers of fabric and skin fuse forever into one impenetrable, optical plane. (2009, 63)

While there are other authors who agree with Hartzell's interpretation of Vuillard's work, Partricia Pringle offers an alternative explanation for Vuillard's numerous depictions of *faire tapisserie*:

His paintings of the decade when his involvement with theatre was at its height used the techniques of his theatre sets to hint at psychological complexities beyond the physical planes of the interior, as for example 'Interior, Mother and Sister of the Artist' (1893) … . I suggest that this conjuror's act, in telling an inconsequential story while producing its character from a flattened screen of thick and coloured air, had – in its own way – the potential to bring an audience's attention to the unstable surface of existence. (2010, 8)

Pringle's provocation is that there is some greater meaning to be drawn from assimilations between the subject and the surface. This chapter departs from this position to create a new lens for capturing the patterned surface. Rather than thinking of the subject as absorbed by the patterned surface, I propose that the subject occupies the surface for refuge; rather than being manipulated by the surface, the pattern might be a method through which the subject can manipulate their social setting. The patterned surface does not consume and suffocate its subjects, it provides space to inhabit, in turn bringing the surface to life. As Léger writes (1973, 49) 'A blank wall is a dead, anonymous surface. It will take life only from shapes or colours that will give it life or destroy it. A coloured wall becomes a living element'. The relationship between the subject and the surface can be viewed as one of reciprocity, simultaneously taking from the subject and giving from the surface.

Sylvia Lavin builds a case for a 'superarchitecture' that engages in a reciprocal relationship between its surface and its subjects (2011, 4). Lavin illustrates this relationship of what she terms kissing architecture through video installation artist Pipilotti Rist's description of her 2008 work titled 'Pour Your Body Out' at the Museum of Modern Art (MoMA), New York. Rist suggests that the basic provocation of her digital installation, projected onto the walls of Taniguchi's voluminous MoMA foyer, is not to dominate the architecture, but to 'melt into it, as if to kiss the architecture' (Rist, quoted in MoMA 2008a). Rist goes on to say that, as the title suggests, the work is a physical engagement between the body and the surface of the art gallery; its purpose is to physically draw people into the space and not deliver the work through the media, internet or other channels of mass communication through which digital video works are often displayed and disseminated (Rist, quoted in MoMA 2008a). As MoMA curator Klaus Biesenbach explains, Rist's work is one that you have to experience through physical contact with the surfaces of MoMA's foyer, touching cushions, the floor, walls and the light of the projections onto the skin; it is a physically immersive experience. It is an experience that the visitor may become lost in; Biesenbach portrays the installation as an experience where 'you could be lying on the floor and losing yourself time wise and space wise' (Biesenbach, quoted in MoMA 2008b).

To 'lose oneself' in the surface of the interior is a paradoxical concept. For Rist and Biesenbech it is a celebration of freedom, liberation from the banalities of the everyday and the socially constructed expectations of identity. On the other hand, to lose oneself is an occasion of lament for the loss of self, especially in the case of transference of identity from subject to surface. Defining the relationship as one of reciprocity shifts the study of wallpaper and assimilation between subject and surface away from the interpretations of Charlotte Perkins Gilman's 1892 novella, *The Yellow Wallpaper* (Gilbert and Gubar 2000, 67). Most of the analysis of Gilman's novella is focused on the absorption of the female subject into domesticity, where the patterned surface suppresses the subject (Gilbert and Gubar 2000, 32). This portrays the interaction between the subject and the surface as singular in direction. These interpretations limit critical discussions of the wallpaper to binary ideologies, where the surface is simply thought of as a flat plane covering some space, matter, or substance underneath it. But there is space *in* the patterned surface; space created by the pattern lines that divide the wall plane into a number of parts. For Florence Broadhurst and Jim Thompson, as will be argued later, these geometries created the segmented surfaces that were manifestations of their creators' divergent personal histories. They represent the multiple 'becomings' underpinning their designers' existence. The patterns have compelling biographical agency, such that they are capable of revealing the lives of Thompson and Broadhurst as a whole from a distance, as well as becoming a series of divided fragments when studied at close encounter.

The phenomenon of the close encounter with the wall papered surface can also be observed in Leos Carax's film *Holy Motors* (Carax 2012). The film's opening scene depicts the body of the director pressed against the wallpapered plane, searching the surface with his hands and one ear, until he finds the keyhole. The wall then opens to an empty cinema. The surreal non-linear narrative that follows involves a constant metamorphosis of subjectivity, as one actor plays a multiplicity of characters in different Parisian locations. *Holy Motors* portrays the correlation between the patterned and divisible surface, and subjectivity as both a state of becoming and a multiplicity of personal histories, echoing the multiple personae played by Thompson and Broadhurst. Both Thompson and Broadhurst moved through a series of different careers, resided in several countries, moving from one situation to another, and playing a different character to reflect each situation. In *Holy Motors*, too, a male character interacts with wallpaper, countering the fixation on women and patterned surfaces. Another male filmic character engaging in a close encounter with wallpaper and embracing the *faire tapisserie* is Sherlock Holmes in the 2011 film *Sherlock Holmes: A Game of Shadows* (Ritchie 2011). In this film, Holmes develops a chameleon-like attack mechanism, an 'urban camouflage' where he visibly assimilates with interior surfaces. The film includes a striking optical illusion reminiscent of the interiors painted by Vuillard, when, in the final scene,

Holmes is hidden amongst the wallpaper and tapestry of a chair where he utilizes his assimilation with the surface to his advantage. This encapsulates two important points in this chapter: that the patterned surface is not a menacing element waiting to consume its inhabitants; and also that neither the patterned surface nor its inhabitation are exclusively the domain of the feminine, as evidenced in the work of Jim Thompson.

PATTERNS WITHIN PATTERNS: JIM THOMPSON

Broadhurst and Thompson's works share a number of commonalities in their design production, even though their work in print design commenced a decade apart. Both designers opted to work more with traditional methods of pattern making. Broadhurst used hand-operated screens, and Thompson outsourced work to local weavers and refrained from operating out of a factory. Despite humble beginnings, Broadhurst and Thompson each enjoyed international success, with their wall patterns featured in a number of renowned international hotels in Bahrain, Singapore, Sydney and London in the 1970s and 1980s. Their patterns were also transferred to fabric for soft furnishings and clothing. Thompson's patterns were used for costumes in films including *The King and I* and *Ben Hur*. Broadhurst's patterns were also widely used by fashion designers and artists, as in Akira Isogowa's costume design for *Salome*, a 1998 production by the Sydney Dance Company. Most recently, her print designs have been used by skin illustrator Emma Hack, in a series of works where female bodies are painted into Broadhurst's patterns. Hack's work camouflages the models' bodies in the patterned surface, assimilating subject and surface, hinting at something living within the patterned wall. More than four decades after Broadhurst's murder and five decades since Thompson's disappearance, their print designs persist as more than just a legacy. They are applied as surface finishes with the same fervour as when the designs were first released. This orientation to surface is relevant to the analysis of Thompson's pre-occupation with the pattern within the pattern, which was influenced by the traditional patterns used in the Thai Kingdom's Court. The infinite divisions created by the pattern accommodate the multiplicities of Thompson's personal history.

William Warren's *Jim Thompson: The Unsolved Mystery* (2007) is the only publication that really addresses the work and life of Jim Thompson. Warren is a writer and lecturer in Bangkok and was a personal friend of Thompson's in Thailand. He originally penned Thompson's biography three years after his disappearance and then re-released the book in 1998 to much critical acclaim. As he was a close friend as well as the only author to write about Thompson, what is known about Thompson is largely uncontested, but if other biographical sources were available, his history might well read in a similar fashion to the conflicting documentation of Broadhurst's life. Like Broadhurst, Thompson 'played out' three main characters in his life. First, he was an architect. His next chapter saw him enlist in the US Army, which led him to Thailand, where he started his business trading Thai silks with traditional motifs. Also, as in Broadhurst's personal history, there are a number of gaps in the Thompson story. He enjoyed a short, successful career as an architect, despite never completing his studies in architecture after repeatedly failing the technical units of the course. Furthermore, during his time with the US Army working for the French armed services in North Africa, he spent a number of years on a highly classified project that remained a secret, and he never spoke about this to friends or family. The enigma around his sexuality is also addressed in Warren's biography. It was rumoured that he was homosexual, but he was never known to have a significant relationship with either a man or a woman. There is also the unexplained falling out he had with a potential business partner, Germaine Krull, in his initial business venture in Thailand owning and running the Mandarin Oriental Hotel in Bangkok. The greatest mystery of Thompson's life remains his unsolved disappearance (death) in the Malaysian highlands in 1967, aged 61.

Thompson invested significant time and energy in rigorous research into the Thai silk business. According to Warren:

> *Thompson consulted his Thai friends on the subject; he studied a collection of rare old pieces in the national museum; he tracked down some of the weavers through the shops in which they sold their material. He discovered the weaving enclave at Bangkrua – little suspecting that one day he would be living across from it – and talked with some of the families who lived in its crowded houses. (2007, 97)*

Thompson worked with traditional weavers, saving a trade that was close to extinction because of a lack of interest in Thai silks both locally and internationally. He refrained from establishing large factories with mechanized looms and instead encouraged the weavers to work in traditional methods from their homes (Warren 2007, 99). Not unlike Broadhurst, who maintained traditional silk screen printing practices to create her wallpapers instead of modern mechanical printing techniques, Thompson valued the working methods of traditional weavers. Thompson, like Broadhurst, enjoyed significant international success, and this is due to his exceptional sensibility for colour, as he created intricate designs that endured as much-admired patterns. Thompson greatly admired the costume and set designs by Russian painter Leon Bakst for the Ballet Russes in Paris, and derived inspiration from them. In a press release on the Jim Thompson website, the depth of his admiration for the Baskt Ballet designs is expressed: 'Mr. Thompson, an architect by training, became so mesmerised by a book of Leon Bakst's visionary scenic and costume designs for the Ballet Russes, that he became a supporter of one of the original company's post-Diaghilev descendants, the Ballet Russe de Monte Carlo' (Jim Thompson and Associates 2011). Drawing inspiration from designers such as Bakst, Thompson would adapt the designs for print in subtle ways, using coloured thread as the painter would use palette, experimenting with many combinations until he found the ones that worked (Warren 2007, 81). In the early 1960s, Thompson turned his hand to printed silks, using traditional designs derived from paintings, porcelains, and textiles. These prints became an instant success, and were soon seen in the designs of high-fashion houses in Europe and America, and copied by other silk companies in Bangkok (Warren 2007, 11).

A visit to Thompson's house on the Klong River in Bangkok (now known as the Jim Thompson House) reveals his love for early print techniques. Exhibited as wall hangings in the house are collections of ancient Thai hand-printed scripts as well as original timber blocks for printing. Set on a large parcel of land just across the river from the local weavers, the house was built by reassembling traditional Thai houses. Using all of some, and parts of others, Thompson created the house, an interconnected whole, linked by external walkways. In building the house, Thompson's fixation with the wall surface and pattern persists. Thompson developed a unique new application for traditional Thai walls. The design of the Thai houses was such that the timber panels were hung from the structure, acting as walls. Ornamentation was traditionally hand carved into these timber panels, which was a decorative device for the external façade of the building. In Thompson's design he inverted these panels so that the ornamentation faced the interior of the house. The outer cladding becomes the inner surface, so it could be admired from the inside. This careful and sensitive design decision anchors the surface pattern to the interior.

Thompson's dedication to traditional Thai weaving lives on through his Foundation. In 1999, the Jim Thompson Foundation hosted a symposium on South East Asian textiles, 'Through the Threads of Time' (Puranananda 2004, ii). In this symposium, John Guy drew attention to the tradition in Thai Court weaving that conceals one pattern within another pattern. He described the tradition thus: 'A typical Thai decorative device of concealing one motif within another, often suggesting a visual metamorphosis is underway before the viewer's very eyes' (Guy 2004, 105). This visual metamorphosis was a device referenced by Thompson in his print designs, including his signature 'Ikat' design, in which the motif inspired by the central Asian nineteenth century, one of 'flowers in a vase' mirrors and unfolds. This enfolded patterning also informs the building of the house on the Klong. A whole made of a seamless connection of parts created an architecture that echoes the surface condition of duality, as being both a singular entity, and composed of individual and intersecting parts. Here too there is a connection with Thompson's life, where in one lifetime he lived three unrelated lives – American architect, army officer in North Africa and Thai print designer. In this way, the house, the surface, and the subject come into conversation. They can be read as a whole from a distance, but also studied to discern their divisible parts and the dividing patterns in a close encounter.

THE STRUCTURE BENEATH: FLORENCE BROADHURST

Broadhurst's earliest endeavours with the visual medium, painting Australian landscapes, were described by a Sydney art critic at the time as being preoccupied with the surface: 'She does not understand the true character of the landscapes she paints, indeed, … her eye only devours surface beauties, skin deep at best without realising the structure beneath … '. (O'Neill, 2006, 79). However, for Broadhurst, the surface was not a shallow realm, as demonstrated in the rich, complex patterns of her wallpaper designs.

Biographical research is incapable of pinning down the fluidity of Broadhurst's life. Siobahn O'Brien's *A Life by Design: The Art and Lives of Florence Broadhurst* (2004), Helen O'Neill's *Florence Broadhurst: Her Secret and Extraordinary Lives* (2006) and Gillian Armstrong's documentary film, *Unfolding Florence: The Many Lives of Florence Broadhurst* (2010) reveal a number of biographical discrepancies. While this lack of consistency and completeness does not call into question the accuracy of O'Brien's, O'Neill's and Armstrong's research, it is indicative of the part Broadhurst played in fabricating and curating her own life story. There are three things that we can be sure of. Firstly, despite Broadhurst's denial of both her origin and her age, she was born in 1899 in Mount Perry, Queensland. Secondly, she commanded a successful wallpaper and printing firm, and finally, she was brutally murdered in her wallpaper studio in Paddington, Sydney in 1977. Her murder remains an unsolved mystery, almost complementing the confused series of invented tales that shroud her life.

There were three main characters that Broadhurst played out in her life, beginning with Bobby Broadhurst, the Shanghai contralto singer and dancer with short dark bobbed hair. It was as Bobby that Broadhurst first learned to adopt a British lilt. Her next role was as the seemingly French Madame Pellier, a fine clothing and homewares retailer to the upper classes in London before the Second World War. Broadhurst's final act was as the bright red-haired Florence Broadhurst, a Sydney-based English artist and designer of fine handcrafted wall papers. In 2009 Christine Schmidt explained these re-iterations of personality as 'a means of bypassing social conventions and surpassing her peers' (2009, 487). These performances were deliberate and intentional, intended to manoeuvre herself towards her desired destination. She was conscious of this and manipulated the performance to her benefit. While in London, under the guise of Madame Pellier, Broadhurst wrote in her personal journal: 'Progress of civilisation is made possible only by vigorous sometimes even violent lying; … the social contract is nothing more or less than a vast conspiracy of human beings … lies are the mortar that bind the individual man into the social masonry' (O'Brien 2004, 59).

If the lies were the mortar in the wall functioning as the underlying structure, is it possible that Broadhurst's wallpapers were a device that concealed her own embellishments? Within her work her past truths manifested in the last act of her life, where she devised a diversion tactic through creating complex colourful surfaces. O'Neill writes that the difficulty in sorting the facts from the fictions of Broadhurst's life is compounded by the distractions created by her colourful existence, supporting Schmidt's argument that even before creating her line of wallpapers, 'she began creating images so bold that few thought to question anything about them' (Schmidt 2009, 486). It has even been noted that Broadhurst would apply the paint used for printing her famous wallpapers to her face as eye shadow or blush at parties she hosted in her warehouse (O'Neill 2006, 81). While the use of vivid and metallic colours has been attributed to Broadhurst's deteriorating eyesight due to cataracts, her bold application of colour sought to also camouflage her colourful personal history with the surface.

Mark Wigley notes that to be faced with the white wall is to be lost (1995, 287). For Broadhurst, the wallpapered surface was an opportunity to be discovered and yet remain concealed, to hide that which she did not want revealed.

5.1 Florence Broadhurst's pattern Cranes (26) in olive/green
Source: Image courtesy of Signature Prints, Sydney, Australia.

It was a paradoxical relationship between the very public life she led, and all the falsities she could bury in the structure beneath the surface. However, the concealment is not complete. Wigley correctly notes that surface facilitates a reciprocal relation. He argues that where the 'flatness' of architecture is seen as 'space restricting', the modern painter's reduction of 'corporeality to flatness' is seen to produce spatial relationship (Wigley 1995, 302). The painted surface, or the patterned surface under investigation in this chapter, might be seen as merely decorating the surface, a seemingly reductive, two-dimensional act. However, as Wigley points out, the patterned surface introduces a new spatial relationship. There is a space within the surface for the subject to occupy.

Despite all of her misgivings, Florence Broadhurst made a significant contribution to the Australian design scene. Undoubtedly, her performances as Bobby and Madame Pellier contributed to the spectrum of images and colours in the Broadhurst range. At a time when interior designers were still perpetuating Australia's ship-fed culture by relying solely on imported textiles and soft furnishings from Europe and Britain, Broadhurst established original Australian motifs that featured on walls in Paris, Bahrain, London and Singapore (O'Brien 2004, 8). In fact, a Broadhurst wallpaper features in the character Casper's house in the 2006 Australian film *Candy* directed by Neil Armfield. The olive and green print of Broadhurst's '26. The Cranes' can be seen stretching across the expansive wall of Casper's living room. The wallpaper was brought in by the set decorator to symbolize the age and stature of the house and its sole inhabitant (Davis, Armfield and Mackie 2006). To support the analysis of Thompson and Broadhurst's assimilation with the surface through their creative endeavours, the following section of this chapter investigates examples of more literal assimilations between subject and patterned surface in both film and visual art.

THE WRITING ON THE WALL – FILMIC AND PAINTED INTERIORS

In the opening scene of Australian film *Candy*, two lovers, Dan and Candy, enter an open top 'Gravitron' amusement ride (Davis, Armfield and Mackie 2006). From a platform above, their fatherly friend Casper watches as the Gravitron begins to spin and the centrifugal forces created by this movement push Dan and Candy into the padded surfaces of the ride's walls. Perhaps the film's director was using the ride to symbolize the two characters spiralling or spinning out of control; but more than this, there is a sense of joy and liberation between Candy and Dan as the two are gently forced onto the wall's surface. As their bodies are freed of the corporeal weight of gravity and forced into the walls of the ride – the soft and flesh-like surface of the Gravitron's padded interior absorbing Candy and Dan's skin and clothing – there is a fluid and dynamic assimilation between bodies and surface.

As the film progresses, the audience is an intimate witness to the demise of the young and vibrant couple in love to a series of tragic events driven by their addiction to heroin. Throughout the film Candy and Dan move in and out of a series of houses, with Casper's house, featuring Broadhurst's 'Cranes' wallpaper, providing their one constant base. Towards the end of the film Candy and Dan attempt to make a new start in an abandoned house in a rural town. This is the last house that they share together. It is in this house that Candy's ultimate undoing is acted out through her assimilation with the wall's surface. Dan wakes up one morning to see Candy inscribing the cream walls of their bedroom with vibrant red lipstick. The lipstick with which she stains her wall also stains her face and her clothes, so that her body becomes just as much a part of the walls as her scrawled words. Candy's hands grip the walls and her head leans into its surface of stained statements. When Dan leaves the room in frustration, Candy sits in front of a mirror and stares at her reflection. The camera zooms in on Candy and her fragile connection with her reflection as she smears lipstick over her image in the surface. Through these gestures, Candy has become surface, a visible representation of what lies below her façade. Sylvia Lavin captures this interplay between the surface and inner being:

> From the face that mirrors the soul, to the magic writing tablet that reveals subconscious drives, the surface, any surface, all surfaces, have been considered worthy of attention insofar as they are the top layer, the outermost skin, the merely visible envelope of more particularized and specific under and inner depths. (2011, 38)

While this scene paints the all too familiar picture of the wall's surface and the insane female character, it is also the scene where Candy begins her journey towards a recovery from addiction, as though her close encounter with the wall's surface is a method through which she can come to terms with her material reality.

In the climactic scene in the house, Dan returns home to find the writing on the wall. Candy is absent and her physical presence has become the surface of the walls, as Dan stands awestruck, reading the poem chaotically sprawling across the surfaces of the house. An excerpt from the poem reads: 'Danny the daredevil. Candy went missing … . A vase of flowers by the bed. My bare blue knees at dawn. These ruffled sheets and you are gone and I am going too' (Davis, Armfield and Mackie 2006).

The wide span image in this scene suggests that Candy is not present as a bodily entity, although she is present within and behind the surface: we are left imagining that she is present in space, she has transformed into the wall's surface. Dan begins to clean some of the writing off the wall until he resigns in despair; he pins a message written on the back of one of Candy's paintings to the wall, as though communicating to her through the wall's surface, and leaves for Casper's house.

At Casper's house, Dan hears that Candy has experienced a 'nervous breakdown' and has been taken to hospital. Dan goes to visit Candy; in this scene there is different, visible, assimilation between Candy and the surface conveyed in the close up shot, which focuses on Candy's pale face and white hair that blend into the white walls and translucent curtains behind her. This assimilation between subject and object through the 'close up' is explicated by Simone Brott (2008, 6) who uses Deleuzian theory to describe the effect of the architectural surface becoming an entity. Examining three films, *Through a Glass Darkly*, *Repulsion*, and *Barton Fink*, Brott writes: 'the close-up is not primarily scopic but a bodily bringing close, a visceral merging of subject and object' (Brott 2008, 10). This device is used throughout the filmic portrayal of Candy's downfall and ultimate recovery. Similarly, this merging of subject and object is evident in the work of the Australian body illustration artist, Emma Hack.

Inspired by the German supermodel and pioneer of body painting, Verushka, who painted herself into rustic walls in the 1960s and 1970s, Hack went in search of a new medium in which she could blend the female body with the surfaces of walls (Hack 2010). Initially, Hack's work was concerned with altering the outline of the female figure by camouflaging sections of the body, painting them into the surface of a wall (Hack 2010). In 2005, after finding a Broadhurst wallpaper in an Adelaide homeware store, she began using Florence Broadhurst wallpapers as the background to her work. For Hack, Broadhurst's wallpapers had a special quality; she felt that 'every time I look at the wallpaper I see there is a character in there' (2010). Hack's work exemplifies a reciprocal relationship between wall surface and subject. Broadhurst's wallpapers, as discussed earlier in this chapter, bring some of her own identity to the work, and Hack's painting of the female body brings a new life to Broadhurst's wallpapers. David Lennie of Signature Prints – the owners of the Broadhurst range of wallpapers – describes Emma's work as a 'joint venture' and something that Florence Broadhurst would have loved (Hack 2010). Broadhurst and Hack both chose to work with traditional applications of their crafts, and Broadhurst maintained the processes of hand-printing wallpapers at a time when machine-produced wallpapers were filling the market; while Hack hand-painted the designs onto live models' bodies, refusing to use projection or post-production editing to create 'flat images' (Hack 2010). This three-dimensional quality of the work draws the viewer into the image to decipher the borders between subject and object, becoming a voyeur of the architectural close-up in a close encounter with the surface.

This close-up view was utilized by Hack when, in 2010, she was commissioned to work on a film clip for a collaboration between Australian musician Gotye and New Zealand singer Kimbra (Hack 2010). The film clip involves the musicians being painted into and out of a wall's surface through a series of close-up shots in a stop animation. The idea for the film clip arises from the song's title, 'Somebody That I Used to Know', a song about a couple breaking up, and depicts the artists blending with, but not disappearing into, the wall's surface, creating a sense of a shadowing of their identities (Pincus 2010). This film clip is of particular interest because it is a male body that is painted into the surface and the female body is painted out of the surface, as though liberated from the wall. The assimilation of the male body with surface is also highlighted in Simone Brott's analysis of the film *Barton Fink*, where the actor John Turturro has a close encounter with the wallpaper in his room (2008, 8).

My interpretation here departs from existing literature on the body and the wall's surface that has developed from critical analysis of *The Yellow Wallpaper* (c. 1892). Rather than the subject being trapped or captivated by the surface, I argue that it is a reciprocal relationship between surface and subject, and that in the process of being lost or losing oneself in the surface, the subject may come to terms with his or her material existence; it is a reflexive relationship that develops from a close encounter with the surface.

5.2 Image from Australian artist Gotye's music video, 'Somebody that I Used to Know' (feat. Kimbra). From the album *Making Mirrors*. Video directed by Natasha Pincus. Body artwork by Emma Hack

CONCLUSION

The one theme that brings all the elements of this chapter together is the intimate, perhaps secret, relationship between living body and inanimate surface. Broadhurst and Thompson's unresolved endings, Candy's nervous breakdown, and Gotye's song about the disappearance of a relationship – all of these tragedies are both concealed and revealed by the patterned surface. The patterned surface is, as Fernand Léger (1973, 49) describes, a living surface, and as the subjects in this chapter demonstrate, the animation of the patterned surface accommodates the subject. There is an important distinction that this research makes from the existing literature on wallpaper and decorative surfaces; the subject is not occupied by the patterned surface, but rather the surface provides a space within it for the subject to occupy. The pattern as a living element draws the subject in for a close encounter and is an agent through which the subject can come to terms with their material existence and the physical environment. The plain white surface offers no such deviation, no space within its surface to occupy, whereas the patterned surface divides the wall, creating a space to harbour divergent histories and multiple characters, a space to occupy.

Beyond this, the occupation of the patterned surface is not one reserved solely for female characters, as demonstrated through Thompson's work and the painting of Gotye's body into the wall's surface. Neither is the act of occupying the patterned surface one of capitulation and submission by the female subject, as can be seen in the way Florence Broadhurst used wallpaper to climb the social ladder to notoriety, and the character Candy arrived at a new becoming through a close encounter with the patterned wall's surface. That patterned wall can be read as space itself;

creating space within the planar surface through its capacity to divide and animate the anonymity of the white wall's surface (Léger, 1973, 47). This space can be read as the singular whole, as one identity, or, as exemplified in Thompson's Bangkok house, as a series of interconnected individual parts, a multiplicity of contained identities within the larger whole. It is this faculty of the patterned wall that relates to subjectivity and brings the wall to life.

ACKNOWLEDGEMENTS

Thanks to Anuradha Chatterjee for her careful feedback in the initial attempts to turn this work into something more than a conference paper. Thanks to Jill Franz for her support to get this work to the IDEA 'State of Becoming' symposium; I am also grateful to the reviewers, organizers and convenors of that symposium. Lastly, thanks to David Toussaint for guiding me to Jim Thomspon on our travels in South East Asia, and thanks to Elle Trevorrow for making such keen observations of the film, *Candy*.

REFERENCES

Armfield, Neil (director). 2006. *Candy*. Motion picture. Sydney: New South Wales Film and Television Office.

Armstrong, Gillian (writer/director). 2010. *Unfolding Florence: The Many Lives of Florence Broadhurst*. Documentary film. Australia: Icon Film Distribution.

Brott, Simone. 2008. 'Close Encounter, Withdrawn Effects'. *Journal of Architectural Education* 61 (4): 6–16.

Carax, Leos (writer/director/producer). 2012. *Holy Motors*. Motion picture. Paris: Icon Film Distribution.

Gilbert, Sandra and Susan Gubar. 2000. *The Madwoman in the Attic: The Woman Writer and 19th Century Literary Imagination*. New York: Yale University Press.

Guy, John. 2004. 'Fit for a King: Indian Textiles and Thai Court Protocol'. In *Through the Thread of Time; Southeast Asian Textiles,* edited by J. Puranananda, 97–111. Bangkok: Riverbooks.

Hack, Emma. 2010. *Interview with Artist, Emma Hack*. Video file. http://emmahackartist.com/documentaries.php. Accessed 20 June 2012.

Hartzell, Freyja. 2009. 'The Velvet Touch: Fashion, Furniture, and the Fabric of the Interior'. *Fashion Theory* 13 (1): 51–82.

Jim Thompson and Associates. 2011. *Jim Thompson's Magical Space by Douglas Little Takes 'Paris Deco Off' by Storm*. http://k2designassociates.com/Portals/0/PARIS DECO OFF 2011.pdf. Accessed 12 November 2013.

Lavin, Sylvia. 2011. *Kissing Architecture*. United Kingdom: Princeton Architectural Press.

Léger, Fernand. 1973. 'The Wall, the Architect, the Painter'. In *Functions of Painting,* edited by Edward F. Fry, 45–53. London: Thames and Hudson.

MoMA. 2008a. *Behind the Scenes with Pipilotti Rist, Pour Your Body Out* (7354 Cubic Meters). Video file. http://www.moma.org/explore/multimedia/videos/28/233. Accessed 30 January 2012.

———. 2008b. *Curator Klaus Biesenbach discusses Pipilotti Rist: Pour Your Body Out* (7354 Cubic Meters). Video file. http://www.moma.org/explore/multimedia/videos/28/233. Accessed 30 January 2012.

O'Brien, Siobhan. 2004. *A Life by Design: The Art and Lives of Florence Broadhurst*. Melbourne: Allen and Unwin.

O'Neill, Helen. 2006. *Florence Broadhurst: Her Secret & Extraordinary Lives*. Sydney: Hardy Grant Books.

Pincus, Natasha (director), Gotye (artist), Emma Hack (artist), Kimbra (artist), 2010. *Somebody that I Used to Know*. Motion picture. Melbourne: Richmond Studios.

Pringle, P. 2010. 'Haunting the Stage: Performances Beyond the Veil'. In *Audience, the XXVIIIth SAHANZ Annual Conference, July 7–10, 2011, Brisbane, Australia*. The Society of Architectural Historians Australia and New Zealand.

Puranananda, J., ed. 2004. Through the Thread of Time; Southeast Asian Textiles. Bangkok: Riverbooks.

Ritchie, G. (director), J. Silver (producer), M. and K. Mulroney (screenwriters). 2011. *Sherlock Holmes: A Game of Shadows*. Hollywood: Warner Bros.

Schmidt, Christine. 2009. 'Undressing Kellerman, Uncovering Broadhurst: The Modern Woman and "Un-Australia"'. *The Journal of Dress, Body & Culture* 13 (4): 481–98.

Suvarnabhumi Airport New Bangkok Airport Guide. 2006. http://www.bangkokairportonline.com/node/182. Accessed 15 March 2013.

Warren. W. 2007. *Jim Thompson: The Unsolved Mystery*. Bangkok: Archipelago Press.

Wigley, Mark. 1995. White Walls, Designer Dresses: the Fashioning of Modern Architecture. Cambridge: MIT Press.

6

Ordinary Things, Domestic Space and Photography: Takashi Yasumura's Interiors

Jane Simon

INTRODUCTION

This chapter is concerned with the things that fill domestic interiors. Takashi Yasumura's photographs in his photographic series (and book of the same title) *Domestic Scandals* (2005) provide an opportunity to think about the relationship between ordinary things, domestic spaces and photography.[1] The domestic is usually imagined through the lens of the intimate, the familial and the human subject. Rather than identifying domestic space through its human occupants, I reframe the focus to the occupation of domestic space by things. This chapter uses *Domestic Scandals*' foregrounding of domestic things to consider the insights of 'thing theory'. Thing theory is a term for the diverse attempts by scholars across multiple disciplines to grapple with the representation of things, the materiality of things, and the value and significance of things, and for a general focus on the world of inanimate objects. My attention to thing theory in this chapter is primarily concerned with the work of Bill Brown, a cultural theorist whose approach to thing theory relies on a distinction between objects and things. I use thing theory here as a way to think about the distinction between objects and things as always in flux, depending on how they are framed and perceived. Drawing on Yasumura's book *Domestic Scandals*, I consider how photography and the camera can reframe our attention to the objects that occupy the interior domestic world, and ask what happens when we finally catch 'a glimpse of things', rather than 'look *through* objects' (Brown 2001, 4, original emphasis). Arguably, the concerns of thing theory are examined in visual form through still life: that quiet genre of painting and photography that levels its gaze at things. Through a close examination of Yasumura's photographs, this chapter brings the concerns of thing theory into conversation with still life, photography and the domestic.

PHOTOGRAPHIC ART AND THE DOMESTIC

Yasumura is a photographer who lives and works in Tokyo. His work is focused on the ordinary or the everyday. His photographs pay attention to the odd moments and unlikely juxtapositions that occur in daily life. His series *Nature Tracing*, for example, shows representations of nature that are combined with the mass produced or the built environment (Yasumura 2009). These 'interior landscapes' highlight the oddity of man-made attempts to recreate nature. *Nature Tracing* includes images of a framed puzzle of a forest scene hung on a wood-panelled wall; a decorative crystal in front of a painting of mountains and clouds; and a stuffed toy animal in front of a sliding door painted with a nature scene. *Domestic Scandals*, in a similar mode, asks us to *look again* at banal aspects of the domestic interior that we might normally take for granted (doors, heaters, table settings and so on), and to notice what might be odd or unusual or compelling about them.

Yasumura's photographs in *Domestic Scandals* can be positioned in the context of photographic art which explores domestic interiors. Attention to domestic spaces and things has a range of registers in the context of contemporary photographic art (Cotton 2009). Some photographers ask us to observe the overlooked – or the underside – of domesticity. For example, Moyra Davey photographs dust gathered underneath furniture and the mess of a work desk in her book *Long Life Cool White* (2008), and Anna Fox focuses on the mess of daily home life, photographing, for instance, the cockroaches that fill her large London shared house in *Cockroach Diary* (2000). Other photographers, such as Bert Teunissen, focus on the history of a building's interior and the lives of its residents. Teunissen's photographic project *Domestic Landscapes* (2007) is dedicated to photographing occupants in domestic interiors that were built in the pre-electricity era when daylight was the main source of light. Other artists such as Laurie Simmons (2003, 2007) and James Casebere (1996) attend to interior spaces through carefully constructed dollhouses or architectural models which are then photographed. These examples speak to the need, as Colin Painter (2002) describes, to consider the relationship between contemporary art and the home, and specifically the relationship between the domestic interior and art photography.

Yasumura's project is distinctive amongst various representations of domestic interiority in contemporary photographic art practice. There is no mess or dust or dirt in his photographs. Unlike Davey's and Fox's emphasis on the daily mess of domestic life, Yasumura's interiors are flawlessly clean, and while two photographs (out of a total of 36 images) in the monograph feature people ('A Father' 1998 and 'A Man' 1998) these portraits are far from the humanism of Teunissen's portraits in domestic interiors. Yasumura's carefully composed photographs are, as Shino Kuraishi describes, 'a space where the quirky qualities of "things" are radically unfolded with shivering calmness' (2005, 88). The photographs feature simple daily things, including red and blue patterned slippers (Figure 6.1), a glass ashtray, a bright pink stapler, floral curtains, nail clippers, a telephone, toilet paper (Figure 6.6) and a kitchen cupboard. Where the photographs feature humans, they are observed coolly as though they too are inanimate objects. We are asked to look at them just as we look at the ashtray, or the stapler – an acknowledgement that 'the human is a thing among things' (Brown 2010, 200).

Domestic Scandals was produced over a period of seven years. Yasumura's photographs of domestic things against the backdrop of the wooden textures of floors and tabletops and printed fabrics of curtains were made at his parents' house in the Shiga Prefecture of Tokyo, but the photographs are not autobiographical. The photographs don't ask us to look at domestic things as meaningful because of any personal attachment or historical importance – this is not a sentimental gaze. The photographs don't portray the domestic things and spaces as though they were saturated with personal memory. The title of each photograph is telling: for example, 'A Father' (Figure 6.2) or 'A Pair of Slippers' (Figure 6.1), is not a statement *about* Yasumura's relationship to his father, and it doesn't matter *whose* slippers are represented. As Norman Bryson has argued in relation to still life painting, this is 'the world minus its narratives or, better, the world minus its capacity for generating narrative interest' (1990, 60). There is nothing confessional about these images and as a collective they do not generate a cohesive narrative (although the sequencing of the photographs in the book does encourage the viewer to make connections between shapes, colours and backgrounds). Yasumura's project is about asking us to view both people and objects as things that occupy space and to attend to the materiality of the domestic realm.

6.1 'A Pair of Slippers' 1997, from the series *Domestic Scandals*
Source: © Takashi Yasumura, courtesy of Osiris.

6.2 'A Father' 1998, from the series *Domestic Scandals*
Source: © Takashi Yasumura, courtesy of Osiris.

Yasumura's interiors – despite the fact that he is photographing his parent's family home – represent a break from a nostalgic or reminiscent approach to home spaces (Kuraishi 2005, 89). My reading of his photographs departs from approaches to domesticity and photography which understand the domestic interior through personal memory and autobiography. This linking of the domestic, photography and life narrative is exemplified by Kathy Mezei (2005). In her reading of Gregory Crewdson's art photography alongside literary examples of domestic interiority, she writes: 'Interior domestic spaces (furniture, rooms, doors, windows, stairs, drawers – familiar, everyday objects) which … could be perceived as banal and ordinary, and hence insignificant, are vital to the shaping of our memories, our imagination, and our "selves"' (2005, 82).

While Mezei positions Crewdson's photographs as having the ability to 'transpose the home into the unhomely' (2005, 89), her discussion of the domestic is very much concerned with the symbiotic relationship between the home and the self. Mezei's approach to domestic interiority is useful for its attention to how seemingly insignificant, banal domestic things can influence the stories of one's life. However, her approach retains focus on the human's relationship to the domestic interior and its objects. Yasumura's project asks for a very different examination of the domestic – one that considers the domestic *outside* of the significance the objects hold for our 'selves'.

Yasumura's photographs of the interior of his parents' home juxtapose the mass produced with traditional Japanese decorations and ornaments. In 'A Tape Recorder' (2002) (Figure 6.3), for example, a silver cassette tape player sits in front of a *fusuma* sliding door, or room divider, its panels painted with a nature scene, and on top of tatami flooring. Another photograph, 'A Bonsai Tree and a Watering Hose' (1999), features the miniature tree at the same height as the coiled plastic blue and white hose. For Martin Jaeggi, the scandal that the English title of Yasumura's series refers to is the cultural 'occupation' of Japan by the West: 'the slow erosion of traditional Japanese ways of living, the global triumph of the trappings of Western middle-class lifestyle and its promises of modernity and convenience' (2005, 85). This idea that there is a pre-existing Japanese culture that is eroded by, or 'borrows' from the trappings of the West is too simple and remains blinkered to the dynamic nature of what Ofra Goldstein-Gidoni describes as the 'constant shift of hierarchies of the "Western" and the "Japanese"' in Japanese contemporary material culture (2001, 86). Rather than focusing on the juxtaposition of Japanese tradition and 'Western' objects, my reading of Yasumura's photographs is much more concerned with the photographs' flattened attention to how things occupy the domestic interior.

I say *flattened* attention, because the photographs offer an equal attention to the human and the inhuman, to the plastic mass-produced and the traditional, to the decorative and the useful, and to nature and its artificial imitations. The gaze of the camera shifts our usual patterns of recognition that position humans as subjects and material things as objects. 'A Father' (1998) (Figure 6.2), for example, presents the human figure as an inanimate statue – the man appears stiff and gazes, unaware of the camera. In the book that particular photograph sits between a photograph of a bright blue coat hook and a wood-panelled wall ('A Coat Hook' 1998) and a photograph of a phone which sits – mysteriously – on the floor in the

6.3 'A Tape Recorder' 2002, from the series *Domestic Scandals*
Source: © Takashi Yasumura, courtesy of Osiris.

very corner of a room ('A Phone' 1999). A coat hook, a father and a phone all appear to be as important and as elusive in meaning as each other. It is this flattening of attention that compels a reading of Yasumura's *Domestic Scandals* through the insights of 'thing theory'.

ON 'THING THEORY'

The increasing attention to material culture, things and objects is regularly rehearsed in scholarship which tackles the nebulous nature of thing theory (Brown 2004, Connor 2010, Plotz 2005, Breitbach 2011). *Things* have been the concern of sociologists, anthropologists, designers and philosophers for many years. For example, the 1920s is a period when things became an important theoretical focus for writers such a Walter Benjamin, Martin Heidegger and Georg Lukács (Brown 1999, 3). However, 'thing theory' is distinct in its attempt to tackle the 'thingness' of the material world without necessarily being concerned with unveiling the deeper meaning or cultural importance of a material object. Instead, things are positioned as having a life of their own beyond – or regardless of – their utility to the human subject. Thing theory, therefore, is an umbrella term for the recent accumulation of critical work that engages with 'the problem of where an object's "meaning" ended and its "materiality" began' (Plotz 2005, 118).

Brown's essay 'Thing Theory' (2001) is a cornerstone of recent literature on things. Brown's exploration of things and thing theory has explored a range of cultural texts, including modernist literature (1999); toys and popular film (1998); and more recently contemporary art and museum/heritage practice (2010). Brown's discussion of things rests on a distinction between objects and things. Objects are those things that we understand – they have a clear role in our daily lives and a circumscribed use. Because of this we don't look at the material thingness that lies beyond the functionality of an object. According to Brown, objects are perceived according to their utility for human use, or for what they tell us about our own history or culture. This gaze at objects through the lens of what makes them meaningful for us means that we 'look *through* objects … but we only catch a glimpse of things' (2001, 4). We only notice the materiality of objects when they become dysfunctional: 'We begin to confront the thingness of objects when they stop working for us: when the drill breaks, when the car stalls, when the windows get filthy, when their flow within the circuits of production and distribution, consumption and exhibition, has been arrested, however momentarily' (Brown 2001, 4). Objects become things when their relation to the human subject changes, when they no longer perform the role that the human subject has ascribed to them.

The distinction between objects and things, therefore, is not about essential qualities or properties, but is rather a question of framing and perception: an object becomes a thing, and a thing becomes an object. This flipping between recognizing objects and noticing things is made clear in Yasumura's photographs. In the case of 'A Fan Heater' (Figure 6.4), for example, the heater is positioned just off-centre and is photographed at a level angle. This framing of the heater encourages the viewer to look *directly* at the heater and to notice its shape and colour.

6.4 'A Fan Heater' 1999, from the series *Domestic Scandals*
Source: © Takashi Yasumura, courtesy of Osiris.

This positioning also draws attention to the patterns of lines and the form of both the heater and the wall behind it. The eye is drawn to notice how the horizontal lines of the air vents parallel the lines of the skirting board, and the darker fake wood of the heater's casing stands out against the lighter wood panelling behind it. In other words, the photograph – by drawing attention to the materiality of the heater – highlights its *thingness*. In paying attention to the form of the heater we can forget – at least momentarily – that the heater is an object with a use: to warm the human body. This shifting between objects and things depends on how they work (or don't work) in particular contexts and in relation to the human subject that perceives them; *looking* is important here. As Julia Breitbach notes, 'Things precede and exceed objects, and objects are what the human intellect makes of things' (2011, 33). An object becomes a thing when it is out of place, when it stops working or being useful, or when it sits outside our usual patterns of recognition (for example when noticing the surface of a mirror rather than the reflection captured in it) and, sometimes, when objects are employed in the still life they also become 'things'.

STILL LIFE, THINGS, PHOTOGRAPHY

Photography 'deprives things of their uses' (Kuraishi 2005, 89), and photographers 'have a special relation to the mystery of thingness' (Warner 2004, 10). Photographs allow us to look at things outside of their use-value and to re-frame the quotidian outside of our normal modes of perception. It is this ability of photography to draw our attention to the qualities – textures, shapes, forms, surfaces – of everyday things that Yasumura practices in *Domestic Scandals*. Yasumura's photographs ask us to meditate on the thingness of a stapler, a fan heater, a cupboard, toilet rolls, piles of neatly tied newspapers and other daily materials beyond their mere functionality for human purpose. Yasumura's attention to the material presence of the quotidian seems to ask us to look *at* things, rather than look *through* objects.

One of the compelling aspects of the still life genre – which maps onto Yasumura's project in *Domestic Scandals* – is its 'radical decentering that demolishes the idea of a world convergent on the person as universal centre' (Bryson 1990, 145). That is, because the still life focuses on the materials of human life that are needed for sustenance and the daily ritual (food, domestic utensils and so on) the individual or personal body is not addressed, because of the generic function of the materials that could 'service' anybody. The still life also moves beyond the anthropocentricism of other genres of painting and photography by assaulting the 'centrality, value and prestige of the human subject', and while the human figure is absent from the scene of the still life, it is also not lurking nearby, indeed '[h]uman presence is not only expelled physically: still life also expels the values which human presence imposes on the world' (Bryson 1990, 60). Of course, the photographic or painted still life is still produced by a human subject who chooses what to paint or photograph, how to frame it, and it is a human subject who looks at the end product. The human figure, therefore, can be excluded from the image, but human presence can never be totally absent. The removal of the human figure in all but two of the 36 photographs in *Domestic Scandals* echoes (albeit not entirely, given the brief appearance of the human figure in 'A Man' and 'A Father') the still life's reframing of our focus on the overlooked, the unimportant, but at the same time very familiar things and forms which are part of daily life (Williams 2006). For these reasons, I would argue that the genre of the still life in both painting and photography has explored the concerns of thing theory long before the term was coined. The aims of thing theory are captured in Bryson's description of the still life:

> *In its quality of attention, still life possesses a delicate and ambiguous instrument. Its whole project forces the subject, both painter and viewer, to attend closely to the preterite objects in the world which, exactly because they are so familiar, elude normal attention. Since still life needs to look at the overlooked, it has to bring into view objects which perception normally screens out.* (1990, 87, original emphasis)

Brown himself acknowledges the capacity of art to propel our understanding of things when he writes of his interest 'in what works of art teach us about the otherness of objects as such, the differentiation between subject and object, as between human and nonhuman' (1990, 186), and his reference to how some artists 'evoke the long and global history of how things are absorbed into the field of cultural production' (194).

The unsettling quietness of Yasumura's photographs – what Kuraishi describes as 'shivering calmness' (2005, 88) – is also akin to the sense of strangeness that is achieved through still life paintings' representation of everyday materials such as food. Bryson highlights how the deliberate arrangement of materials and the careful use of light in still life paintings can make ordinary objects appear 'radically *un*familiar and estranged' (1990, 87). Playing with the conventions of still life, Yasumura's 'Japanese Oranges' (Figure 6.5) features a plastic strainer bowl atop a table that is covered with a green and white striped tablecloth. The photograph is framed to exclude the surroundings in the room: the surface of the table meets the background surface of a wood-panelled wall and the oranges glow from the centre of the image as light hits the dimpled skin of the fruit. The careful manipulation of light and the arrangement of the fruit in the plastic latticed bowl defamiliarizes the bowl of fruit. Estranged from their function as food, the oranges instead become extraordinary forms to admire.

'Japanese Oranges' (Figure 6.5) makes a feature not only of the oranges, but also of the gridded texture of their container and the slightly rippled surface of the tablecloth whose stripes lie adjacent to the (fake-looking) panels of wood. 'A Pair of Slippers' (Figure 6.1) pays similar attention to the texture of the domestic interior. The photograph features a red and blue pair of slippers that sit just inside a door (we see a stripe of curtain), and atop wooden floorboards. The slippers seem to be on their way somewhere, they appear as if caught mid-shuffle across the wooden surface, a visual response to the question Ernst Bloch poses in his book *Traces*: 'Do inanimate objects play-act?' (quoted in Parlati 2011, 76). This plays with the idea that things have their own form, essence and lives outside of their utility to humans. In other words, the focus for Yasumura is on the life of objects themselves.

Domestic Scandals draws attention to the dysfunction of objects – thereby allowing us to glimpse *things* – through their careful arrangement. 'Rolls of Toilet Paper and a Plastic Flower' (1998) (Figure 6.6), for example, shows 12 stacked rolls of toilet paper next to a plastic vase containing a fake red rose. Things occupy unlikely places in many of the photographs. For example, in 'A Shortcake' (2002), the dessert sits inexplicably inside an empty kitchen cupboard; in 'A Candy Bar' (2005), a wrapped chocolate sits alone inside an empty, dark cabinet; and in 'A Stuffed Pheasant' (1998), the stuffed animal sits in an improbable area of display – perching on the carpet facing towards a floral curtain. The tongue-in-cheek positioning of 'Rolls of Toilet Paper and a Plastic Flower' speaks to Yasumura's habit of juxtaposing the banal and useful with the decorative. And, as with all of the images in *Domestic Scandals*, the photograph draws attention not just to the quotidian things featured, but also to the texture of the domestic interior walls: the green and beige checkered bathroom tiles are in focus, as is the surface of the painted wall. But most importantly, the collocation of the toilet rolls on the bathroom floor next to the fake rose adds to the odd sense that these things have their own purpose

6.5 'Japanese Oranges' 2002, from the series *Domestic Scandals*
Source: © Takashi Yasumura, courtesy of Osiris.

that is unrelated to the functions of the human world. Ordinary domestic things, when they appear in Yasumura's photographs, begin to seem strange. As Akihito Yasumi describes:

> Under the meticulous direction of the photographer they even begin to show humorous and sometimes grotesque qualities, as though they had long forgotten about a 'nature' that might have existed sometime somewhere; and thus they make us feel as if they existed according to their own logic, in a world without humans and out of touch with any functions related to humans. (2005, 86)

This 'logic' or quality of a vase or a cupboard or a curtain is a logic of 'things' – one that is, despite being arranged by a human, completely unconcerned with having a functional relationship to humans.

'A Fan Heater' (1999) (Figure 6.4) shows a heater, complete with wooden surface, sitting solidly in the centre of the image. A white electrical cord crawls out of the heater's side and out of the side of the image. Beneath the heater is a red-brown carpet, and behind the heater are wooden panels to the left, and to the right, pale yellow flowered wallpaper. According to Kuraishi, it is these surrounding domestic interior textures that are crucial to Yasumura's photographs:

6.6 'Rolls of Toilet Paper and a Plastic Flower' 1998, from the series, *Domestic Scandals*
Source: © Takashi Yasumura, courtesy of Osiris.

> Yet more important than the 'objects' situated at the centre of the image and the emphasis on their surface appeal are the 'things' in the 'background', such as wallpapers, screen doors, linoleum-covered floors, tiled walls and curtains. In contrast to the 'objects' whose position is easily changed, these backgrounds are basically immovable and can only be photographed as they are. (2005, 89)

Yasumura's photographs draw attention not only to the things featured in the title of each photograph, but also to the materiality of the interior setting of each artefact. In his photographs the focus is not only on the bowl of oranges (Figure 6.5) or the heater (Figure 6.4), it is extended to the patterns, textures and qualities of the surrounding surfaces of the domestic interior. This mode of attention is akin to 'still life's fascination with effects of intense focusing, frequently amounting to glare' (Bryson 1990, 169). This 'glaring' intensity of attention that Bryson describes in relation to the majority of still life paintings prior to the 1700s is, interestingly, positioned in relation to the technology of the camera lens: 'still life seems to have been a camera with only one, unadjustable lens, with the sole property of rendering all objects in the scene in brilliant and drilling clarity' (169).[2] Yasumura's project takes on the challenge of rendering the domestic space and the things that occupy it with the same 'drilling clarity' and flattened non-hierarchical mode of looking.

SEEING OBJECTS, LOOKING AT THINGS

Attention to framing and modes of perception is the concern of still life art photography. It is precisely this concern with framing and the act of looking which allows us to glimpse the thingness of domestic things but this can also fold back into seeing objects. While Yasumura's photographs highlight the qualities of things, the very act of *looking* at the domestic things in the photographs – the toilet rolls, the plastic vase, the fake rose and so on – means that they might shift from being things to objects. For Brown, our attention to things turns them into objects. He makes this point by drawing on Vladimir Nabokov, who writes in *Transparent Things* that 'When we concentrate on a material object, whatever its situation, the very act of attention may lead to our involuntarily sinking into the history of that object' (quoted in Brown 2001, 4). This means that our ability to perceive things in their full thingness is always a slippery one. As Brown writes: 'We don't apprehend things except partially or obliquely (as what's beyond our apprehension). In fact by looking *at* things we render them objects' (4). If '[o]bjects and things are really two sides of the same coin – with either face up, depending on their reception by an interpreting subject' (Breitbach 2011, 34), then Yasumura's photographs move between both sides of the coin: offering a glance at things while at the same time we perceive them as recognizable objects. *Domestic Scandals* reframes what we see, recognize and notice in the domestic interior and in doing so, allows us to catch a glimpse of domestic things.

Marina Warner reminds us that 'there is the quiddity of things which photographs explore' but, she goes on to add, 'photographs have their own being, are themselves a subject with their own quiddity' (2004, 10). In other words, all this attention to things *in* photographs sidesteps the point that photographs themselves *are* things (Edwards and Hart 2004, Breitbach 2011). To focus our attention too narrowly on the hide-and-seek nature of seeing the thing-ness of things represented in *Domestic Scandals* means we ignore the thing-ness of the photographs before us. The very act of looking at things in photographs also produces the elision between objects and things: focusing on the things in the photograph can mean the viewer doesn't notice the materiality – the thingness – of the photographs themselves. As Yasumi writes, 'if there is something we should find in Yasumura's photographs, it is not to the meanings behind his subjects, but the "photographs themselves" that have become invisible by overlapping with their subject matter' (2005, 86). While the bright domestic surfaces, interiors, and things *in* Yasumura's photographs compel a thinking about the material existence of those things, the photographs' ability to mediate our relationship to things are further questions to be considered in the light of thing theory. Warner argues that photographers 'have a special relation to the mystery of thingness' (2004, 10). This is because photographers are able to seize upon and 'still' the material world and to notice what is usually overlooked. Photography, in other words, can act as a visual tool for redirecting our attention to the material world.

If thing theory opens up more questions than it provides answers, then Yasumura's photographs with their flattened attention to the animate and inanimate, the useful and the decorative, the traditional and modern, and the alive and the inert, provide us with a visual tool for thinking about the thingness of the domestic object world, and for thinking about occupation in terms outside of the human subject. Yasumura's project in *Domestic Scandals* calls for an examination of the domestic outside of the personal, the sentimental and its significance for our 'selves'. The flattening of things in Yasumura's photographs allows us to notice their thing-ness. It confounds our attempts to imbue things with significance and indeed prompts a reconsideration of the notion of significance as a human projection onto things. In doing so it makes strange the domestic interior and the items, surfaces and materials which occupy it.

REFERENCES

Breitbach, Julia. 2011. 'The Photo-as-thing'. *European Journal of English Studies* 15 (1): 31–43.

Brown, Bill. 1998. 'How to do Things with Things (A Toy Story)'. *Critical Inquiry* 24 (4): 935–64.

———. 1999. 'The Secret Life of Things (Virginia Woolf and the Matter of Modernism)'. *Modernism/Modernity* 6 (2): 1–28.

———. 2001. 'Thing Theory'. *Critical Inquiry* 28 (1): 1–24.

———. 2010. 'Objects, Others, and Us (the Refabrication of Things)'. *Critical Inquiry* 36 (2): 183–217.

Bryson, Norman. 1990. *Looking at the Overlooked: Four Essays on Still Life Painting*. London: Reaktion.

Casebere, James. 1996. *Model Culture: Photographs 1975–1996*. San Fransisco: The Friends of Photography.

Connor, Steven. 2010. 'Thinking Things'. *Textual Practice* 24 (1): 1–20.

Cotton, Charlotte. 2009. *The Photograph as Contemporary Art*. London: Thames & Hudson.

Davey, Moyra. 2008. *Long Life, Cool White: Photographs and Essays*. New Haven: Yale University Press.

Edwards, Elizabeth and Janice Hart. 2004. 'Introduction: Photographs as Objects'. In *Photographs, Objects, Histories: On the Materiality of Images*, edited by Elizabeth Edwards and Janice Hart, 1–15. London: Routledge.

Fox, Anna. 2000. *Cockroach Diary*. London: Shoreditch Biennale.

Frow, John. 2001. 'A Pebble, A Camera, A Man Who Turns Into a Telegraph Pole'. *Critical Inquiry* 28 (1): 270–85.

Goldstein-Gidoni, Ofra. 2001. 'The Making and Marking of the "Japanese" and the "Western" in Japanese Contemporary Material Culture'. *Journal of Material Culture* 6 (1): 67–90.

Jaeggi, Martin. 2005. 'The Calm Surfaces of Scandal'. In *Domestic Scandals*, by Takashi Yasumura, 85. Tokyo: Osiris.

Kuraishi, Shino. 2005. 'Family Home, or the Stage of Representation: Takashi Yasumura's Domestic Scandals'. In *Domestic Scandals*, by Takashi Yasumura, 87–9. Tokyo: Osiris.

Martineau, Paul. 2010. *Still Life in Photography*. Santa Monica: J. Paul Getty Museum.

Mezei, Kathy. 2005. 'Domestic Space and the Idea of Home in Auto/biographical Practices'. In *Tracing the Autobiographical*, edited by Marlene Kadar, Linda Warley, Jeanne Perreault and Susanna Egan, 81–95. Waterloo: Wilfred Laurier University Press.

Painter, Colin, ed. 2002. *Contemporary Art and the Home*. Oxford: Berg.

Parlati, Marilena. 2011. 'Beyond Inchoate Debris'. *European Journal of English Studies* 15 (1): 73–84.

Plotz, John. 2005. 'Can the Sofa Speak? A Look at Thing Theory'. *Criticism* 47 (1): 109–18.

Simmons, Laurie. 2003. *In and Around the House: Photographs 1976–78*. New York: Carolina Nitsch Editions.

———. 2007. *Color Coordinated Interiors 1983*. New York: Skarstedt Fine Art.

Teunissen, Bert. 2007. *Domestic Landscapes: A Portrait of Europeans at Home*. New York: Aperture.

Warner, Marina. 2004. 'Introduction'. In *Things: A Spectrum of Photography, 1850–2001*, edited by Mark Haworth-Booth, 7–12. London: Jonathan Cape; Victoria and Albert Museum.

Williams, Val. 2006. 'Death, Disorder and Melancholy in the Contemporary Still Life'. In *Stilled: Contemporary Still Life Photography by Women*, edited by Kate Newton and Christine Rolph, 6–8. Cardiff: Ffotogallery.

Yasumi, Akihito. 2005. 'Friendship with the World of Things'. In *Domestic Scandals*, by Takashi Yasumura, 86. Tokyo: Osiris.

Yasumura, Takashi. 2005. *Domestic Scandals*. Tokyo: Osiris.

———. 2014. *Nature Tracing*. Accessed 10 March, http://takashiyasumura.com/site/nature_tracing_1e.html.

NOTES

1. The Japanese title of the book is 日常らしさ and the literal English translation is 'Everyday-like-ness', (Kuraishi 2005, 88). When exhibited in galleries Domestic Scandals consists of large 94 × 122 cm C-prints. In this chapter I'm focusing on the book version of *Domestic Scandals*. The photographs can be viewed on Yasumura's website: http://takashiyasumura.com/site/domestic_scandals_1e.html. Accessed 10 March 2014.

2. Bryson is making this point in relation to a specific period of still life painting (prior to the 1700s). He also discusses many examples of still life painting from the 1900s where painters upturned the allegiance to 'high focus' realism.

7

Seeing the Unseen: This is Not an Interior

Vanessa Galvin

INTRODUCTION: ORDERING THE RUINOUS SPACE

At the touch of a screen, flawless interiors roll continuously, presenting an assortment of considered, enviable responses to our fundamental need to dwell. These kinds of immaculate interiors, such as the one in Figure 7.1, are neat, luxurious, appealing and contain no detectable trace of authentic occupation or experience: no remnants of yesterday's celebrations, no hair brush by the basin, no utensils in the sink, not a crumb to be seen. Furthermore, the gleam of uncluttered surfaces, polished stone and considered furnishings induce the desire to inhabit in an idealistic, traceless way. To divert one's attention from the image is unsettling, as we are awakened to the consciousness of our own imperfect surroundings, which are disordered by the effects that everyday living imposes. Occupation ruins space.

Positively, traces of occupation validate spatial intention – the room is after all in use. Yet, to include signs of occupation in the image compromises adherence to interrelated social and institutionalized ideals of design practice, morality, and cleanliness. It is a fastidious task to maintain the ideal order of the interior by erasing the traces of life. Simone de Beauvoir laments that 'Few tasks are more like the torture of Sisyphus than housework, with its endless repetition' (de Beauvoir 1997, 470). It is, however, a far simpler task to frame these ideals permanently through the interior's image, instead alluding to the potential for occupation, which the act of viewing and imaginative inhabitation of the image invokes.

By disowning and repudiating the evidence of living, the image presents what is perceived to be the interior's ideal condition: unoccupied. A consequence of this paradoxical yet conventional idealization is the normalized understanding of how we are bound to present interior environments. This knowledge of the interior is accepted without question and dominates our thoughts, words and actions. Foucault describes this paradox in relation to similarly opposed conventions:

> And perhaps our life is still dominated by a certain number of oppositions that cannot be tampered with, that institutions and practices have not ventured to change –

7.1 KENZO-inspired apartment. Design by Olga Akulova
Source: Olga Akulova DESIGN. Photography by Andrey Avdeenko (2013).

oppositions we take for granted, for example, between private space and public space, between the family space and social space, between cultural space and useful space, between the space of leisure activities and the space of work. All these are still controlled by an unspoken sacralization. (Foucault 2000, 177)

The oppositional relation between idealized and actual occupation as evidenced through image articulates an accepted duality of the lived environment, indicating an understanding of the interior that is divided. Despite this dichotomy, it is a dominant practice to repudiate occupation through the erasure of life in the interior's image.

The aim of this chapter is therefore to challenge the normalized relation between occupation and the conventional representation of space. It is a discussion of oppositions and contrasts, order and conventions: the paradoxical consequence of institutionalized practices and understanding. The intention is to identify the idealized image as a construction which is more than just a model for optimal living, by positioning it instead as a discursive site for further contemplation, as a product of the 'techniques and procedures' of 'exclusion' and as what Foucault would describe as a material condition of knowledge (Foucault 1980, 101).

Such a pursuit allows us to confront how and what we do in terms of conventional representations of the interior: the way we passively see, actively consume and, in a combination of passive and active states, produce images of lived space. This is not a quest for the truth of interiors, nor is it a search for idealistic origins. Rather, it is a call for a contemporary mode of representing the interior to be problematized and questioned so that it can be contemplated in new ways.

Foucault's critical positioning facilitates the evaluation of our present reality and enables us to question what we are today, as well as awakening us to the possibility of what we might become. His mode of analysis elucidates the contingency and 'forms of rationality' (Foucault 1991, 48) surrounding what people presently do, the way that they do it, and helps us to 'recognize ourselves as subjects of what we are doing, thinking, saying' (Foucault 1991, 46). The idealized image presents an extension to our own material condition. In questioning the image, we are also questioning ourselves – what compels us to produce these images without signs of occupation? The Foucauldian ethos provides a framework to question these normalized understandings and practices of the interior so that we might conceive of it in other ways.

This research seeks to move beyond the widespread and critical acknowledgement of current thought and attitudes towards the way the interior is depicted. Stanley Abercrombie, for example, recalls Bruno Zevi's description of such traceless images that 'appear to be little more than dead-looking mineral formations left standing after the destruction of the human race, for whom, however, those spaces and chairs were obviously intended' (Zevi 1974, 216, quoted in Abercrombie 1990, 164). Witold Rybczynski, too, as part of his greater argument on comfort and the home, addresses

> *the kinds of sterile and impersonal homes that appear in interior-design and architectural magazines. What these spotless rooms lack, or what crafty photographers have carefully removed, is any evidence of human occupation. In spite of the artfully placed vases and casually arranged art books, the imprint of their inhabitants is missing. (1987, 17)*

The significance of Rybczynski's comment is not in the familiar observation that the rooms are intentionally uninhabited, spotlessly clean or staged for the camera, nor in the questioning of the practicality of living in such fastidiously maintained rooms: 'How do they manage without toothpaste tubes and half-used soap bars in their bathrooms?' (Rybczynski 1987, 17). More crucial to this argument is the insight it gives to disciplinary thinking, evidenced by the author's spontaneous response to the image, 'These pristine interiors fascinate and repel me' (Rybczynski 1987, 17). He describes the incompatibility between the signs of everyday living and their absence from the photographs as he compares these interiors to the contents of his own personalized office space; but it remains just that – a point of contention.

A further insight to disciplinary thought is evidenced when Abercrombie warns of the 'perilous situation' caused by disregarding the practical needs of the client during the design process (1990, 164). Kevin Melchionne recalls Abercrombie's claim that 'we cannot live *in* art or even in a "white cube"' (Abercrombie 1990, 135, original emphasis). He explains that 'Of course, what Abercrombie means is that we cannot live in interiors entirely given over to an aesthetic vision and, consequently, divorced from all consideration of what it might really mean to inhabit them' (Melchionne 2006, 228). The famous tale of Adolf Loos's *Poor Little Rich Man* (1900) is a testament to this disproportionate subjectification and subordination of the client. The anecdote describes a wealthy client's desire for a house of art, which he resplendently receives: 'When he turned a door handle he grabbed hold of art, when he sank into a chair he sank into art, when he buried his tired bones under the pillows he burrowed into art, his feet sank in art when he walked across the carpet' (Loos 2003, 18).

The resulting home was comfortable, but the poor little rich man was soon to discover that living in art 'was hard mental work' (19).

> In the first weeks the architect guarded the daily life, so that no mistake could creep in. The rich man put tremendous effort into it. But it still happened, that when he laid down a book without thinking that he shoved it into the pigeonhole for the newspaper. Or he knocked the ashes from his cigar into the groove made for the candleholder. You picked something up and the endless guessing and searching for the right place to return it to began, and sometimes the architect had to look at the blueprints to rediscover the correct place for a box of matches. (Loos 2003, 19)

There was no flexibility for the client in this interior entirely given over to the architect's aesthetic vision. This became an unbearable constraint for the poor little rich man, who soon 'tried to be home as little as possible' (Loos 2003, 19), seeking respite from so much art in restaurants, cafes and friends so that he could face his own home. He dejectedly accepted the aesthetic limitations as his life's fate, from where 'He was shut out of future life and its strivings, its developments, and its desires' (Loos 2003, 21), a perilous fate indeed.

The story makes explicit the conflicting needs and desires of occupation and aesthetics in the context of professional practice. A struggle for domination is described in the relation between the client and the designer. The client's 'invasion' of their own home with unrefined occupations in the form of clutter, refuse, personal possessions or unsuitable furnishings is perceived as the inevitable deterioration of aesthetic vision. Conversely, what this familiar scenario actually represents is the insurrection of the client, in a revolution of ownership. Despite this struggle, it is aesthetic vision which continues to dominate our scheme of rationalizing the interior, which is evidenced through the unoccupied image.

In an allusion to the contentious relation between client and designer, Abercrombie reminds us that 'the quality of the uninhabited interior is of no consequence' (1990, 164). Significantly, this sentiment does not extend to his consideration of the interior's image, as indicated by his lapse into naturalized understanding:

> … an unpeopled photograph is not the same as an unpeopled room; in the former, the absence of people, opaque as they inevitably are, lets us see the designer's work more clearly. Further, the illustrated room's emptiness is an invitation, allowing us as voyeurs an easier projection of ourselves into the space. (Abercrombie 1990, 164)

Abercrombie's conclusions are defensible in the context of conventional knowledge, but there is little challenge in his justifications. What Abercrombie's warning does reveal however, is his personal acknowledgement of the significant relation between occupation and the interior, despite the disciplinary inclination to conceal the former through the image. In saying this, of particular interest is his slippage to the understanding that empowers him: the disciplinary reasoning for the suppression of occupation by which his response is structured.

Foucault describes the kind of knowledge which has been concealed in a formal systemization, as, in this case, authentic occupation is concealed in the discourse of architecture and design, as a subjugated knowledge. 'When I say "subjugated knowledges" I am also referring to a whole series of knowledges that have been disqualified as nonconceptual knowledges, as insufficiently elaborated knowledges: naïve knowledges, hierarchically inferior knowledges, knowledges that are below the required level of erudition or scientificity' (Foucault 2003, 7).

Abercrombie's examples make visible ways in which the profession subjugates occupation by positioning it as external to disciplinary knowledge. This exclusion is what makes authentic occupation of the interior so difficult to express in erudite ways – there is no way of describing it professionally. It is these suppressed, subjugated knowledges that have played a significant role in Foucault's interrogation of what we are, through his histories of sexuality, the clinic and the prisons. He explains that it was the 'reappearance' of these 'unqualified or even disqualified knowledges' through historical contents that 'made the critique possible' (Foucault 2003, 7–8).

Foucault's tools of scholarship enable the search for reappearances of disqualified knowledges, which form part of the 'differences, transformations, continuities, mutations' that constitute Foucauldian histories (Kendall and Wickham 2003, 24). These transformations reveal points of insurrection or revolution, where what has been suppressed is released into disciplinary or systemized knowledge. They also reveal the contingency of our present understanding, and make visible the possibility for change in a system largely perceived to be immutable. Seeing the interior's image in this way enables a test of 'the limits that we may go beyond' (Foucault 1991, 47), and leaves open the possibility of its transformation. The idealization of the interior can therefore be seen as a contingent, material condition of disciplinary knowledge, which presents 'the possibility of no longer being, doing, or thinking what we are, do, or think' (Foucault 1991, 46).

(UN)OCCUPIED–(UN)INTERIOR: RATIONALIZING THE INTERIOR

Beatriz Colomina posits that 'The perception of space is produced by its representations; in this sense, built space has no more authority than do drawings, photographs, or descriptions' (1996, 369, n.3). This insight is critical to attributing disciplinary and social value in terms of the way the images are rationalized, and the authority they uphold. Significantly, the domestic interior's representation is historically limited to the recognition of its emergence in the nineteenth century (Rice 2007a, 2007b), as it is only through the surfacing of the interior as a conscious subject that it forms a possible object of representation. For this reason, the current relation, posed as problematic, between the interior and its image is historically constrained and contingent. Charles Rice acknowledges this contingence and therefore changeability when he claims 'the interior conceptualized a particular emerging and developing consciousness of and comportment to the material realities of domesticity, realities which were actively formed in this emergence, and which … could also become transformed and destabilized through it' (2007a, 3). This possibility for change is critical to the interior's revolution, that is, its potential to be conceived of in other ways.

Our current understanding that the interior is more than just the inside space of architecture is born from this cultural construction that coincided with the emerging social value of the domestic in terms of home and family life (Rice 2007a, 2007b, Rybczynski 1987). Our personal and everyday experiences of living 'inside' supplement this knowledge, and provide an intimate understanding of occupying the interior. The interior localizes the enactment of daily encounters and experiences, providing a place for ordinary traces to manifest; these may be no more monumental than spilled water on the bench, a discarded wrapper on the desk, finger prints to cabinet doors, or dishes in the sink. The way we live is evidenced through our occupation of built space and constitutes our localized knowledge of the interior.

Professionally, this localized understanding is 'present' but 'masked' (Foucault 2003, 7) by concealing any trace of authentic occupation through the representation of the interior. However, this does not preclude professional practice from intimating occupation through the interior's image in ways that are deemed acceptable. For example, a chair intentionally positioned to gesture an imminent arrival, or a pair of slippers placed neatly by the bed, are evidence of the profession's proclivity to aestheticize occupation, which raises an important distinction between the notion of authentic lived experience, and its euphemized but more acceptable forms. The act of representation, in its ability to manipulate, idealize and frame (Rice 2007b), provides the means through which the evidencing of occupation is moderated and made acceptable.

While this idealization increases visual disparity between the room and its image, a representation will always draw an analogy to real space. This inseparable relation extends to the understanding of interior, which renders both image and spatial formations interchangeable in their classification (Rice 2007a, 2). Coinciding with this semantic development of the word 'interior', Rice identifies the theme of 'doubleness', which 'involves the interdependence between image and space, with neither sense being primary' (2007a, 2). This free exchange between three-dimensional space and its image is significant, because the mutuality imposed by coincidental naming neutralizes the distinctions that enable us to accept as normalized the problematic relations between the interior's two forms.

Despite the disjuncture between actual circumstances and visual evidence, the regularity with which the interior's 'unlived' image is encountered, combined with the mechanisms of legitimate production and distribution, positions these highly visible idealizations as rational depictions of lived space. At the heart of these legitimizations are the institutions: architecture, interior design, the publishing industries and the internet, as institutions 'which acquire authority and provide limits within which' thoughts, practices or objects such as the ideal image can be thought of or exist (Kendall and Wickham 2003, 26). These institutions implement mechanisms or techniques of legitimization which extend to ideological outputs such as morals, laws, or theories, and determine particular social behaviours, accounting in part for the way the interior is rationalized.

Through their social authority, institutions promote their outputs as valuable. Gillian Rose advises that an output originating from an authoritative institution is 'likely to be more productive' and therefore more visible 'than one coming from a marginalized social position' (2007, 166). The ubiquity of the interior's image, as evidenced and disseminated through media channels such as Instagram, websites and design blogs which now accompany the traditional magazine formats, is a testament to the authoritative standing of the institutions from which they are both produced and circulated. The voracity of production and consumption results in these sterilized depictions of the interior being the only kind we see.

Roland Barthes, in his discussions on photography, alludes to this monopolization when he describes a violence of the photograph, 'not because it shows violent things, but because on each occasion *it fills the sight by force*, and because in it nothing can be refused or transformed … ' (2000, 91, original emphasis). Barthes' existential reflections offer an insight into the viewer's subjectification to the domination of institutional outputs. As authoritative and therefore productive entities, these outputs are highly visible, and for this reason, dominate what can be seen. Further, the assertion of the interior's portrait through its authoritative standing and seemingly immutable appearance makes it impossible to 'refuse' or 'transform'.

In addition, specific technologies or practical techniques implemented by these institutions articulate rationale in themselves. For example, the practice of representing the interior through photography is not accidental. The medium's likeness to reality supposedly presents a mirroring of the way things actually *are*, despite the ease of manipulation photography affords. Susan Sontag explains in relation to this understanding that photographic images 'are indeed able to usurp reality because first of all a photograph is not only an image (as a painting is an image), an interpretation of the real; it is also a trace, something directly stenciled off the real, like a footprint or a death mask' (Sontag 2008, 154). More than this, however, institutional techniques and mechanisms are able to legitimize the representational limitations of the photograph, which extend to processes such as content manipulation. John Tagg describes a kind of institutional reprieve in the rationalization of 'the legal record', which he explains as being:

> *an image produced according to certain institutionalised formal rules and technical procedures which define legitimate manipulations and permissible distortions in such a way that, in certain contexts, more or less skilled and suitably trained and validated interpreters may draw inferences from them, on the basis of historically established conventions. It is only in this institutional framework that otherwise disputable meanings carry weight and can be enforced.* (1988, 2–3)

While this analogy refers to more formalized rules of convention in terms of image production and the law, the understanding that institutions are able to define 'legitimate manipulations and permissible distortions' is significant to the way the interior's idealizations are rationalized and associated 'problematics' ignored. These institutional mechanisms provide a means for understanding the interior's photographic image as a constructed or alternate reality that stands in contrast to actuality. Tagg advises that:

> we have to see that every photograph is the result of specific and, in every sense, significant distortions which render its relation to any prior reality deeply problematic and raise the question of the determining level of the material apparatus and of the social practices within which photography takes place. (1988, 2)

In a similar way, Lindsay Prior describes institutional constructions, such as those relating to the interior's image, not as accurate reflections of an external world but rather as manifestations of 'the discursive rules and themes that predominate in a particular socio-historical context', resulting in a representation of what is understood to exist (1997, 70) and which Foucault describes as understanding 'The fundamental codes of a culture' (2002, xxii). These cultural codes provide the means through which the world is viewed, understood and engaged with, but which 'do not simply elucidate the world but establish regimes of knowledge and truth that regulate our approach to ourselves, each other and our surroundings respectively' (Anderson 2003, 3). The interior's image is therefore a material condition of knowledge, which we accept with little contention.

However, Foucault states that naturalized understandings which are accepted without question

> must remain in suspense. They must not be rejected definitively of course, but the tranquillity with which they are accepted must be disturbed; we must show that they do not come about by themselves, but are always the result of a construction the rules of which must be known, and the justifications of which must be scrutinised … . (2002a, 28)

Suspending the way the interior's image is rationalized challenges the assumption that pervades these constructions as neutral positions of communication (Anderson 2003), and consciously foregrounds the relation between the authentic occupation of the interior and its representational counterpart.

SUSPENSION AND REPUDIATION

> The first version, that of 1926 I believe: a carefully drawn pipe, and underneath it (handwritten in a steady, painstaking, artificial script, a script from the convent, like that found heading the notebooks of schoolboys, or on a blackboard after an object lesson), this note: 'This is not a pipe'. (Foucault 2008a, 15)

Here, Foucault describes a calligram: an arrangement of words reinforced through image. Foucault uses this simple example to illustrate the suspension of normalized understandings which is applicable to the interior's image. He uses what James Harkness describes as the 'visual non sequitur' (2008, 4) of Magritte's *Ceci n'est pas une Pipe* (1926), in a critique of language, to challenge concepts of perception, semantics and the mimetic. Magritte depicts common objects whose recognition is contested by '"impossible", "irrational", or "senseless" conjunctions' (Harkness 2008, 8). Through the very simplicity of the image, we are disconcerted (Foucault 2008a, 15). Magritte presents a realistic image of a pipe, and below it the words, 'This is not a pipe'. 'Nothing is easier to recognize than a pipe, drawn thus; nothing is easier to say – our language knows it well in our place – than the "name of a pipe"' (Foucault 2008a, 19). The positive image asserts that it is indeed a pipe; the familiarity of the object, the realism of representational form and semantic understanding produces a perceptive invisibility of the image. Despite this transparency, the caption beneath advises otherwise, enabling the oppositional statements of image and text to exist discordantly on the space of the page: ' … it's just a representation, is it not? So if I had written on my picture "This is a pipe", I'd have been lying … ' (Magritte, quoted in Basson 1999, 183). This conscious process of clarification suspends one's instinctive thoughts, and challenges the viewer to actively distinguish between the axiomatic relations of the object, its naming and its representation, disrupting the ordinary apprehension of the image.

This juxtaposition of incompatibilities to suspend normalizations extends to the spatial. Foucault identifies particular places that, like the calligram, disrupt the understanding of ordinary spatial arrangements. He recognizes these places as 'spaces' of knowledge, existing in a series of relations 'we live inside' and 'that define emplacements that are irreducible to each other and absolutely nonsuperposable' (Foucault 2000, 178). That is, their particular contextual relations define and determine both how they interrelate and how we understand them within these relations.

Foucault emphasizes those emplacements which 'have the curious property of being connected to all the other emplacements, but in such a way that they suspend, neutralize, or reverse the set of relations that are designated, *reflected*, or represented [*réflechis*] by them' (2000, 178, original emphasis). The suspension of trace, the neutralization of life as lived and the reversal of the relation between actuality and representational content are qualities attributed to the interior's image, aligning it directly to this spatial analogy. Foucault explains these emplacements as existing in two major forms: utopias and heterotopias. 'Utopias are emplacements having no real place. They are emplacements that maintain a general relation of direct or inverse analogy with the real space of society. They are society perfected or the reverse of society, but in any case these utopias are spaces that are fundamentally and essentially unreal' (Foucault 2000, 178).

The interior's image can be interpreted directly as a utopia: by representing the space in which we live, a direct correlation with real space is maintained; however, the erasure of the human trace alters this by elevating the image to an idealized state. While the image in itself is tangible, the non-habitable space of the image renders it placeless, thereby qualifying the interior's idealized image as a utopia.

Like utopias, heterotopias represent, contest and reverse institutionally embedded emplacements, but significantly stand in contrast as localizable, habitable places (Foucault 2000, 178). Heterotopias are, essentially, realized utopias.

Between the regions of the utopias and heterotopias, Foucault identifies an intermediate space, which functions as both the chimerical and the actual, and this, he explains, is the mirror:

> *The mirror is a utopia after all, since it is a placeless place. In the mirror I see myself where I am not, in an unreal space that opens up virtually behind the surface; I am over there where I am not, a kind of shadow that gives me my own visibility, that enables me to look at myself there where I am absent – a mirror utopia. But it is also a heterotopia in that the mirror really exists, in that it has a sort of return effect on the place that I occupy … . The mirror functions as a heterotopia in the sense that it makes this place I occupy at the moment I look at myself in the glass both utterly real, connected with the entire space surrounding it, and utterly unreal – since, to be perceived, it is obliged to go by way of that virtual point which is over there. (Foucault 2000, 179)*

The understanding of the mirror as both a utopia and a heterotopia, but also as an intermediate emplacement, can be compared to the photographic depiction of the ideal interior. The duplicating effect of the mirror's reflection can be likened to the mirroring effect of the documenting photograph. Further, the representational image is localizable, as it exists (albeit placeless), and through a process of imaginative projection it can be 'inhabited'. Understanding the ideal image as an 'other' place renders it 'a kind of contestation, both mythical and real, of the space in which we live' (Foucault 2000, 179).

Foucault explains that in primitive societies, heterotopias were reserved for people in states of crisis in relation to the society they inhabit. Foucault cites 'Adolescents, menstruating women, women in labour, old people and so on' as examples (2000, 179). These crisis forms, although identifiable, are no longer relevant in the same ways. This results in the replacement of crisis heterotopias with heterotopias of deviation: 'those in which individuals are put whose behaviour is deviant with respect to the mean or the required norm' (2000, 180). People are usually forced into these heterotopias, which surface in such forms as psychiatric hospitals and prisons; he also cites nursing homes as heterotopias which fall on the borderline of crisis and deviance, 'seeing that in our society, where leisure activity is the rule, idleness forms a kind of deviation' (2000, 180).

Significantly, the interior's image can be drawn into this combined context of 'crisis deviation': the act of occupation renders the occupant in a state of moral, organizational and hygienic disorder (crisis) and the taboo associated with tolerating the residue of daily living signifies a perceived social deviation. The interior's image as heterotopia functions in relation to the 'real' space by 'creating a different space, a different real space as perfect, as meticulous, as well-arranged as ours is disorganized, badly arranged and muddled. This would be the heterotopia not of illusion but of compensation …' (Foucault 2000, 184). The heterotopia materializes social values and ideals, which accentuate the comparative deficiency of ordinary space, for which it then compensates. Like the conscious clarification of the calligram, the active recognition of the heterotopia's compensatory relation to remaining space incites disruption to our normalized perceptions.

The heterotopia, like the idealized image, can be understood as product of the 'techniques and procedures' of exclusion (Foucault 1980, 101), and as a material condition of knowledge. Foucault identifies an absence, such as occupation, as that which reflects a rationale of social arrangements, and Rose advises that these 'Absences can be as productive as explicit naming; *invisibility* can have just as powerful effects as visibility' (2007, 165, original emphasis). In saying this, the absence of any trace of authentic occupation is just as productive in its promotion of a particular reasoning as its positive image. However, it is the institutional techniques and mechanisms of this exclusion which produce and continue particular regimes of thought; this production is illustrated earlier in this chapter in the exclusion or subjugation of authentic occupation in the claim to professionalization. This exclusion is physically evidenced through the heterotopia, which stand in contrast to the chimerical utopia. Heterotopias are, then, institutionally embedded, material conditions of knowledge evidenced through built space.

Foucault explains that 'heterotopias have the role of creating a space of illusion that denounces all real space, all real emplacements within which human life is partitioned off, as being even more illusory' (2000, 184). This designates the image as the frame through which the actual conditions of the 'real world' masked by the heterotopic illusion can be interpreted. In interpreting this difference, what is excluded through the heterotopian image is key. These forms of exclusion function in multiple ways. For example, through the imaginative habitation of the image, one can permissibly enter a private realm, such as a depicted bedroom or bathroom, and envisage what it would be like to live *there*. 'Everybody can enter these heterotopian emplacements, but actually this is only an illusion: one believes he is going inside and, by the very fact of entering, one is excluded' (2000, 183). Of encountering Aldof Loos's photographs, Colomina writes: 'Looking at the photographs, it is easy to imagine oneself in these precise, static positions, usually indicated by the unoccupied furniture. The photographs suggest that it is intended that these spaces be comprehended by occupation, by using this furniture, by "entering" the photograph, by inhabiting it' (1996, 234).

The concept of heterotopic exclusion is revealed through this example, and in this case is obvious and varied; firstly, it is not possible to physically occupy the two-dimensional space of an image, nor can the object of the image actually be entered. What's more, any authentic sense of the real occupants is erased in favour of providing a public view of their private existence. This shields the occupant from revealing their 'true' privacy, to the viewer's exclusion, which is evidence of a particular social value relevant to our perceptions of occupation: the shift of the private into the public realm made possible through institutional technologies of the media, film and photography. Barthes' reflections capture this point: 'the age of Photography corresponds precisely to the explosion of the private into the public, or rather into the creation of a new social value, which is the publicity of the private: the private is consumed as such, publicly … .' (2000, 98).

Despite this shift in social value, so relevant to the way we perceive other people's lives today, the level of intimacy revealed through the interior's image remains dominated and limited by the institutional ideals to which we are bound. Through the image we are presented with a diffused, public face of private life.

7.2 KENZO-inspired apartment. Design by Olga Akulova
Source: Olga Akulova DESIGN. Photography by Andrey Avdeenko (2013).

To contextualize this particular concept, and the heterotopia more generally to both the spatial and representational realm of current practice, consider the image of Akulova's KENZO apartment bedroom in Figure 7.2, alongside the following anecdotal example which conveys a similar ideological sentiment.

There is a well-known and long established Italian design house, which offers immaculately designed, highly desirable furniture, and whose design inventory, intended for architects, designers, and clients alike, is openly accessible via the internet. Their furniture is presented as pièces de résistance to imposing rooms of indisputable architectural reverence boasting contemporary framing, requisite transparency, luxurious finishes, restrained palette; and now, on account of the furniture, the enviable package is realized in total. On reading the bedroom catalogue, something conspicuously out of the ordinary surfaced: a perfectly un-made bed in an otherwise impeccably presented room. It is notable and somewhat jarring to encounter subversion in this disciplinary realm. However, this understanding is in itself an illusion. The contrivance of the un-made bed deludes us into thinking an ideological shift has been embraced, when in reality all this gesture essentially provides is an allusion to the real that is still unreal – and which functions as nothing more than a reinforcement of the ideal. In tribute to Magritte, the perfectly imperfect bedroom image should perhaps be captioned, 'This is Not an Interior'.

CONCLUSION

In conclusion, this chapter has sought to challenge the conventional and continuing rationalization of the interior by foregrounding the oppositional relation between authentic occupation and the interior's image. Paradoxically, *occupation* – the principal objective of spatial design, is perceived as a contaminate to aesthetic agendas: occupation ruins space. In a revolution of ownership, the client's domination is conceded, as unrefined and disordered occupations infuse designed space. To counter this entropy, the profession subjugates occupation, which is evidenced through the interior's ideal and sanitized image.

Foucault's theory reveals that the largely unquestioned idealization of the interior needs to be challenged – not to be repudiated definitively – but to be understood as historically contingent, and therefore transformable. This changeability presents the possibility for the conventional aestheticization of occupation no longer being something which limits our practices, thoughts and actions, but as something which enables the interior's image to exist in new or other ways, making possible a revolution of perception and/or form.

The analysis of Magritte's calligram reveals the tacit nature of incongruous yet normalized understandings. The active deciphering of common object and corresponding text suspends and alters our intuitive response to the image. This recognition provides an analogical lens through which the interior image can be evaluated and then identified as something other than it was previously thought to be. Foucault's concept of the heterotopia provides a further means to challenge conventional thoughts and practices in relation to the interior. As an ideal mirroring of actual space, it has been possible to interpret the interior's image as a heterotopia, that is, a realized spatial ideal.

Of significance to this argument are the two functions heterotopias perform in relation to the remaining space of our occupation. The first, enacted through a process of exclusion, censors signs of authentic occupation from the image. This results in a combination of aesthetic, sanitizing and idealizing effects on the image of occupiable space, and presents an archetypal modelling of our current schema of institutional ideals. These idealized images then compensate for the deficiencies of our own actual and imperfect conditions, that is, the disordered conditions imposed by occupation.

The second function of the heterotopia in relation to the remaining space is the creation of a space of illusion – one which 'denounces' the real space in which we live (Foucault 2000, 184). In this case, the image as heterotopia makes explicit the difference between actual conditions and ideal form. The effect of this juxtaposition results in the interior's ideal portrait presenting something even more illusory than initially realized. The heterotopia suspends our current thoughts and challenges us to see what we do, say and think in relation to the interior as something other than we had previously considered. This destabilizes our conventional understandings of the interior and its image, and presents an alternative viewpoint.

These illusory depictions of the interior, while recognizable as such, are validated by the authenticating techniques and mechanisms of the institutions. The subjugation of authentic occupation by the profession, and its exclusion from the image in favour of euphemized and more acceptable forms are combined with the use of photography; these strategies function as 'truth' mechanisms. These same techniques further enable the adherence to social values, such as morality, hygiene and legitimate exposure of the most private intimations into the public realm.

Unravelling the interior's image in these ways disturbs the relative composure with which it is ordinarily apprehended, and reveals the contingency of current thoughts and practices. This positions the interior as a discursive site for further contemplation and repudiation. New ways of perceiving and conceiving of the interior are suggestive of the possibility for transformative revolution. This could extend to the disclosure of what is conventionally subjugated or repressed in the interior's image – that we could think, do and say what is currently unthinkable, undoable, unsayable: that we could see the unseen.

This unfurling of new possibilities has wider implications for the consideration of spatial representation and interiors more broadly. A transformed understanding of the interior would reflect a shift in the perceptions and values that presently shape the thoughts, words and actions defining it. This would incite the need for different approaches to professional practices and design education to perpetuate these new values, thereby revolutionizing our approach to occupied space and in turn the interior's image in the context of our everyday lives.

ACKNOWLEDGEMENT

The support of the Australian Postgraduate Award and Curtin Research Scholarships are acknowledged in the publication of this research.

REFERENCES

Abercrombie, Stanley. 1990. *A Philosophy of Interior Design*. Boulder: Westview.

Anderson, Niels Akerstrom. 2003. *Discursive Analytical Strategies: Understanding Foucault, Koselleck, Laclau, Luhmann*. Bristol: The Policy Press.

Barthes, Roland. [1980] 2000. *Camera Lucida*. Translated by Richard Howard. London: Vintage Books.

Basson, Steve. 1999. 'On the Perceptual Edge of Autonomy: The Problematics of Expressing the Needs of Others'. *Urban Policy and Research* 17 (3): 179–90.

Colomina, Beatriz. 1996. *Privacy and Publicity*. Cambridge, MA: MIT Press.

de Beauvoir, Simone. [1949] 1997. *The Second Sex*. Translated by H.M. Parshley. London: Vintage.

Foucault, Michel. [1977] 1980. 'Two Lectures'. In *Power Knowledge: Selected Interviews and Other Writings 1972–1977*, edited by Colin Gordon, 78–108. New York: Vintage Books.

――. [1984] 1991. 'What Is Enlightenment?' In *The Foucault Reader: An Introduction to Foucault's Thought*, edited by Paul Rabinow, 32–50. London: Penguin Books.

――. [1984] 2000. 'Different Spaces'. In *Aesthetics, Method and Epistemology*, edited by James D. Faubion, 175–85. London: Penguin Books.

———. [1966] 2002. *The Order of Things*. New York: Routledge Classics.

———. [1969] 2002a. *The Archaeology of Knowledge*. Translated by A.M. Sheridan Smith. London: Routledge.

———. 2003. 'Lectures at the College De France, 7 January 1976'. In *Society Must Be Defended*, edited by Arnold I. Davison, 1–21. New York: Picador.

———. [1983] 2008a. *This Is Not a Pipe*. Translated by James Harkness. Los Angeles: University of California Press.

Harkness, James. 2008. Translator's Introduction to *This Is Not a Pipe*, 1-12. Los Angeles: University of California Press.

Kendall, Gavin and Gary Wickham. [1999] 2003. *Using Foucault's Methods*. London: Sage.

Loos, Adolf. [1900] 2003. 'The Poor Little Rich Man'. In *Adolf Loos 1870–1933 Architect, Cultural Critic, Dandy*, edited by August Sarnitz, 18–21. Cologne: Taschen.

Melchionne, Kevin. 2006. 'Living in Glass Houses'. In *Intimus: Interior Design Theory Reader*, edited by M. Taylor and J. Preston, 228–32. Chichester: John Wiley & Sons, Ltd.

Prior, Lindsay. 1997. 'Following in Foucault's Footsteps: Text and Context in Qualitative Research'. In *Qualitative Research: Theory, Method and Practice*, edited by David Silverman, 63–79. London: Sage.

Rice, Charles. 2007a. *The Emergence of the Interior*. London and New York: Routledge.

———. 2007b. 'Imagined Interiors: Representing the Domestic Interior since the Renaissance', edited by Jeremy Aynsley and Charlotte Grant [Book Review]. *Journal of Architecture* 12 (3): 340–44.

Rose, Gillian. 2007. *Visual Methodologies: An Introduction to the Interpretation of Visual Materials*. 2nd edn. London, Thousand Oaks, New Dehli, Singapore: Sage.

Rybczynski, Witold. 1987. *Home: A Short History of an Idea*. New York: Penguin.

Sontag, Susan. [1977] 2008. *On Photography*. London: Penguin.

Tagg, John. 1988. *The Burden of Representation*. Basingstoke: Macmillan Education.

Zevi, Bruno. [1957] 1974. *Architecture As Space*. New York: Horizon Press.

PART III
Revolution

Plate 4 'Palimpsest'. 2014

8

Occupying Utopia: Collusion, Persuasion, Revolution

Lynn Churchill

UTOPIA DYSTOPIA

The focus of this chapter is the mutable concept of utopia's inextricable symbiosis with revolution. Since Thomas More's detailed account of a perfect society was first published in 1516 in his influential *Utopia* (2009) there seems always to be something unnerving about the concept of utopia and the slipperiness of its proximity to dystopia. While initially aimed at corruption within his contemporary world, More's provocative vision endures as a potent work for its exposé of human weakness and our inevitably flawed attempts to straddle the objectives of living well, not only within some or other form of community, but also of thriving as individuals.

Utopia tells the story of a mysterious place and its inhabitants, as relayed by the fictional character Raphael, who, it is said, spent some time on the crescent-shaped island called Utopia, a name taken from the Greek *ou topos*, meaning 'no place'. What the reader is primed to contemplate throughout More's critique of social and economic systems is his lampooning of our Western foundation: ownership, excess, accumulation and wealth (More 2009, 71–4). He is incisive in his review of society's food supplies, the killing of animals, the structure of governance and the rules of family life (40–43). Everything is considered: the formation of community, social cohesion, the role and rights to education, the morality of aged care and the viability of healthcare. More conceptualizes religion, war, law or lore, work, leisure, international relations, clothing and punishment (92–7).

While remaining uncannily and perhaps antagonistically relevant hundreds of years later, this work is frustrating to read, because as More tracks the consequences of what may appear to be ideal, there is always a looming question (presumably planted by More): 'at what cost?'. What are the economics of the utopian vision of an ideal life, and who pays? In *Utopia*, the creation and maintenance of the ideal life depends on people being contained, and human drives being sublimated. In More's societal portrait, the revolutionary spirit of human creativity as well as the desire for experiencing extreme sensation – pleasure and or pain – remain absent.

The patriarchal organizational structure of More's fictional island has strict laws requiring a high degree of human compliance, that could only result in individuals remaining more or less unfulfilled and lodged in stasis, unable to re-position themselves. But what of those troublesome internal forces or instincts that so occupied Sigmund Freud in the development of his psychoanalytic theory? Where is human desire or the urge to take risks? Where is the sense of prospect, creativity, innovation and metamorphosis?

When Freud considered the problem of individuals working together for the benefit of the group, he acknowledged the economics of sacrifices made by individuals. For each individual within a group there are expectations that the benefit gained by being within a strong and cohesive group will at least equal the necessary cost of suppressing individual desires and characteristics. Sometimes, however, when there are imbalances between the costs and the benefits, humans will find ways, perhaps subversive, to regain a sense of equilibrium. Hence, in Freudian terms, the occasional 'irresistibility of perverse instincts', and 'the attraction in general of forbidden things' (Freud 1969, 16). There is much pleasure in illegal indulgence and transgression.

In addition to the lampooning, More's reader is also led to contemplate a dystopian antithesis, an ever-present tendril of his provocation that there is always a dark side to liberation. This is exemplified by Utopia's reliance upon slavery, which is only made acceptable by creating an unequal society in which some are more or less worthy or valued than others. So it was outcasts and outsiders who were enslaved and forced to undertake particular tasks that involved facing the ugly realities of life (More 2009, 92). Slaves worked in the abattoir, for example, so as to protect the good Utopian carnivores from the unbecoming physical and mental experiences of blood, filth and violence (83). As we see, it is within More's seminal work that we find confronting dark truths that remain at the heart of the contemporary struggle for human occupation.

Perhaps the island of Utopia is analogous to that not so far away place in the sky, the Earth's moon that sometimes appears as a crescent. What we only ever see is the portion of the moon's truly spherical body that at any particular time is reflecting the sun's light from the other side of the Earth. Meanwhile, however, we are always aware of the inevitable waxing and waning of light and shadow that continually re-forms our perception of the moon both in reality, and in our imaginations – performing as both a beacon and a mirror.

Visions of utopia (and its antithesis) that speculate on ideas and schemas addressing the complexity of human habitation are the natural territory of architecture; forever complicit in spatial propositions and manifestations of every conceivable form of every aspect of human occupation: the physical, spiritual and psychical; the social, political and economic. Placing the breadth of human experience, from the intimate to the colossal, is the business of architecture.

Peter Zumthor recollects the intimate pleasure of his young hand sensing the metal door handle of his aunt's house: 'That door handle still seems to me like a special sign of entry into a world of different moods and smells' (2006, 7). From Zumthor's sensuous memories of close acquaintances with architecture to Richard Weller's 2009 utopic/dystopic proposition for the city of the future, human occupation is a complex network of interdependent and antagonistic relationships. Weller's vision of the future of human occupation is to design for better management of the overloaded planet's struggle to survive unsustainable population growth with its consequences for food, water, transportation and energy supplies (Weller 2009). Architecture and design are at the forefront of repudiation and revolution.

Much of architecture is a negotiation with utopia that takes place on a precipice overhanging dystopia. If only human occupation were as simple as Yoko Ono's utopian installation 'Imagine Peace' suggests: 'If one billion people in the world think peace – we'll get peace'(Ono and Kellein 2008, 8–9). Ono invites us to alter our position, to pay attention to shifting, in this instance, our passive acceptance of the condition of war to thinking and imagining the condition of peace. Revolution is the focus of this chapter. It is about the imagining, shifting, re-positioning and altering of the condition of occupation.

Drawing from works by theorists, including Jean Baudrillard and Guy Debord, this chapter reflects on a period of time, the 1950s to 70s, when architecture, art and design were not only inspired by, but symbiotic with the space race, the arms race and the Cold War. It was new technology that drove new physical realities, shifts in political dynamics and new utopic visions. And capitalism capitalized on the prospect of social and economic 'mobility'.

A series of built and unbuilt works embodying these new utopic visions are discussed here, including a number of politicized spatial scenarios: the 1959 American National Exhibition Moscow, the Situationists' Babylon project, Jacques Tati's 'Playtime', and alterations by architect/artist Gordon Matta-Clark.

These various iterations of the concept of utopia provide the context for critique and analysis of two recent YouTube videos, produced by Corning Incorporated in 2011 and 2012 to promote future visions of early twenty-first-century lives, made virtually ethereal by interactive glass surfaces and two- and three-dimensional augmented reality.

Corning's story of glass portrays the evolving synergy of information and communication technologies. Their now almost obsolete YouTube videos, *A Day Made of Glass* and *A Day Made of Glass 2: Same Day* portray a vision of ethereal life experienced elsewhere via omnipresent interactive devices, and surfaces capable of both two- and three-dimensional real time and time lapse projection. Such ethereality is something of an advance on the Situationists' mid-twentieth-century visions in which the concept of mobility that was predominantly a physical reality had been catalyzed by a mix of Cold War tension and Space Age euphoria.

Corning's videos show characters blissfully gliding through daily life filled with elation and wonderment, enriched by mental mobility and illusion as glass surfaces everywhere reveal the multiplicity of their personal connections to elsewhere.

Throughout, glass dominates; it is the technological evolution of glass as a conductor of energy that positions this material as most powerful. Not only has glass always been a catalyst for connection, it has also always been a medium and a network through which we both seek and disseminate information across space and time. It mediates interior and exterior, illusion and truth.

Essentially, glass's fundamental properties of transparency and reflection simultaneously generate reality, mobility and illusion. Arguably, while steel, concrete, glass, and later plastic, defined the material reality of the nineteenth and twentieth centuries, it is glass (and plastic) that are formulating the twenty-first century, utopic or otherwise. Glass has always taken us somewhere where our body is not.

UTOPIA + MOBILITY

In the 1960s, Baudrillard found himself surrounded in everyday life by inherent obsolescence, and noted the rapid redundancy of many common objects such as ballpoint pens, cars and paper, and became interested in the bigger idea of fleeting urban experiences and the concept of ephemeral buildings. Turning to the built environment, Baudrillard (2011, 76–91) questioned the value of 'durability'. 'The ephemeral is undoubtedly the truth of our future habitat', he wrote in the journal *Utopie*:

> If clothes, objects, appliances, and automobiles increasingly obey … the norms of the ephemeral, nothing says that they do not, taken together, oppose 'inhabiting' … . Their symbolic schema is that of ventilation and expenditure, the symbolic schema of inhabiting is that of provision and investment.
> (Baudrillard 2011, 77)

Within Baudrillard's dichotomy lies the implicit truth that, driven by social and economic imperatives, we have mostly preferred to prevail over entropy. Similarly, we have preferred our buildings and cities to be 'solid and durable' (Baudrillard 2011, 77), particularly in terms of the benefit to our physical and economic security. So it is spectacular that Baudrillard proposed the containers of our everyday activities could be ephemeral, arguing that, since the physical structure of a building is frequently intended to prevail over a period of 60 or 100 years, there is an obvious and inevitable problem of 'obsolescence'.

Still, although clearly extravagant, the idea of an ephemeral building is intriguing and valid, because it is clear that even within a decade, modes and ways of occupation will shift and re-form, technologies will develop and values will change. Together with human (cultural) migration, these factors create flux that effectively renders old habitats redundant, as they lose synchronicity with the evolution of our everyday habits.

According to Baudrillard (and the Situationists) the problem with durable space in stasis is that it serves to constrain rather than enable metamorphosis. Whereas ephemeral, portable, dynamic space more effectively accommodates the shifting ideas and practices that continually challenge and re-position our lives. If our relationships, leisure, work, rituals, luxuries and material and temporal realities are always in a state of flux, why not our buildings?

The experimental works by visionaries such as the Situationists, Baudrillard and Matta-Clark draw our attention to the value of re-formation, alteration and mobility. Between 1957 and 1972, the Situationists International (SI) produced a body of work, including theory, art, events and urban speculation, that continues to be influential. Much of their work, which aimed to improve life for the masses, stemmed from Marxism, moved towards anarchism and was fundamentally anti-ideology, anti-capitalist and anti-culture.

Urbanism, as the organized structure of ownership, control, access to and activities within public space, was central to their interests. SI's key theorist, Guy Debord (1977), railed against urbanism, which in his view had arisen as a means by which 'established powers' used suppression to quell uprisings and impose order in the streets following the French Revolution. Debord's critique of modern urbanism came in repudiation of Corbusier's utopian blueprint for a city, its complicity with capitalism and its 'pseudo community that follows the isolated individual right into the family cell'(1977, par. 172).

Published as *The Radiant City* in 1935, Corbusier's vision for an ideal city was inspired by the potential of cars, airplanes and high rise buildings, much of which occupied shared amenity, for example, parklands and roads. For this vision, Corbusier drew on Ebenezer Howard's influential 'Garden City Model', in which Howard advocated a semi-rural healthy environment with shared amenities for ordinary workers. Howard argued against private ownership, which in his view 'led to inflation of property values'(quoted in Friedman 2002, 8).

Howard's *Tomorrow: a Peaceful Path to Real Reform*, first published in 1898 and widely taught internationally throughout the twentieth century and beyond in architectural schools, has significantly influenced the concept of suburbia. Howard's influence can be seen, for example, in the famous post-Second World War veterans' housing estate Levittown.

However, unlike Corbusier, Debord was not inspired by technology, but rather, worried that the technological evolution and rising domination of the capitalist transport system was on a dystopic rather than utopic trajectory:

> *The present is already the time of the self-destruction of the urban milieu. The explosion of cities which cover the country with 'formless masses of urban residues' (Lewis Mumford) is directly regulated by the imperatives of consumption. The dictatorship of the automobile, pilot-product of the first phase of commodity abundance, has been stamped into the environment with the domination of the freeway. At the same time … enormous shopping centres built on the bare ground of parking lots; and these temples of frenzied consumption, after bringing about a partial rearrangement of congestion, themselves flee within the centrifugal movement which rejects them as soon as they in turn become overburdened secondary centres. (Debord 1977, par. 174)*

UTOPIA + REVOLUTION

In 1967, around the same time as Debord's protestation, the French film director Jacques Tati paralleled Debord's prophecy in images. Almost silent, Tati's film *Playtime* portrays a never-ending and frenetic trafficking of cars and people as a metaphor for another type of traffic congestion generated by twentieth-century politics and economics, that of consumerism. The metaphorical image that lingers at the conclusion of Tati's film suggests that we are becoming what we are consuming.

From the film's beginning and under Tati's direction, the camera follows a group of American women on a shopping spree in Paris, showing us (the spectators) a range of goods that serve to distance humans from the reality of life. The upright vacuum cleaner, for example, affords us the dignity of remaining upright when we remove dirt from the floor. Similarly, the pedal-operated garbage bin and the washing machine keep our hands clean. Living the ideal modern life, we need never actually touch dirt.

Then as night falls and Paris darkens, we find ourselves via the camera lens on the street before an apartment block looking in through the fully glazed façade. The view in is acute. We see domestic life completely exposed: husbands are fussed over by perfectly-groomed wives, spotlessly clean children play quietly to one side, politeness reigns, modern rooms are beautifully decorated and televisions and slide projectors take the family elsewhere.

Although calm and reassuring, this domestic perfection is disquietingly unnatural, particularly as the camera pans out to reveal the apartment façade functioning as a multi-screen television transmitting numerous replications of living advertisements for ideal modern living. Where is the residue, the fatigue and the mess?

But Tati does not leave us there, stunned by the perfection; he goes on to show us the downfall (or the liberation, the ruin and revolution) that takes place in a restaurant. At first we see the polite rituals of entry, seating, ordering and eating. However, this containment soon degenerates, morphing into something more primitive as the guests respond to a raw, throbbing jungle beat. Quickly they form a conga-line of bodies becoming more and more excited. As the intensity escalates, the animal within becomes unleashed and the restaurant building, perhaps as a metaphor for the capitalist structure, begins to fray, crack and collapse (quoted in Churchill 2007, 147).

In the final scene – one in which Debord's readers may experience déjà vu – Tati leaves us to contemplate another metaphor – that of a gorging traffic roundabout where vehicles go around and around again, being consumed rather than released by this device that ironically was designed to regulate traffic. The drivers are apparently oblivious to the cumulative effect and seem unaware that being caught on the roundabout is limiting, mindless and repetitive, with those affected becoming followers of others who are in the same rut (quoted in Churchill 2007, 147).

This capitalist rut is what the Situationists encouraged people to free themselves from. They encouraged action such as the *dérive* – long, random, drunken, wandering experiences of urban terrain – and the *détournement*, which, like graffiti, is an act of makeover that effectively repudiates various existing cultural, artistic or urban forms. Debord explains:

> The literary and artistic heritage of humanity should be used for partisan propaganda purposes.... Since the negation of the bourgeois conception of art and artistic genius has become pretty much old hat ... the appearance of new necessities outmodes previous 'inspired' works. They become obstacles, dangerous habits. The point is not whether we like them or not. We have to go beyond them. (1956, pars 3 and 4)

Debord and Wolman (1956) advocated that ordinary people exercise their sovereignty in everyday life by becoming involved in constant movement and alterations to shift their positions, find new sensations and discover other ways of seeing and feeling. By taking various and possibly completely diverse elements, perhaps poetry, a play and a painting, to create new combinations through appropriation, the new relationships may well alter the meaning of the original.

Such was the New Babylon Project, the Situationists' proposition for urban development and social interaction that speculated on a world-wide city of the future that would be a dynamic collective, a community project alive with psychological and emotional states built into spatial incidents. Although Debord initiated the project, it was Constant Nieuwenhuys who continued to create an extensive series of drawings, models and texts for ten years after their alliance split in 1960 (Hemmens 2012).

Technology was crucial to New Babylon, where work was to be fully automated and the masses were free to roam and play all day. However, because SI believed automation to be essential but socially destructive, it was necessary to completely separate it from social life, and so New Babylon was designed to be vertically stratified, with social life on the upper levels and automation at the base.

The concept of New Babylon's physical construct was that of an immense structural framework elevated above the ground and then divided into smaller sectors of up to five to ten hectares. Nieuwenhuys described 'a complicated, netlike pattern interspersed with remnants of landscape and crisscrossed by a traffic grid, which runs independently below the built up areas' (quoted in Ball 1995, 195).

It was a world formed by continuous, ever evolving spatial situations, 'a world in which nature will have been totally superseded by technology, fixed communities by nomadic flows, work by leisure' (Colquhoun 2002, 228). Light, colour, volume, sound, climate and ambience could be altered at any moment. Time, a commodity highly valued by capitalists, was there to be spent, even wasted in the extravagance of New Babylon – a 'deterritorialized city' (Ball 1995, 199). Edward Ball described New Babylon as:

> *directed at the lived experience of the urban, its psychosomatic textures and phenomenal effects. Taking the city as the aim and end of industrial society, New Babylon understands urbanism to be the only sensual knowledge that an ethnically and culturally divided world might share; therefore it presumes that architecture is the only place to attempt a 'universal' intervention. (Ball 1995, 197)*

In 1961, Nieuwenhuys explained the project:

> *[It] theorises the activation of the enormous creative potential … present in the masses. It theorizes the disappearance of non-creative work as the result of automation … . But it also theorizes facts like the rapid spread of the world population, the perpetual growth of traffic, the cultivation of the whole planet, and total urbanization … . (Quoted in Ball 1995, 195)*

When Nieuwenhuys deployed automation to liberate New Babylonians from work, his intentions were similar to those of More, who used slaves to save Utopian citizens from the terrible realities of war and other violence. The intention was to facilitate the ideal life. However, there were dark sides to the people's liberation. In More's Utopia, it was the suppression of creative impulses that was the problem, whereas in New Babylon the almost diametrically opposite problem was the individual's abdication from responsibility, a state of mind that would diminish the New Babylonians' opportunity to empower themselves.

New Babylon's flaw lies in the strategy for liberation that was an endless, unregulated roaming, forming, dissolving and re-forming of both physical and psychological 'situations'. Ultimately, this would weaken and disempower individuals and society, because the endless mobility denies opportunities for both the individual and the collective to be tested in stasis by the consequences of their actions, and to aspire and to endure the challenges of maintenance, consolidation and cohesion. SI failed to recognize the value of work, which offers opportunities to develop command and to evolve through humility and reflection to become something more.

UTOPIA + CAPITALISM

A decade earlier in July 1959, during the early stages of the intense and competitive era of the Cold War, US Vice President Richard Nixon famously wowed Muscovites with his capitalist ploys. It was during the six weeks of the American National Exhibition in Moscow (ANEM) (Masey and Morgan 2008, 154–8) that Nixon and his cohort of American designers, notably Charles and Ray Eames (1959), flaunted another version of utopia: the ideal image of the everyday abundance, ease and pleasure typically enjoyed by American consumers of domestic suburban life.[1]

Known as 'the Kitchen Debate' (Watergate.info 1959), this was a political manoeuvre by Nixon, who was attempting to captivate the hearts and minds of the 2,700,000 ordinary Russians who attended the American exhibition, and for whom a stark awareness of their own comparatively austere lives became painfully apparent. By presenting his case for capitalism, Nixon intended to shift attention away from Russia's rightly felt pride and glory after their successful technological advance in the space race – the launch of their satellite Sputnik.[2] His strategy was to tap into the Russian housewife's feelings of envy and desire.

Prosecuting the case for capitalism, Nixon argued that inherent redundancy and constant refreshment was not only economically advantageous, but exciting, affordable and widespread in America. What he was advocating was the ever new and improved: new ideas that manifested as dynamic, progressive ways of living. In response to Nixon's provocations, an energetic debate ensued. Alongside the kitchen that was part of the full-scale typical American house exhibit, Nixon and the USSR First Secretary Nikita Khrushchev debated the topic of durability versus expendability.

The General Electric kitchen showcased a stunning display of appliances promoted as 'labour saving', including refrigerators, cooking appliances, washing machines, vacuum cleaners and televisions. Susan Reid positioned the American strategy: 'The American suburban kitchen was the supreme symbol of the imagined

America, the chief site of individual family-based consumption, where the advances of modern science and technology were placed at the service of peaceful domestic life, and – in the rhetoric of the time – of 'making women happy' (2008, 154).

Nixon argued that most American veterans from the Second World War and 'any steel worker could afford this [six-room] house', (Watergate.info 1959) and that capitalism and consumerism provided freedom to suburban America: 'Diversity, the right to choose, the fact that we have 1,000 builders building 1,000 different houses is the most important thing. We don't have one decision made at the top by one government official. This is the difference' (quoted in Colomina 2007, 244).

In response to Nixon, Khrushchev argued for durability: 'We build for our children and grandchildren' (Watergate.info 1959). He continued: 'Some things never get out of date – houses, for instance, and furniture, furnishings – perhaps – but not houses. I have read much about America and American houses, and I do not think that this is exhibit and what you say is strictly accurate' (Watergate.info 1959).

Mixed responses were received from the Russian people, who understood life from a different perspective to that of the Americans. Unemployment, basic survival and in particular acute housing shortages created daily struggles for millions of Russians. However, policies were in place to develop more efficient construction systems, and by 1957 progress was underway towards the socialists' ideals of raising the standard of living across the collective.

During the ANEM, the writer Marietta Shaginian published a critique of American domestic space and technology in the Soviet state newspaper, *Izvestiia*. Sceptical of claims that the accumulation of labour saving devices would be liberating, Shaginian predicted the 'countless domestic devices' would effectively 'anchor' the 'woman in perpetuity [to] her mission as "housewife", wife and cook' (quoted in Reid 2008, 155). Echoing something of More's vision, she continued: 'But we love innovations that actually emancipate women – new types of houses with public kitchens with their canteens for everyone living in the house; with laundries where vast machines wash clothes not just for one family alone' (quoted in Reid 2008, 155).

Shaginian was concerned that individual ownership of an ever-increasing abundance of things 'creates a kind of power over man' (quoted in Reid 2008, 155), effectively a fetish for private possessions. Even in those early days, television with its particularly seductive and influential affects was proving to be a pervasive force with the potential to control the hearts and minds of entire populations. At the time this was a source of concern, as was the alienating and 'de-humanizing' effect of computers.

The early 1960s lexicon became suffused with the language of technology – 'networks', 'feedback', 'systems' and 'software' – even though it was derived from the Cold War's pervasive, competitive and intimidating race to the future via technology. This was of interest to Jane Pavitt and David Crowley, who wrote: 'Cold War anxieties were frequently triggered by high-tech advances: the computer set off concerns about dehumanization; the fast spread of television led to discussion of the pervasive effects of new media; and communication systems were imagined as instruments of surveillance' (2008, 165).

Therefore, due to ambient conditions and values, the ANEM was perceived through mixed emotions. The exhibition visitors' books included comments such as 'I wish that our housewives had the chance to own such things', and 'I especially liked the Miracle Kitchen. It would be nice if such kitchens were mass-produced. And if we could trade with you'. Others were more critical: 'We expected that the American Exhibition would show something grandiose, some earthly equivalent to Soviet Sputniks. But you Americans want to amaze us with the glitter of your kitchen pans and the fashions which do not appeal to us at all'. And, 'I feel sorry for the Americans, judging by your exhibition. Does your life consist really only of kitchens?' (quoted in Reid 2008, 160–61).

The Americans had clearly tapped into Russians' individual desires and collective values. An image of feelings generated by the ANEM emphasis on home-based consumerism and the politics of envy was captured for the August 1959 cover of *Life* magazine, which featured a photograph of the wives rather than their politician husbands. Beatriz Colomina describes the image as follows:

> Pat Nixon appears as the prototype of the American woman depicted in advertisements of the 1950s: slim, well-groomed, fashionable, happy. In contrast, the Soviet ladies appear stocky and dowdy, and while two of them, Mrs. Khrushchev and Mrs. Mikoyan, look proudly toward the camera, the third one, Mrs. Kozlov … cannot keep her eyes off Pat Nixon's dress. (2007, 244)

ENVY + UTOPIC VISIONS OF EVERYDAY LIFE

Eliciting awe and envy was instrumental in the creation of the Eames's film *Glimpses of the USA* (1959); it was so popular when shown to the Russians at the ANEM that the floor to the geodesic dome in which it was screened was re-surfaced three or four times (Colomina 2007, 251).

Inside the Buckminster Fuller-designed dome, the Eameses hung seven 6 × 10 metre screens onto which they projected seven reels of film from seven projectors. Composed of both still and moving images collected from various sources including popular cinematography, newspapers, sports magazines and photographers' collections, the film deployed 'telescopes, zoom lenses, airplanes and night-vision cameras' (Colomina 2007, 252) to cleverly re-position the spectator, offering extraordinary images of ordinary, idyllic American life on earth.

The film opens with the narrator explaining reassuringly: 'From the sky it is difficult to distinguish the Russian city from the American city. … People live in this land, and as in Russia they are drawn together into towns and cities. Here is something of the way they live' (Eames and Eames 1959). Following the first series of images from the awe-inspiring perspective of outer space which evoked the mystery of the universe, the spectator is then shown dramatic glimpses of North America's magnificent, vast and extraordinarily diverse landscape. But what comes next would have been confronting for the Russians.

Drawn in closer again, although still from an aerial perspective, the spectator is then faced with a seemingly endless expanse of individual suburban houses, many with swimming pools; enormous, busy freeways; huge car parks full of fabulous cars; impressive engineering feats such as bridges; and then, as the tempo of the background score rises sharply, the screens are filled with images of cities tightly composed of many high rise buildings. Now on street level, footpaths are filled with well-dressed people enjoying life's exhilarating speed and excitement as they head off to work or shop.

The American strategy throughout the ANEM, as *Glimpses* exemplified, was to convey a utopian vision: American capitalism. The intent was to portray American abundance and liberation in everyday life directly to the Russian people via their own sensations of desire and envy.

This utopian vision was deployed as a weapon. It was a Cold War attack on Russia at a time of intense anxiety and competition, when the nuclear arms race and the space race were imposing real and terrifying threats to life on earth, while at the same time exercising the real and exhilarating thrills of human potential. Images of the technology and design of everyday life were used to undermine the ordinary Russian housewife's faith in her government. This was seen as important because keeping the housewife happy was central to the American Dream, in which the heart of suburban (political, economic and social) life was the kitchen. As Susan Reid writes:

> … [T]he full–time housewife reigned supreme, keeping a serene home in which the male breadwinner could retreat from the nervous strains and alienation of the public sphere. With the effort and dirt of housework carefully hidden, everyday family life was constructed as a space of leisure and freedom from anxiety and work. (Reid 2008, 154)

Of course, the Russians were astute in their criticism of the images presented by the Americans, and accurate in their suspicions that the reality for American women was not quite as portrayed by either the ANEM or by American television programs. Advertising in general could be especially cruel in portraying ridiculously high standards for the quality and extent of service to be provided by the housewife.

The well-known TV program *Bewitched*, created by Sol Saks and produced by Screen Gems between 1964 and 1972, portrayed the perfect housewife, Samantha, married to Darrin, an advertising executive. Samantha, beautiful and serene, manages herself, her children, her house, her husband and his boss perfectly through any situation. Even though Samantha was actually a witch, she admirably showed the moral fortitude to resist using her magical powers. With grace and beauty, Samantha kept her house and children spotless, her husband happy and their guests entertained.

Reality was different. As demonstrated by journals such as *House Beautiful*, American households were under significant pressure from all directions to acquire more and more appliances and products to be stored in larger houses with additional garages (Barry 1953). With such an array of cleaning products on sale, the average housewife felt compelled to maintain spotlessly clean clothes, floors and bench tops and so on; while at the same time sewing, making beds, chauffeuring children, cooking, looking fabulous and keeping her husband happy. But as Betty Friedan exposed in 1963, the American suburban housewife lay by her husband at night and asked 'Is this all?' She lay silently because American women 'were taught to pity the neurotic, unfeminine, unhappy women who wanted to be poets or physicists or presidents' (Friedan 1963, 15–16).

Remarkably however, as the world teetered on nuclear obliteration, optimism ran rampant. By the 1960s, technological advancement had dramatically vivified prospects for life on earth. Affluence, leisure, health, mobility and access to knowledge became more widespread and accessible. As the 1968 student protests and workers' strikes in Paris demonstrated, ordinary people came to believe they could change the world. Slogans like 'We want structures that serve people, not people serving structures' (Bureau of Public Secrets 1968) expressed an unleashing of people power actions aimed at creating a better world.

Like the Situationists, who had identified urbanism as the culprit in systemic control of the masses (and who had to some extent inspired the 1968 strikes), Manfredo Tafuri explicitly identified the role modern architecture played in the rise of capitalism. Recalling Giovanni Battista Piranesi's prophecy of the bourgeois city as an 'absurd machine', (1976, 42) Tafuri wrote:

> Being directly related to the reality of production, architecture was not only the first to accept, with complete lucidity, the consequences of its own commercialization, but was even able to put this acceptance into effect before the mechanisms and theories of political economy had furnished the instruments for such a task. Starting from its own specific problems, modern architecture as a whole had the means to create an ideological situation ready to fully integrate design, at all levels, with the reorganization of production, distribution, and consumption in the new capitalist city. (1976, 48)

ALTERATION AS REVOLUTION

Seeing modern architecture's complicity in the rise of capitalism is what drove much of Gordon Matta-Clark's critical body of work, his extremist alternative art/architecture that could well be categorized as a serialized détournement. It was during the 1960s and 70s that Matta-Clark rebuked architects like Richard Meier, whom he saw as working in collaboration with big business to profit from development known to be responsible for reducing ordinary people's basic social amenity.

Their crime was the misappropriation of virtuous modernist ideals. In Matta-Clark's view, these collaborations had 'not only failed to solve the problems but [had] created a dehumanized condition at both domestic and institutional level' (quoted in Diserens 2003c, 188). He talked of an everyday conspiracy that everywhere controlled the lives of ordinary people contained by 'suburban and urban boxes as a context for ensuring a passive, isolated consumer – a virtually captive audience' (quoted in Diserens 2003c, 187).

Aligned to SI thinking, Matta-Clark similarly intended to awaken his audience from their complacency, empowering them by physically altering the material world, which for him often involved the wielding of his chainsaw while suspended mid-air from a beam or some other structural element in a disused building.

It was through his reading of philosophical alchemy (Diserens 2003b, 22–37) that Matta-Clark believed he was affecting 'a kind of psychic alteration' (quoted in Celant 2003, 168) in those who experienced the work. He was interested in sculpting new ways in which to experience existing buildings, space and objects so as to affect people's sense of sovereignty. Firstly, he altered the physical material of a thing, and consequently, he shifted perceptions of that thing.

Memorial for Marcel Duchamp (1968), *Photo-Fry* (1969), *Window Blow-Out* (1976) and *Splitting* (1974) (all quoted in Diserens 2003a) are some of many works in which Matta-Clark cooked, entombed, cut, and or flayed objects, rooms, photographs, food and abandoned buildings. He explained, 'the spiritual focus of my work is connected to those traditions that have always dealt with the preparation and transformation of materials' (quoted in Diserens 2003a, 28).

Window Blow-Out happened when he was invited to exhibit work at the Institute of Architecture and Urban Studies in New York alongside three members of the renowned New York Five: Michael Graves, Richard Meier and Charles Gwathmey. It was in the middle of the night before the exhibition was to open that the 'wrecked' Matta-Clark turned up with an air rifle and shot out all the windows all the while ranting abuse at the Institute and their ideologies. 'These are the guys I studied with at Cornell, … these were my teachers. I hate what they stand for' (quoted in Atlee and Le Feuvre 2003, 67).

Less revolutionary was *Memorial for Duchamp* for Matta-Clark's godfather who had passed away earlier in that year. A room with an overlooking balcony set the scene for the event that began when a woman dressed as Duchamp's female alter ego read poetry from the balcony. As the poetry held the upward gaze of the 'bemused' audience, Matta-Clark 'began filling the room with an inflatable structure, which progressively grew in volume until it occupied the entire floor. When the last spectator had been forced from the room, the memorial was over' (Diserens 2003a, 22).

Splitting was a work that took place after Matta-Clark gained access to an abandoned house, a remnant of a poor black neighbourhood that had been reclaimed and evacuated to allow for high-density development. Effectively, he altered the house by cutting it in half. He cut it right through the middle vertically and then sliced a horizontal wedge-shape from one half of the foundation, and removed the wedge. When that half of the house lowered onto the now sloping foundation, a vertical 'v' shaped gap opened up between the two halves of the house. Filled with daylight, the gap was half a metre wide at the top.

When *Splitting* was completed, that is to say when the house was cut in half, a busload of invited guests were driven to the site at 322 Humphrey Street, New Jersey, for a risky tour through the house and up the stairs. As they climbed higher and the daylight gap widened, the audience became the work as they negotiated crossing the gap. Reflecting on the feeling of altering the building, Matta-Clark said: 'what I mean is that the realization of motion in a static structure was exhilarating' (quoted in Celant 2003, 168). 'The first act of doing is moving. Giving it a good heave' (169).

Rich in analogy, Matta-Clark's alterations of physical space were intended to affect the audience's psyche. In terms of a utopian vision, his work was less about a pre-determined or directed design outcome and more about a process in which individuals and groups who experienced the 'alterations' were then empowered to make their own alterations, thereby (re)claiming some aspect of sovereignty.

Throughout the thrilling drama and danger of Matta-Clark's prolonged détournement, there is a strong anticipation of vivacity in close proximity to death. His work is about the body, summonsing bodily responses and sensations from fear to exhilaration that linger even now after 40 years, imagining the roar of the chainsaw, the smell and feel of the dust, and the penetrating stench of the fried photos (Diserens 2003a, 25).

NEW UTOPIAS: BEYOND BODIES BECOMING ETHEREAL

The 2011 and 2012 YouTube videos, *A Day Made of Glass* (Corning Inc. 2011) and *A Day Made of Glass 2: Same Day* (Corning Inc. 2012), present visions of a not so distant or unlikely future in which everyday life appears smooth, seamless and uncomplicated, as only very well-designed software will deliver. This iteration of utopia is made possible by an omnipresence of glass surfaces incorporating edge-to-edge interactive technologies and touch-sensitive displays.

Corning's videos conjure the image from Tati's *Playtime*, in which full-height windows across the apartment building façade serve as a multi screen, advertising a series of ideal domestic lives made possible by the economics of consumerism. Of course, since the 1960s, technology in the home has moved on from the slide projector, and many have confessed to the imperfections and variations of family life. But what Corning has now articulated is another reality – one where our body is not.

Similar to Tati's characters, those of Corning's videos appear perfect. They are beautiful, instantly responsive, their movements are agile, they appear light, thin and they are in control. These qualities are the aspirational attributes in twenty-first-century life. Most importantly, they exude mastery over their environments. Their material world appears to be enabling and anticipating the characters' next move so as to rapidly progress them through richly engaged and informed lives. What distinguishes them is firstly their tranquillity, but most significantly, that they are elsewhere.

The power is magical, almost of another dimension and it belongs to everyone, young and old. What is quite remarkable is the absence of stress. Even when, in the 2011 video, Jennifer (the central figure) wakes at 7 am and glides to the bathroom mirror on which she discovers amongst her messages that her 9.30 am meeting has been brought forward an hour to 8.30, her bliss remains undisturbed then, and as her day unfolds, is brightened by being constantly connected via many glass devices.

Meanwhile, Jennifer's partner prepares a breakfast in their shiny white kitchen where most surfaces seem to be 'display enabling'. While Dad instantly converts the kitchen's white work surface to a cook surface, his young daughters, Amy and Sarah, slide images from their portable display unit onto the same work surface to have a fun conversation with their grandmother, who is calling in from elsewhere.

Jennifer lightly breezes through to the car, where more messages and directions await her. Later, when, surprisingly, she visits an actual clothing store, the large glass, high impact, multi-functional, interactive display panel is emblazoned by a welcome for her return to the store.

Posted in 2012, Corning's second video opens with the magic of Amy's tablet that 'captures, organises and displays all her favourites things' (Corning 2012a), waking her at 7.04 am, in her bedroom lined with soft cuddly toys. Ignoring them, Amy walks across to the glass doors of her closet to find her day's schedule displayed. There are a few reminders and the weather report. Rather than rummaging through the textures, fragrances and mementos of her closet, Amy selects her clothing for the day by navigating the electronic menu on the surface of the door.

Later, in the car with moments to spare before Dad joins them, Amy and Sarah use their tablets to select 'pinkified' as the dashboard theme for the morning. When Dad slides in he discovers the car's dashboard has been 'pinkified' by little hearts swirling across its thin durable glass surface. Dad is so proud! But immediately converts the dash to the manly grey he prefers.

At school the roof is lined with next generation (concealed) solar panels. Inside, wall-to-wall interactive glass screens are connected to small mobile devices on each of the children's desks.

At work, Dad, who appears to be a neuropathologist, is video conferencing in an all-glass room formed by wall-sized, durable, seamless interactive displays. The patient, who is in a scanning machine, and his medico are actually somewhere else, but for Dad, they appear to be on the other side of the glass. When a three-dimensional image of the patient appears in the middle of Dad's room, he is able to select a location to take a sectional image through the brain and then lift the virtual image up out of the virtual patient's head into the air so as to examine it more closely.

Back at home, evening has fallen, the house dims its glass optical fibre lighting, Sarah uploads her homework and prepares for bed, and Dad has snuggled up in bed with his tablet. Things seem very cosy.

OCCUPYING THE DREAM

In July 2012, after millions of hits on their videos, Corning posted a third video, *A Day Made of Glass 2: Unpacked*. The narrator explains:

> *Of course, this is not just a story about glass. It's a story about a shift in the way we will communicate and use technology in the future. It's a story about ubiquitous displays and operating systems, shared applications, cloud media storage and unlimited bandwidth .... But at Corning, we believe in this vision and we're not waiting. Care to join us? (Corning 2012b)*

To some great extent we have already joined, begging the question 'what is happening to us in this hypermedia state?'

Back in the 1960s, when Marshall McLuhan speculated on how each new technology shifts ways in which we humans occupy the world, he found the significant impact was less a consequence of what we were consuming from television (in particular), and more that we had moved away from other aspects of our lives. McLuhan found the family unit had been completely revolutionized by technologies that enabled new views out into the world: no longer dependant on the social, economic and intellectual limitations of the parents, 'now all the world's a stage' (McLuhan and Fiore 1989, 14).

Essentially, he perceived all forms of media as physical or psychological prosthetic devices that effectively extend our human faculties. McLuhan's concern was for the effects media have on the human sensorium:

> All media work us over completely. They are so pervasive in their personal, political, economic, aesthetic, psychological, moral, ethical, and social consequences that they leave no part of us untouched, unaffected, unaltered. The medium is the massage. Any understanding of social and cultural change is impossible without a knowledge of the way media work as environments. (McLuhan and Fiore 1989, 26)

McLuhan's incisive questioning of media remains as pertinent today in the age of the hypermedia as it was in the 1950s and 60s. Today, these are the big questions: How do today's media change the way we live in the world? How do they affect the sensorium? What are the consequences of occupying space defined by interactive, display-enabling technology that, rather than harbouring us, takes us somewhere our body is not?

Citing the alphabet as an earlier example of media influence, McLuhan argued it is the means of communication that is the predominant influence on the form of human environments, rather than the content of the message. He writes: 'Words and the meaning of words predispose the child to think and act automatically in certain ways' (McLuhan and Fiore 1989, 8). Always interested in the effects any particular medium has on modes of perception and resultant behaviours, McLuhan says:

> We associate the uniform modular structure of the printed page with the classroom itself, with the seating plan – the grid system .... Visually, the classroom is the exact counterpoint of the book page, with the teacher like the page heading, and the lines underneath ... the moveable types being the students. (McLuhan 1969, 149–50)

In 2015, hypermedia is the environment we occupy. When intuitive information technology is ubiquitous, we feel increasingly dependent on our electronic connections. From birth, children learn to walk, talk and connect. They emerge at ease with hypermedia – but at what cost? Connected to hypermedia, we have moved towards being light and fast, fuelled with endless information, virtual friends, schedules and lists, but in McLuhan's terms, what have we moved away from? What is the dark side of the new vision of the ideal world of extreme mental mobility and continuous transformation? Is a longing for the deep dark cave of respite and contemplation nothing more than a Freudian archaic desire?

CONCLUSION

Reading Corning's utopian vision in the context of More, Baudrillard, Debord, SI, Tati, the ANEM, Matta-Clark and McLuhan, what do we see? More's politically motivated proposition for an ideal world is undermined firstly by its structural necessity to suppress the individual's realization of selfhood, and secondly by Utopia's justification of their reliance upon slavery. We have also seen various reactionary provocations from Baudrillard, the Situationists and Matta-Clark that more or less generated political action from their audiences. New visions of liberation and transformation that were catalysed and popularized by the Cold War and the space race were adopted as human-centred weapons by the ANEM, an event which seductively emphasized the value of capitalist innovation, technology and obsolescence.

To some extent, many of us living in 2015 have experienced something of each of these ideals as well as their antitheses: suppression of the individual for the benefit of the group; the downfall of excessive play; and the dark sides of perfection, for example, beauty or cleanliness.

While we are yet to fully occupy the reality of elsewhere as articulated by Corning, most of us have certainly come to live most of our lives through instant endless virtual mobility connected to somewhere else. Connectivity is the new place of utopic/dystopic occupation. Heeding McLuhan's warning, that the aspect of our lives we have moved away from in this technological revolution is respite – we are being worked over completely.

It is in this moment of revolution, knowing our human sensorium is being altered by the hypermedia environment, that I turn to the early Buddhist concept of *Anatta* or No-Self (*Anatman*), which urges us to 'become aware of the process of continuous change' (Jayaram 2000–2014). Nothing is permanent. Everything is ephemeral, relatively, and ownership is an illusion. We may delude ourselves that we own our body or our car, but in reality a virus or an accident may claim these within an instant. If we let go of the fixation to cling on to things, accepting our constant evolution, then we rid ourselves of anxiety and sorrow in relation to less or to loss.

> *It is like the identity of a river which flows continuously and maintains a semblance of an entity, though not a single drop of yesterday's water remains at the same place today. When a man realizes that he has been changing continuously every moment, he grieves neither for what he has lost nor for what he has not gained. (Jayaram 2000–2014, n.p.)*

We are constructs of our environment. We are the result of symbiosis.

REFERENCES

Atlee, James and Lisa Le Feuvre. 2003. *Gordon Matta-Clark: The Space Between*. London: Nazraeli Press.

Ball, Edward. 1995. 'Case Study: New Babylon'. In *Sites and Stations: Provisional Utopias: Architecture and Utopia in the Contemporary City*, edited by Stan Allen and Kyong Park, 193–9. New York: Lusitania Press.

Barry, Joseph. 1953. 'Report on the American Battle Between Good and Bad Modern Houses'. *House Beautiful* May: 172–3, 266–72.

Baudrillard, Jean. 2011. 'The Ephemeral'. In *Utopie: Texts and Projects, 1967–1978*, edited by Craig Buckley and Jean-Louis Violeau, 77–90. Los Angeles: Semiotext(e).

Bureau of Public Secrets. 1968. *May 1968 Graffiti*. http://www.bopsecrets.org/CF./graffiti.htm. Accessed 15 May 2014.

Celant, Germano. 2003. 'Gordon Matta–Clark, L "Architettura E" Un Ready–Made'. In *Gordon Matta–Clark*, edited by Corinne Diserens, 162–9. London: Phaidon Press.

Churchill, Lynn M. 2007. 'Architecture "Doing" Body: An Architectural Proposition Inspired by an Analysis of Francis Bacon's Paint "Doing" Body'. PhD diss., Curtin University of Technology.

Colomina, Beatriz. 2007. *Domesticity at War*. Cambridge: MIT Press.

Colquhoun, Allan. 2002. *Modern Architecture*. Oxford: Oxford University Press.

Corning Inc. 2011. *A Day Made of Glass*. YouTube video, 5.32. http://www.youtube.com/watch?v=6Cf7IL_eZ38. Accessed 23 March 2013.

——. 2012a. *A Day Made of Glass 2: Same Day*. YouTube video, 5.58. http://www.youtube.com/watch?v=jZkHpNnXLB0. Accessed 23 March 2013.

——. 2012b. *A Day Made of Glass 2: Unpacked*. YouTube video, 11.24. http://www.youtube.com/watch?v=X-GXO_urMow. Accessed 23 March 2013.

Debord, Guy-Ernest. 1956. 'Methods of Détournement'. *Les Lévres Nues* 8 (May). http://library.nothingness.org/articles/SI/en/display/3. Access 15 May 2014.

Debord, Guy, and Gil J. Wolman. 1956. 'A User's Guide to Détournement'. *Les Lévres Nues* 8 (May). http://www.cddc.vt.edu/sionline/presitu/usersguide.html. Accessed 15 May 2014.

Debord, Guy. 1977. *Society of the Spectacle*. Detroit: Black & Red.

Diserens, Corinne, ed. 2003a. *Gordon Matta–Clark*. London: Phaidon Press.

——. 2003b. 'Alchemy and Anthropology 1962–71'. In *Gordon Matta–Clark*, edited by Corinne Diserens, 22–37. London: Phaidon Press.

——. 2003c. 'Interview with Gordon Matta-Clark, Antwerp, September 1977'. In *Gordon Matta-Clark*, edited by Corinne Diserens, 187–90. London: Phaidon Press.

Eames, Charles and Ray Eames. 1959. '*Glimpses of the U.S.A*'. YouTube video, 4.24. http://www.youtube.com/watch?v=Ob0aSyDUK4A. Accessed 20 April 2014.

Friedan, Betty. 1963. *The Feminine Mystique*. London: Victor Gollancz.

Friedman, Avi. 2002. *Planning the New Suburbia: Flexibility by Design*. Vancouver: UBC Press.

Freud, Sigmund. 1969. *Civilization and its Discontents*. Translated by J. Riviere. London: Hogarth Press and the Institute of Psychoanalysis.

Hemmens, Alastair. 2012. 'A Portrait of Guy Debord by Constant Nieuwenhuys', *Marblepunk*, July 14, http://www.marblepunk.com/2012/07/portrait-of-guy-debord-by-constant.html. Accessed 16 May 2014.

Jayaram, V. 2000–2014. *The Buddhist Concept of Anatta or No-Self (Anatma)*. http://www.hinduwebsite.com/buddhism/anatta.asp. Accessed 28 June 2014.

Masey, Jack and Conway Lloyd Morgan. 2008. *Cold War Confrontations: US Exhibitions and Their Role in the Cultural Cold War*. Baden: Lars Müller.

McLuhan, Marshall, William Blissett, Harley Parker and Robert Shafer. 1969. 'Part Three: Explorations in the New World'. In *McLuhan, Hot and Cool: a Primer for the Understanding of and a Critical Symposium with Responses by McLuhan*, edited by Gerald Emanuel Stearn, 114–63. New York, NY: The New American Library Inc.

McLuhan, Marshall and Quentin Fiore. 1989. *The Medium is the Massage*. New York: Simon & Schuster.

More, Thomas. 2009. *Utopia*. Translated by Paul Turner. London: Penguin.

Ono, Yoko and Thomas Kellein. 2008. *Yoko Ono: Between the Sky and My Head*. Köln: Cornerhouse.

Pavitt, Jane and David Crowley. 2008. 'The Hi-Tech Cold War'. In *Cold War Modern Design 1945–1970*, edited by David Crowley and Jane Pavitt, 163–91. London: V&A Publishing.

Reid, Susan E. 2008. '"Our Kitchen is Just as Good": Soviet Responses to the American National Exhibition in Moscow, 1959'. In *Cold War Modern Design 1945–1970*, edited by David Crowley and Jane Pavitt, 154–62. London: V&A Publishing.

Tafuri, Manfredo. 1976. *Architecture and Utopia: Design and Capitalist Development*. Translated by Barbara Luiga La Penta. Cambridge: MIT Press.

Watergate.info. 1959. *The Kitchen Debate: Nixon and Khrushchev*. http://watergate.info/1959/06/24/kitchen-debate-nixon-khrushchev.html. Accessed 20 July 2012.

Weller, Richard. 2009. *Boomtown 2050: Scenarios for a Rapidly Growing City*. Crawley, W.A.: UWA Publishing.

Zumthor, Peter. 2006. *Thinking Architecture*. 2nd edn. Basel: Birkhäuser.

NOTES)

1   Charles and Ray Eames worked in collaboration with George Nelson who had been commissioned to design the exhibition, film director Billy Wilder, architects Eero Saarinen and Buckminster Fuller, and Mildred Constantine, the Museum of Modern Art's associate curator of design.

2   On 4 October 1957 Russia's 7 metre diameter satellite, Sputnik, was the first successfully launched into orbit.

9
Hypersexual Occupations

Nicole Kalms

INTRODUCTION

> *The visual (and verbal) discourses of public femininity come to occupy an increasingly spectacular space as sites, events, narratives and occasions within the cultural milieu. The commercial domain provides a proliferation of interpellations directed to young women, with harsher penalties, it seems, for those who refuse or who are unable to receive its various addresses.*
> (McRobbie 2009, 60)

These words of McRobbie (2009) speak exactly to the hypersexualized provocation of femininity which is the theme of this chapter. There has been an increase in sexualized representations of femininity in the cities of North America, Australia and the United Kingdom. This surge indicates how the contemporary city is linked with the infrastructures of new media, so much so that advertising and image often create the primary context for our occupation of urban space, concealing and sometimes replacing the exterior façade and co-opting any available urban surface. These contemporary cities form both the context and also the principal mode for the visual delivery of sexualized images and 'porno chic' representations, signposting a shift in the occupation of the late capitalist city. A post-feminist view suggests that cities are undergoing a territorial transformation that echoes women's expanding sexual empowerment and liberation, with women precariously positioned in the 'context of a wide range of social, political and economic changes of which they themselves appear to be the privileged subjects' (McRobbie 2009, 59). This chapter will consider the tensions of the post-feminist view of individualized sexualized agency against a radical feminist view that offers an entirely different logic. The research questions what constitutes empowerment and advocates consideration of the larger socio-cultural implications of sexualization in the urban realm.

What follows is a discussion of the urban sexualization of space, or what I term 'hypersexuality', which has moved from the private and interior spaces of the city and into the exterior public realm. I examine several case studies that illustrate hypersexualized representations in urban space, with the aim of reflecting on what is presently distinctive about the mutual territory of sexualization, media and architecture. I argue that the public 'stage' of sexualized images and representations contribute to gender stereotypes that currently have negative consequences for both men and women.[1] What, however, is less discussed in architectural discourse is: what opportunities and challenges are offered to designers through the shifting boundaries which produce sexualization, and how might men and women take this knowledge and use it constructively as an opportunity to repudiate, re-imagine and redefine urban space?

I will begin by positioning the city as a 'media city' (McQuire 2008) where new and old media occupy an increasingly privileged position. I will then outline how ethnographic research reveals that commercial representation of women in the city is dominated by sexualized images and will introduce the context of hypersexuality, before discussing several case studies where public 'porno chic' cultural practices expose the tensions around women's agency and identity. The case studies will provide a broad critique of hypersexuality in urban space, and are drawn from the period 2000 to 2014 (the height of 'raunch culture' and the subsequent debate surrounding sexualization). These case studies include: examples of hypersexual billboards and advertising that typify those found in late capitalist urban spaces; sexualized 'phenomena' that reveal how the hypersexual body is now opportunistically deployed in the public realm; and key architectural examples, which include a domestic project that marks the possibility of architecture's critique of hypersexuality, as well as an urban pole dancing event space which implements architectural apparatus from the sex industry.

PIN-UP MEDIA CITY

In the millennium year, a Melbourne architect, Cassandra Fahey, was commissioned by Melbourne footballer and celebrity bad-boy Sam Newman to build a contemporary home on a prominent strip in the lively suburb of St Kilda (Figure 9.1). Scandal erupted when the façade was unveiled to reveal a 9 × 8 metre pixelated image of the Playboy Bunny and actress Pamela Anderson. The project made the front page of a Melbourne newspaper, and on 23 June 2000, the *Herald Sun* quoted a neighbour who suggested that it looked 'like a very big billboard for a high-class brothel'. The sexualized image had expanded its territory, moving from the screen and men's magazines to the residential setting. So prolific was the local interest in the project and the associated media coverage that both the house and the architect have secured a place in the Australian mediascape.

Pamela Anderson's face shimmering on the glazed domestic surface echoes an emerging tension between sexuality, media and urban space, as demonstrated by the 12 July 2000 report in *The Age*, where the architect stated: 'I like to think of it as for the public, it's turning a little bit of Sam's house inside out and showing them a part of it'. And as Kim Dovey wrote: 'the house juxtaposes the real with the reflected; the real house virtually disappears beneath its represented and reflected images', and 'this is an architecture of its time that engages with image, myth and advertising … with global images of consumption and desire' (2005, 236).

Certainly there was a witty – if mysterious – coupling of the two celebrities, but the project exemplified an enfolding of media, sexuality and architecture.

Scott McQuire discusses the collapsed space of media and architecture, noting the significant transformations delivered by new media to urban life:

9.1 The Newman House by Cassandra Fahey
Source: Author photograph.

> Rather than treating media as something separate from the city – the medium which represents urban phenomena by turning it into an image – I argue that the spatial experience of modern social life emerges through a complex process of co-constitution between architectural structures and urban territories, social practices and media feedback. (McQuire 2008, vii)

By suggesting that architecture and media are no longer separate, McQuire proposes a radical shift in architectural urbanism: here, architecture is intertwined with media to the point where the formation and structure of urban events are determined equally and reciprocally by advertising and architecture, screen and infrastructure as well as networks and community. Certainly the contemporary city is no longer defined by glass and steel and, as Beatriz Colomina argues, the engagement 'with the new mechanical equipment of the mass media: photography, film, advertising, publications, and so on' is what presently defines architecture (Colomina 1994, 73) with 'discourses about sex and sexuality across all media forms' (Gill 2007, 150). Certainly, the media city's hypersexual typology potentially provides many exciting opportunities for architects and urban designers, yet it is also the framework in which men and women iteratively perform gender stereotypes, and where they are 'rewarded' for adopting sexualized culture.

Judith Butler suggests that it is through our sexuality and, by inference, our *sexualization* we are able to assert our individual value. And the media city assists in this production, where sex is not a static description of what one *is* but a norm by which one *becomes* viable (Butler 1993, 2). The ethnographic research in this arena tells us that women in media cities are in a particular position. They are confronted regularly with images that map out a *ready-to-wear* gender stereotype.

In 2003 Lauren Rosewarne documented a year in the life of the billboards of Melbourne's Central Business District, and analysed women's representation. Her study revealed that in billboard advertising, younger images of women are dominant, with 79 per cent represented as being between 16 and 30 years of age. Rosewarne analysed the characterization of women in these advertisements and found that over 30 per cent of women were represented in various states of undress or nudity, that is, in lingerie or underwear, in swimwear, naked, or in the process of dressing or undressing. Furthermore, she examined the facial expressions of women represented in this period: 6.5 per cent had an orgasmic expression, 30 per cent an inviting expression, 11 per cent had their eyes closed and 11 per cent had their head thrown back (Rosewarne 2007a, 85).

As cars hurry past, the Newman House conveys an expanding and contentious relationship of how gendered representations occupy public space and, in turn, the viewer. This is a point that Anne Cronin throws light on when she observes a temporal connection between image and viewer that potentially impacts the problematic of sexualized images in urban space:

> '[T]he image' is not a static, fixed container of meanings – these meanings are produced in the time of vision … they reach out for an explicit temporal connection with the viewer. Therefore we must pay close attention to the relation between the temporalities of self in moments of vision and the multidimensional connection of differences (gender, 'race', sexuality, nationality and so on) to the material body of the viewer. (Cronin 2000, 106)

Cronin's positioning of the image as temporally connected to the viewer supports this chapter's understanding that the media are not 'homogeneous, monolithic and all-powerful', (Gill 2012, 738), and that, in the case of sexualization, there are many different kinds of representation of girls and women with varied kinds of interpretations. Yet the media reduces women's image and desire to stereotyped, objectified and heterosexual constructions – as seen in Rosewarne's research. Furthermore, the advertising media's unregulated and highly accessible content means that the audience is producing these images too (albeit with less funding resources and access). Even more complexly, with digital devices and interactive feedback, sometimes these activities may be operating simultaneously. All of which question the levels and forms of empowerment, and the dialectics of individual agency becomes ambiguous territory.

HYPERSEXUALITY

By the mid-nineties, the term 'raunch culture' had become the colloquial term for describing the many and varied sexualized representations that had moved from the private space of the brothel, strip club or screen into the public sphere. The depiction of 'porno chic' practices moved beyond magazines, internet sites and television, and deep into advertising campaigns, social media and other less likely spaces.

In 2005, Ariel Levy published *Female Chauvinist Pigs: Women and the Rise of Raunch Culture*, and a few years later in 2008, an Australian academic, Emily Maguire, followed with *Princesses and Pornstars – Sex, Power, Identity*. Both authors critiqued the tensions of raunch culture and porno chic productions, where 'representations of porn in non-pornographic art and culture' (McNair 2002, 61) circulated. They agreed that young women are increasingly and prolifically engaged with rehearsing a media-driven sexuality where the use of aesthetics from pornography and strip club culture becomes confused with personal power and identity. The raunch phenomena have propelled women from 'once sexualized representations of women in the media presented as passive, mute objects', to the 'active, desiring sexual subjects' (Gill 2008, 42) that Rosewarne's study highlights, as cited above.

My use of the word 'hypersexual' aims to distinguish it from the more fashionable and recognized term 'raunch', and to acknowledge a discursive shift from the early fad of raunch culture to one that is firmly embedded in cultural practice. Sheila Jeffreys discusses the way that everyday language strategically 'adapts' to give the impression of choice and empowerment (1997, 5), suggesting that language can often be manoeuvred to disguise deeper social issues. Phrases such as 'sex worker', 'working girl' and 'sex industry' normalize women's exploitation, and this use of language contributes to making the practices acceptable. In a similar way the terms 'raunch' or 'raunchy' and 'porno chic' help to make the phenomena seductive, whereas 'hypersexuality' denotes a more critical position and problematizes contemporary sexualization as a moment of excess, when visual modes of self-expression are lifted from the practices of pornography and the contemporary sex industry.

While post-feminism continues to debate the transformation of both feminism and media culture and 'their mutual relationship' (Gill 2007, 147), mainstream culture has tended to conceptualize the various choices of individual women who participate in hypersexual practices as empowered and autonomous, and in doing so, expects that these individual views and decisions will be respected. I argue, however, that in advocating for individualistic 'agency', there is a failure to fully problematize the ongoing negotiation of power that takes place in public space between men and women and the larger institutions and infrastructures that they occupy, and in turn to question the individualized proclamations for sexualized empowerment that mask larger issues which affect both men and women. The case studies that follow develop this argument through examining how sexualization has entered the ordinary events of urban life.

THE HYPERSEXUAL BODY IN PUBLIC SPACE

In 2010, the under-16 Broadbeach Cats Football Club, located on the east coast of Australia, publicly defended its sponsorship deal with the American restaurant chain 'Hooters'. On 6 May 2010, the *Brisbane Times* reported the launch of the sponsorship deal, where two Hooters waitresses dressed in the Hooter's uniform of 'tight tank tops and bottom hugging orange shorts' cheered the under-16s on. The article, titled 'Sponsorship Scandal a Storm in a D-Cup', suggested that the wider implications of the presence of the Hooters waitresses at the match sent a message to the young footballer: that they may feel entitled to 'large-breasted women in skimpy outfits bouncing around at your games'.

In the same article, a restaurant spokesperson claimed that the women who are employed to work as Hooter's waitresses represent 'the all-American cheerleader'. Hooters imposes strict guidelines on staff behaviour and appearances, such that a Hooters waitress is required to sign a document acknowledging:

> my job duties require I wear the designated uniform; (2) my job duties require that I interact with and entertain the customers; and (3) the Hooters concept is based on female sex appeal and the work environment is one in which joking and innuendo based on female sex appeal is commonplace. (The Smoking Gun 2014)

One of the outcomes of such requirements of female employees is that they can be discriminated against for stepping outside the company's or even the customers' expectations.

The Hooters example heightens the shift of sexualized practices from contained interior into exterior urban space, with the hypersexualized waitress moving from the relatively private space of the restaurant where 'joking and innuendo based on female sex appeal is commonplace' to the public space of the local sporting field. The already gendered space of the football arena becomes a sexualized site that conflates the controlled sexualization and objectification of women with teenage boys' recreation in a way that indicates public grooming is now considered acceptable, at least on the Gold Coast in Australia.

It is reasonable to suggest that these teenage boys' perception of the role of women will be shaped by this experience. For example, they may stereotype young waitresses as sexualized objects, seeing them as an available support to their aspirations and valuing only their sexual attractiveness. And while the event may be a temporary act, it reveals the entrenchment of masculine positions from institutions that see the use and production of women's bodies as having economic and aesthetic value.

The sexualized waitress who has moved beyond restaurant bounds to sexualize public space furthers the distribution of a range of perceptions and stereotypes about women in urban life. This shift and expansion of territory raises the question of whether the 'agency' that the Hooters waitress may individually assert should be repudiated in order to limit the regulated and disciplined practice that she proliferates.

SEXUALIZED IS RE-CONTEXTUALIZED

If the tensions evident in the Hooter's case study are an example of how hypersexuality assists in cultivating sexist behaviour and attitudes, then the Australian fashion label Ksubi demonstrates the power dynamics potentially present in the sexualized occupation of the public realm.

Sex and advertising have long been expedient allies with the obvious progression towards the sexualization of public shopping districts where advertising, architecture and fashion merge. However, the following description of a Ksubi jeans advertisement (Figure 9.2) displayed in General Pants stores in Melbourne's central business district in 2010 may still surprise some readers: 'A topless young woman with black electrical tape across each nipple. There is a man behind her but you can't see his face and he is in the process of removing her jeans. The word SEX appears above her head in huge bold type' (Advertising Standards Bureau 2014).

On 8 May 2011, the *Daily Telegraph* reported that the Ksubi campaign included their young adult retail staff wearing 'I love sex' badges, and extended to the General Pants Group's linking of erotic online videos to the in-store promotion. In this example we can recognize a more sexually explicit development and provocative evolution of the so-called 'wholesome' sexualization of the Hooter waitress. In the space of the General Pants store, the power hierarchy between the consumer and service provider (in this case the retail assistant) is exploited by the badge the retail worker is required to wear, asserting her (or his) love of sex.

9.2 General Pant Group's advertisement from 2010. Melbourne Central Shopping Centre, Melbourne, Australia
Source: Author photograph.

Ksubi's sexualized campaign 'directs' or instructs a sexualized interaction and impacts the public retail space. The *Daily Telegraph* article continued with reports that the staff were uncomfortable about wearing the badges and felt that it was inappropriate to send this message to the teenage customers who frequent the store and mall, although the CEO of the company offered that it was 'a bit of a stretch' to suggest that the campaign might encourage teenagers to have sex.

In November 2011 a lengthy claim against the poster was submitted to the Advertising Standards Bureau (2014). The complaint began: 'These ads are in public places. They contain explicit and highly suggestive material. The huge size of them in the front windows of the stores make them impossible to ignore thereby removing the choice of the consumer to be exposed to these images … .'

A second complaint was made about the General Pants internet advertising campaign.

Both complaints were upheld by the Advertising Standards Bureau, with the Case Report on 5 November noting that the 'image overall conveyed a strongly sexualized image' (Advertising Standards Bureau 2014). The complaint was registered on 5 November and the ads were removed by 23 November. In those 18 days (and with the associated publicity) it is arguable that the campaign had already had a substantial effect on its target audience as well as on the occupation of the public space where it was displayed.

The Ksubi campaign reveals a move towards a 'porno chic' advertising style in which the tropes of stripping and pornography are deployed, using the rhetoric of 'girl power', and portraying these tropes as agents of women's sexual autonomy. Gill critiques these sexualized tactics and contends that it is often legitimized under a rubric of a 'sexually autonomous heterosexual young woman who plays with her sexual power and is forever "up for it"' (2008, 41).

For the past 60 years, the feminist project has worked persistently to critique the commercial representation of women and, more recently, the increase in the sexualization of these images. Gill has offered extensive critique of the sexualization of culture and its impact on the individual subject; her most recent work asks if it would be 'more productive to talk about sexism rather than sexualization?' (Gill 2012, 741).

Rosewarne uses the evidence from her study of women's representation in public space (as discussed earlier) to carefully analyse the content of sexualized images and then takes Gill's critique a step further by suggesting that sexist public advertising is a form of sexual harassment (2007b, 314). For retail spaces where sexualized images are prevalent, this results in a gendered and hypersexualized territory that excites and reinforces heterosexual masculinity 'marking the space as a male domain' (Rosewarne 2007b, 321).

Together, Gill and Rosewarne's ethnographic research can assist in understanding the trajectory from encountering the image to considering the cumulative and iterative impact of hypersexual urbanism. For example, in the *Reality and Risk* project entitled 'Erotising Inequality – Technology, Pornography and Young People', Crabbe and Corletts (2011) link the pervasiveness of the porno chic aesthetic in the public realm and social life generally to shifts in individual sexual practices.

Their argument states that the pornified aesthetic that is now culturally present in 'billboards, music videos and designer stores shape the desires and imaginations of a younger and younger demographic' (2011, 12).

Crabbe and Corletts (2011) go on to assert that these representations are the key determinant for gender stereotyping and unequal gender relations. Similarly, their research links sexualized and pornographically styled representations like those outlined in the Ksubi advertising campaign with gender stereotyping and unequal gender relations and ultimately to violence towards women (13).

This research suggests that upon experiencing the cumulative effect of sexualized representations in the public realm, young heterosexual men may experience sexual entitlement, which may provoke sexual aggression and even harassment. Further, women may experience a certain pressure to experiment with the porno chic representations that the media routinely displays, in order to feel valued or valuable, and to see these practices as viable. In-depth and long-term research in this arena (indeed, the objectives of my larger research project) will substantiate whether the occupation of public space by sexualized representations contributes directly to violence towards women.

THE STREET IS THE STRIP CLUB

The phenomena of bikini and topless car washes reveal how the media city is not simply borrowing from sexualized practices to represent an image of women; it is *hosting* sexualized practices for commercial ends in the public realm. Both the bikini car wash and the topless car wash are not only prevalent in Australia, but also in North America and the United Kingdom; for example, *All Girl* topless car wash in Darwin, Australia; *Bubbles'n'Babes* topless car wash in Leicestershire, United Kingdom; *Crewe* bikini car wash in Staffordshire, United Kingdom; *TingTing* bikini car wash in Los Angeles, United States. The case of Kitten's Car Wash is drawn on here to exemplify how gender stereotyping and unequal gender relations are outcomes of sexualized representations in public space, and demonstrates how strip club practices are commonly relocated onto the street in order to sexualize an activity formerly unsexualized.

Kitten's Car Wash, with its female staff washing cars year round wearing nothing more than skimpy bikinis, has been operating since 2006 in East Bentleigh, a suburb in Melbourne. The car wash is an extension of a larger organization, a metropolitan 'gentleman's club' (also called Kitten's) that hosts a chain of stripping and lap dancing venues. This public exposure places a large responsibility on the female car wash worker who, like the Hooter's waitress, may have to 'distinguish between paid-for sexual attention and sexual harassment' (Jeffreys 1997, 265).

Over the past eight years, the business has regularly breached its planning permit, indicating that regulation of such practices is challenging. For example, in 2009, the company failed to comply with the on-site staff limit (a maximum of two), and was fined $50,000 AUD for having six women on site. In fact, on 24 March 2009, *The Age* reported that between December 2006 and March 2009,

9.3 Kittens Car Wash 2014, Bentleigh East
Source: Author photograph.

council enforcement officers saw more than two staff washing cars on 12 occasions, stating 'a senior member of VCAT found that up to 'six skimpily clad' girls were hired to spruik for an affiliated strip venue'. The same article claimed that, following an appeal, the company was fined $20,000 AUD.

The Kitten's 'stag' bus had routinely frequented the car wash site and caused tension, as it was seen to perform as a large billboard to supplement the existing and fixed street signage with its bus-sized image of a reclining naked woman. Images of the vehicle's interior are shown on the Kitten's website to advertise party and event hire, and show it lined with seating and fitted with pole dancing apparatus for lap dancing to be performed. The bus continues to appear outside football games where large numbers of potential clients may be exiting, tapping into the 'peak times' around sporting events when businesses are networking (Jeffreys 2010, 275).

In 2010 the Advertising Standards Bureau banned the bus from the Kitten's Car Wash site. On 18 August, a *Herald Sun* reporter declared that the 'giant advertisement … had been banned, five years after it began providing eye candy for passing drivers', yet on 5 March 2013, the same Melbourne newspaper announced an on-site floodlit billboard 10 × 3.5 metres was approved by the Glen Eira Council. The article stated: 'The application stirred fierce debate at last week's council meeting. Deputy Mayor Oscar Lobo told the chamber it would distract drivers, be inappropriate for families and children and he was worried about what might end up on it'.

I contend that the near-naked female body aligned to strip clubs but deployed here to wash cars on this ordinary suburban street means the car wash site acts as a 'stage' with which passers-by become engaged. Water play is commonly used in the strip club interior, and in the car wash this is re-staged, with hoses to wash cars as well as beach umbrellas, lounges and play pools where the female workers are displayed between jobs, indicating 'the primary source of women's capital' (Gill 2008, 42) – her body. On-site music encourages dancing and playful exchange between female workers and patrons, but also for the larger audience in cars and on foot. The single building on site is masked, with no indication of what might occur 'backstage'. Notices and surveillance systems announce appropriate patron behaviour, yet in doing so, indicate that managing this behaviour may be problematic. The explicit sexualized exchange between the client and the bikini-clad employee is an example of hypersexuality in the public realm.

Over 8,000,000 cars per year pass through the intersection[2] where Kitten's Car Wash is sited. Therefore, if we consider the extent of sequential mediated relationships that are unpacked via the 'live billboard' of Kitten's Car Wash, we can perceive further connections to the sexual objectification and exploitation of women. Stark and Whisnant suggest a relationship between the exploitation of women and the way that the sex industry is 'amplified and extended by contemporary technologies of mass communication' (2004, xiv).

The advertising from the car wash leads directly to either the Kitten's website (via the advertised web address) or to the signage which neatly associates the car wash to the Kitten's strip clubs. Once online, the sexualized images and videos of dancers in the interior spaces of the various Kitten clubs appear alongside the offers of a 'virtual stag tour', links to events and shows, login to club membership as well as information about the Kitten's stripping classes where (sub)urban women can learn pole and lap dancing.

The folding of the strip club with the *strip class* indicates a shift towards mainstreaming of stripping and sexualized performance. Brian McNair (2002) tracks the mainstreaming of sexualization through an examination of its meta-discourses, including film, television, books and business, where he finds 'porno-chic' as the link between previously private pornographic incarnations and the normalized deployment of sexually explicit images and mediated sex. McNair opposes feminism's anti-pornography position, arguing that the exposure to pornography does *not* lead to abnormal sexual behaviour or acts of sexual violence – a position that this research contests.

Citing the 'commissions into the subject funded by both the British and American governments' (2002, 54), McNair concludes that 'women throughout the world (homosexuals too) are subject to oppression in direct proportion to the severity of sexual censorship prevailing in their society' (2002, 56). He argues that pornography is a cultural form much like any other, with a range of meaning and worth. However, he overlooks the powerful collusion of social systems that support this 'amazing expanding pornosphere' (2002, 37) and quotes Jackson and Scott to support his argument: 'A man does not rape as a direct reaction to pornographic stimulus; rather pornography contributes to the cultural construction of a particular form of masculinity and sexual desire which make rape possible and which scripts the possibilities for its enactment' (Jackson and Scott, quoted in McNair 2002, 55).

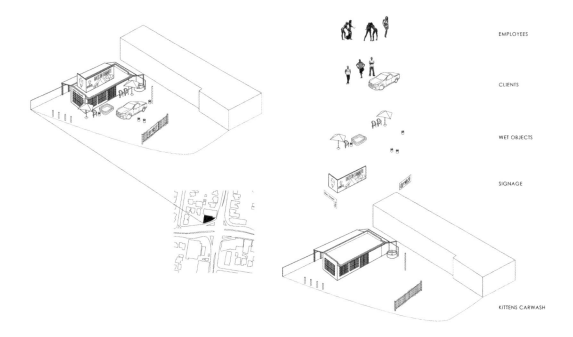

9.4 Axonometric diagram, Kittens Car Wash, Bentleigh East
Source: Author (with Kieren Guerrero)

McNair uses this reference to emphasize the word contributes, suggesting that this reveals pornographic stimulus has minor relevance in the larger sociological systems affecting women. However, I argue that *any* contribution is surely of concern. I suggest that pornography, far from moralizing about sex, is about 'women's subordination, their lack of power and their position as means to male gratification' (Brown 1990, 134). The public presentation of women at the Kittens Car Wash site (and the stereotypes that this encourages) have extended and validated many of the negative consequences of privately consumed pornography that already exist for women.

Similar to Hooters and Ksubi, the significance of Kitten's is its power to legitimize the larger infrastructures of sexual exploitation and stereotypes that oppress women. On the Kittens site 'power operates here not by silencing or suppressing female sexual agency, but by constructing it in highly specific ways' (Gill 2008, 53). And while it may be extreme to suggest that upon viewing Kitten's Car Wash, women are running off to become strippers or find work as bikini-clad cleaners; or alternatively that heterosexual men are participating in the economy of prostituted women; what must be acknowledged is that the longevity and acceptance of the urban phenomenon of Kitten's legitimizes the public acceptance of women in such oppressive and violated roles.

The occupation of public space by 'porno chic' representations of women (as in the Ksubi example) has now been extended in the Kitten's case, where the Kitten's Car Wash is not an *image* of 'porno chic' but an altogether new typology for the public realm, one in which the stripper *arrives* in (sub)urban space. The relationship between the interior occupation of the strip club and the external deployment of these practices from the sex industry has a considerable effect on the public realm.

For example, the tensions of the strip club industry in the late capitalist city are frequently documented in the press media, with *The Age* running regular stories about the notorious King Street. Recent headlines include 'Strip Club Boss Pulled Gun on Wife, Court Told', 'The Business Men who Make their Fortune from the City's Seediest Strip', and 'Curfew could Fuel more Nightclub Violence'. The strip culture's seepage into the public realm via the strip club precinct is at times a dominant and violent part of these cities. On the inside of the club women are engaged by customers 'trained in the commercial sexual use of women' (Jeffreys 2008, 152) and these interiorized behaviours are spilling onto the streets and the surrounding public spaces, where physical violence from crime-related activities associated with strip clubs (Jeffreys 2008, 157) have become common occurrences.

This chapter argues that in strip club culture, various kinds of sexual identities are being rehearsed and reiterated. This view aligns with Butler's position that identity is 'instituted through a *stylized repetition of acts*' (1988, 519, original emphasis). For example, as sexualization gathers ground (literally), the once interior and more private violence becomes external and performed in public space. Through this shift in the occupation of public space by strip club culture with its associated violence, hypersexuality is being legitimized and condoned. Effectively, 'on the street and in the world I am always constituted by other, so that my self-styled gender may well find itself in comic or even tragic opposition to the gender that others see me through or with' (Butler and Salih 2004, 35).

As these case studies exemplify, the occupation of urban space by hypersexual representations play an important role in crafting sexual norms that reflect sexist practices where, for example, women are required to deny aspects of their sexuality or where male sexuality may be forced upon women. For Michel Foucault, acts of power regulate the construction of our identity and actions, encouraging some behaviours while discouraging others. He discusses the tactics of power as a condition capable of masking itself, and suggests that 'its success is proportional to its ability to hide its own mechanisms' (Foucault 1979, 86). The veiling of hypersexuality in ideas of empowerment raises questions about how public space can construct and iteratively form identity, assuming a role in legitimizing our gendered actions and offering rewards for some behaviours while framing others negatively. In most cases, the hypersexualization of urban space works in subtle ways, informing our social relations, self-perceptions and perceptions of others. But as these experiences are reiterated and accumulate, they normalize sexist behaviour and thereby have a negative impact upon women's experience.

DESIGNING HYPERSEXUALITY IN THE MATERIAL CITY

I have argued that the car wash is the public redeployment of the sexualized practices previously confined to the private realm, and that urban space has incorporated sexualized practices. The infiltration of pornography into mainstream culture has transformed pornography's status from belonging outside and beyond mainstream to one that occupies a central position in (sub)urban life.

When McNair (2002) discusses the infiltration of pornography (or, as he refers to it, the 'pornosphere') into mainstream culture: 'This took the form of growing public interest in the nature of all aspects of the pornography industry, accompanied by a flirtation by cultural producers of all kinds with the iconography and conventions of pornography as a genre' (McNair 2002, 63). McNair discusses the meta-pornographies and presumes that all genres and media are able to assume a 'quite sophisticated familiarity with and understanding of pornography' (2002, 63).

As such, an architect's action in hypersexual space potentially marks a shift from phenomena-based observation (an example being the un-designed Kitten's Car Wash) to a constructed and material dialogue with hypersexuality where purposeful and critical designs are implemented. Here I would like to explore a recent architecturally designed example that contributes to my critique.

In June 2010, the Museum of Modern Art (MoMA) in New York announced the winner of its young architects' competition for the outdoor PS1 site. A project entitled *Pole Dance* by a New York firm SO-IL Solid Objectives was installed shortly thereafter. The work consisted of a 5 metre grid of 10 metre tall poles connected by elasticized bungee cords and an open net filled with large coloured balls. The inclusion of a sand pit and play pool emphasized a game-like atmosphere. The grid of poles linked hammocks, pulleys and rain collectors and provided an interface between the visitor and the installation. An iPhone app allowed visitors to interact with the accompanying sound work and to record their own experiences in the space. Once installed, the work was photographed in various incarnations and the architect's media images included the use of dancers performing spins and tricks on the poles, and directly referenced the installation's title: *Pole Dance* (Figure 9.5).

Popular culture has helped to facilitate pole dancing's transition from a sexually orientated activity to one that is marketed as a recreation and aerobic exercise within a discourse of liberation and empowerment. Originated in North America during the 1970s and 80s, pole dancing is historically an extension of exotic dancing with the pole introduced as a prop for a dancer to perform tricks and spins of a sexual nature. The commissioning and installation of the Solid Objectives piece in the MoMA PS1 site signalled that by 2010 pole dancing had become so ritualized as a leisure activity that it was able to assume its place in the public sphere.

The architects of *Pole Dance* describe the project as 'an exploration of sensorial charged environments' and state that they responded to a brief via the 'choreography of situations rather than object making' (Etherington 2012, n.p.). They say:

> *How liberating is it to be an architect these days. Never have the dominant systems been so frail. If one can steer clear of crashing debris of hubris, there is a daunting space dawning to be explored. As we free ourselves from the fascination of the finite, we can start to capture the elastic cloud that our habitation of this planet has become. It was our naïve hope to capture this gigantic cloud of human and environmental turmoil into a walled off little triangle in Long Island City. New ecologies, economies, energies, flows, fantasies, nothing is grounded anymore, foot loose we bounce around on a network of intersections and knots. The limbs need flexing. (Etherington 2010, n.p.)*

9.5 Solid Objectives *Pole Dance*, 2010 Source: Photographer: Iwan Baan. www.so-il.org.

Somewhat reminiscent of Archigram, SO-IL's manifesto optimistically embraces the desire to escape boundaries and to think in revolutionary terms about what might emerge from the collapse of 'dominant systems'. Yet in terms of hypersexual culture their engagement with various apparatuses – for example the poles, the wet-play areas and the use of distributed stages – can be compared with the apparatus that occupies strip clubs and as such provokes the concerns around these contexts for both men and women that are discussed in this chapter.

Pole dancing is viewed by post-feminism as a 'positive' and 'empowering' activity for women and is often cited as the quintessential 'raunch culture' example. Whitehead and Kurz discuss the reinvention of pole dancing and state that 'pole dancing per se positions the female body (at least ideologically) as a sexual commodity to be viewed and consumed' (2009, 227). I maintain that when the apparatus and visualization of pole dancing enter into public space as celebration and 'play', predictable tensions emerge that warrant debate. Donaghue, Whitehead and Kurz contend that there is a perception of pole dancing as empowering and that the exploitation of women's sexuality is masked by displacing pole dancing from its normative context (2011, 445), for example, from the strip club to the gym.

This construction of women's empowerment also relies on the expression of a 'repressed' sexuality that has the potential to emerge in this 'playful' arena and is a key aspect of raunch culture's claim for empowerment and liberation. The redeployment of pole dancing, be it in a gym or an urban design project is, in any case, strongly connected with exotic, erotic and sexual connotations (Donaghue et al. 2011, 443) and the sexualized environment of the Solid Objectives installation. By requiring participants to engage with the rhetoric of the sex industry, the project

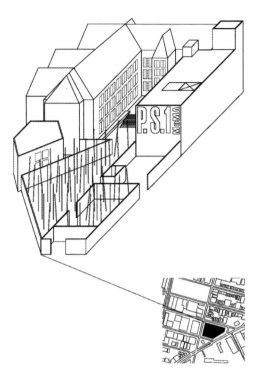
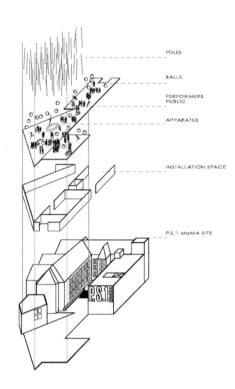

9.6 Axonometric diagram, *Pole Dance*, 2010
Source: Author (with Tess Carpenter).

risks occupying the post-feminist trick of 'undoing feminism while simultaneously appearing to be engaging in a well-informed and even well-intended response to feminism' (McRobbie 2007, 27).

SO-IL's installation shows a further development of the aforementioned case studies: the Ksubi advertising campaign demonstrates how sexualized practices are represented in urban space to stereotype women and men; in the Kitten's case study, sexualized practices become a 'live billboard' for commercial ends that are hosted in the public realm and are a conduit for sexualized engagement with the general public; *Pole Dance* invites the public to assume the role of either the sexualized dancer or the objectifying observer – both performing on and in the provided apparatus.

REFLECTION

Four concepts have emerged from this exploration of hypersexual occupations. Firstly, as Cassandra Fahey's house for Sam Newman exemplifies, we come to occupy the sexualized image that first occupies us. Secondly, in the hypermedia state, the boundary containing sexualization within the interior appears to have become irrelevant. Thirdly, the stage, the performance, the aesthetics and the script for sexual activity have relocated to the public realm. And finally, this playful, public sexualization is seductively presented as liberating.

However, despite feminism's long critique of sexualized representations of women across all forms of media, hypersexualized images occupy the urban landscape of North America, the United Kingdom and Australia, reflecting a narrow presentation of female agency while proliferating gender stereotypes. The interiorized private space is no longer the primary site for sexual acts and performance of sexuality; the case studies indicate that retail space as well as residential and community spaces are sites of sexualization. Sex *and* the city, as a collapsed space of private and public realms, are now the *hypersexualized city* where 'stages' of pornography, play, fashion, flesh, empowerment and repression permeate public space through multi-modal media.

The case studies presented extrapolate the tensions of how hypersexuality occupies urban space: the cycles of ever-present sexualized advertisements; a fleeting glance of the bikini-clad cleaner while jammed in suburban traffic; or a playful spin on a pole installed in a downtown New York City art space. The case studies expand the feminist and post-feminist positions and challenge architects and designers to recognize their roles in reinforcing or reframing the hypersexualized city. Certainly an architectural method engaged with feminist perspectives has the ability to harness critical creative processes and to challenge hypersexual normativity, in order to produce inclusive and engaging occupation of urban space.

The analysis, it is hoped, will cultivate awareness of the implications for the women that occupy and traverse publicly sexualized environments. Furthermore, it is hoped that designers will take up the opportunity to materially critique the constituents of power and liberation brought about by the shifting boundaries of hypersexuality. While further empirical data will quantify the powerful interplay between the temporary occupation of these spaces and the subsequent way these spaces then occupy our own bodily interiors, it is not enough to know how hypersexuality is working; there is a need to advance actions that express alternatives to hypersexual normativity. As revolution is fed by the desire to change the societal frameworks or infrastructure, and suggests 'a particular, radical intent, as well as inferring the use of action as a catalyst for change' (Mosley and Sara 2013, 17), then undoubtedly it is an expanded definition of 'architectural practice' that will take up the responsibility to conceive a response and intervention to hypersexual urbanism.

In closing, I suggest it is productive to understand the hypersexualized occupation of urban space as *sexual residue* offering the potential to stimulate – in women and men, architects and designers – new acts suggestive of other forms of liberation and empowerment. If we are to create a truly emancipating feminist discourse on the occupation of urban space, such interventions need to emerge from critique of the prevalence of hypersexuality. Subsequently the urban excess of sexualization may be *re*-possessed, *re*-built, *re*-written and repudiated.

REFERENCES

Advertising Standards Bureau. 2014. 'Standards Board Cases'. Accessed 2 March. http://www.adstandards.com.au/casereports/determinations/standards.

Brown, Beverley. 1990. 'Debating Pornography: The Symbolic Dimensions'. *Law and Critique* 1 (2): 131–54.

Butler, Judith. 1988. 'Performative Acts and Gender Constitution: An Essay in Phenomenology and Feminist Theory'. *Theatre Journal* 40 (4): 519–31.

——. 1993. *Bodies that Matter: On the Discursive Limits of Sex*. New York: Routledge.

Butler, Judith and Sara Salih, eds. 2004. *The Judith Butler Reader*. Malden: Blackwell Publishing.

Colomina, Beatriz. 1994. *Privacy and Publicity: Modern Architecture as Mass Media*. Cambridge: The MIT Press.

Crabbe, Maree and David Corletts. 2011. 'Erotising Inequality: Technology, Pornography and Young People'. *Redress* 20 (1): 11–15.

Cronin, Anne. 2000. *Advertising and Consumer Citizenship – Gender, Images and Rights*. Routledge: New York.

Donaghue, Ngaire, Kally Whitehead and Tim Kurz. 2011. 'Spinning the Pole: A Discursive Analysis of the Websites of Recreational Pole Dancing Studios'. *Feminism and Psychology* 21: 443–57.

Dovey, Kim and Leonie Sandercock. 2005. *Fluid City*. New York: Routledge.

Etherington, Rose. 2010. 'Pole Dance by SO-IL at P.S.1'. *Dezeen Magazine*. http://www.dezeen.com/2010/06/25/pole-dance-by-so-il-at-p-s-1/. Accessed 1 February 2014.

Foucault, Michel. 1979. *The History of Sexuality Volume 1: An Introduction*. Translated by Robert Hurley. London: Allen Lane.

Gill, Rosalind. 2007. 'Postfeminist Media Culture: Elements of a Sensibility'. *European Journal of Cultural Studies* 10: 147–66.

——. 2008. 'Empowerment/Sexism: Figuring Female Sexual Agency in Contemporary Adverting'. *Feminism and Psychology* 18: 35–60.

——. 2012. 'Media, Empowerment and the "Sexualization of Culture" Debates'. *Sex Roles* 66: 737–45.

Jeffreys, Sheila. 1997. *The Idea of Prostitution*. North Melbourne: Spinifex.

——. 2008. 'Keeping Women Down and Out: The Strip Club Boom and the Reinforcement of Male Dominance'. *Signs* 34 (1): 151–73.

——. 2010. 'The Sex Industry and Business Practice: An Obstacle to Women's Equality'. *Women's Studies International Forum* 33: 274–82.

Levy, Ariel. 2005. *Female Chauvanist Pigs: Women and the Rise of Raunch Culture*. Melbourne: Schwartz.

Maguire, Emily. 2008. *Princesses and Pornstars: Sex, Power, Identity*. Melbourne: Text Publishing.

McNair, Brian. 2002. *Striptease Culture Sex, Media and the Democratisation of Desire*. London: Routledge.

McQuire, Scott. 2008. *The Media City: Media, Architecture and Urban Space*. Melbourne: Sage.

McRobbie, Angela. 2007. 'Postfeminism and Popular Culture: Bridget Jones and the New Gender Regime'. In *Interrogating Post Feminism: Gender and the Politics of Popular Culture*, edited by Yvonne Tasker Yvonne and Diane Negra. Durham: Duke University Press, 27–39.

———. 2009. *The Aftermath of Feminism: Gender Culture and Social Change*. London: Sage.

Mosley, Jonathan and Rachel Sara. 2013. 'The Architecture of Transgression: Towards a Destabilising Architecture'. *Architectural Design* 83 (6): 14–19.

Rosewarne, Lauren. 2007a. *Sex in Public Women Outdoor Advertising and Public Policy*. Newcastle: Cambridge Scholars Publishing.

———. 2007b. 'Pin-ups in Public Space Sexist Outdoor Advertising as Sexual Harassment'. *Women's Studies International Forum* 30: 313–25.

Stark, Christine and Rebecca Whisnant, eds. 2004. *Not for Sale Feminists Resisting Prostitution and Pornography*. North Melbourne: Spinifex Press.

The Smoking Gun. 2014. 'So you Wanna be a "Hooters" Girl?'. Accessed 2 March. http://www.thesmokinggun.com/file/so-you-wanna-be-hooters-girl?page=7.

Whitehead, Kally and Tim Kurz. 2009. 'Empowerment and the Pole: A Discursive Investigation of the Reinvention of Pole Dancing as a Recreational Activity'. *Feminism and Psychology* 19 (2): 224–44.

NOTES

1   The research is limited to analyzing hypersexuality with regard to heterosexual adults. Without doubt the current media-driven sexualized culture has affected those who are not yet adult or those who do not identify as heterosexual (for example lesbian, gay, bisexual and transgender or transsexual and intersex) but the sociological effects are different and would require a different logic.

2   In 2008 the owner of Kitten's Car Wash submitted a letter to the Standing Committee on Environment, Communications and the Arts. The letter stated that between December 2006 and April 2008 over 12,000,000 cars were estimated to have passed through the intersection; data was obtained from Vic Roads. This figure does not account for multiple passengers potentially present in each car. Accessed 16 May: http://www.aph.gov.au/binaries/senate/committee/eca_ctte/sexualisation_of_children/responses/kittens.pdf.

10

With Feet Firmly Planted on Unstable Ground

Jesse O'Neill

LOOKING DOWN

In *Stories of Mr Keuner*, Bertolt Brecht (2001, 9) told of a man who was indifferent to the politics of state identity. Mr Keuner dismissed the idea of belonging to one place, and even though he lived in a city occupied by an enemy army, he put no pride in the rights of citizenship. One day, walking along the street, he found himself faced by one of the foreign soldiers, and following social expectations, he stepped from the footpath into the gutter, allowing the soldier to pass. In doing so, Mr K was momentarily remade with nationalistic fervour and genocidal fantasy, wishing to wipe this soldier's country from the face of the earth. In the story, the Bavarian-born Brecht drew on the connotations of the nineteenth-century German footpath, the *Bürgersteig*, which literally means the 'citizen's step', a ground to be trodden by those deemed to rightfully belong to the place. Being forced from the citizen's step revealed to Mr K his disenfranchisement; and as his unconscious symbol of belonging was taken, he responded with a desire to strip the soldier and his country of origin of any right to a place on the earth. The message I take from this story is that ground surfaces can have great resonance. Where one stands is invested with symbolic meaning that defines who one is able to be.

Physically, all human spaces are equally composed of a ground plane (the field, the street, the floor), a vertical plane (the façade, the wall), and a roof plane (the ceiling, the sky), yet in many discourses of design there is a clear planar hierarchy. In practice, the ground plane holds important material and experiential qualities, but many texts on spatial design suggest the primacy of walls. For example, Francis Ching (1996, 120) states that in defining interiors, 'vertical forms have greater presence in our visual field than horizontal planes and are therefore more instrumental'. His focus on the vertical plane is by extension an emphasis on the visual barriers of space. Katherine Benzel (1998, 239) gives more value to the floor as a binding agent for walls and structure, yet there is still the implication that really the latter are the more important elements.

If this sounds like a trivial concern, we should look at how this focus on vertical planes infuses our theories of architecture's social operation. Our understanding of social spaces is most commonly framed through the division of community and individuality and expressed through the binary of the public exterior where the person hides within the group, and the private interior where they reveal themselves (see Rice 2007; Sparke 2008). The common adoption in architectural discourse of Georg Simmel's work on the detached observer of the industrial city streets (Sennett 2012, 38), and Walter Benjamin's (2002, 220) musings on the collector and the soft and pliable interior residence 'as a receptacle for the person', illuminate the division. This conception of social space is architecturally defined through walls that contain or expose. If looking to the ground seems odd, it is perhaps because we are already so swayed by the allure of walls. The story of Mr K implies there can also be powerful divisions of social space operating without visual distinction, and that the ground plane presents another opportunity to view how people relate to each other through their physical environment.

My aim is to explore the various ways people have discussed the ground plane in its social sense. 'Ground' is used as a general term referring to all types of lower horizontal plane, but as Brecht's story implies, distinctions are of vital consequence in this area, so I begin to unfold different categories of ground. I concentrate on what I refer to as 'earth' and 'floor', which I suggest should not be limited to physical surfaces, but are to be read as symbols invested with meaning. The purpose of categorization is to define what these meanings are and how they explicitly or intuitively guide occupation, which is the manner in which people organize themselves in a spatial context.

CONNECTED SURFACES

The ground is fundamental in orienting spatial experience, providing a divided continuity that ties together countryside, city streets and interior as we step from one surface to another. Ground links spaces when walls divide them. Giambattista Nolli's famous 1748 illustration, the *Pianta Grande di Roma* (or the Nolli Plan) clearly illustrates one common division of the ground plane. Through black and white solids it demarcates Rome's streets and interiors, though since church interiors are combined with the public streets the map's organizing logic cannot be a simple division of inside and outside. The map is composed according to access – places of congregation and retreat. As a starting point, the ground can initially be divided into two general categories that follow current understandings of public and private space: the floor of the interior, and that which it directly covers: the earth itself.

Christopher Alexander (1977, 1009) refers to these categories of earth and floor, proposing their inherent connection. To explain the effect of the interior floor he describes its strong foundations in the earth, and how through these foundations the floor draws on the earth to provide stability in the home. 'Stability' is not used simply for its structural sense, it is the romantic image of the home as an enduring symbol in the occupant's mind – this is the image of home popularly found in the work of Bachelard (1994) and Heidegger (1971, 143–59). Linguist Marie Stenglin

(2004, 252), in her study of museum spaces, similarly describes the floor as anchored in earth, a connection that transfers 'roundedness' and 'stability' into the floor, and fosters the interior's sense of comfort and continuity. Foundations bind floor to earth, therefore connecting the individual home to the enduring landscape.

This line of thinking defines earth and floor as forming a unity, though the interior's social power is ultimately derived from the earth below, and it is seemingly powerless on its own. The private interior is presented not as an escape from the public exterior, but as a product of it. These arguments of stability suggest that the fundamental power of the ground resides in the primary category of earth. But what exactly does 'earth' mean in this case? Is it the soil, the field or the natural plane? Is it the public ground of the city? It seems that to develop understandings of other kinds of ground surface we first need to look at this idea called earth.

EARTH

In relation to social spaces, reference to earth frequently revolves around notions of common ground, community, and long-standing historical tradition. The earth is utilized as a metaphor for the continuation of culture. Taking on this theme of earth, Neil Leach (1998, 33) wrote:

> *Identity … becomes territorialized and mapped on geographic terrain. The individual becomes one with the land in a process of identification which is itself mythic … . Thus we find constant references to natural phenomena – storms, blood, and soil – in fascist ideology … . It is precisely in the context of an identity rooted to the soil that those groups not rooted to the soil become excluded.*

Earth is being shaped into a symbol of archetypal socialization, where individuals first relate to location, and through this to other people. A society's identity is closely linked to terrain, or the earth to which groups believe themselves entitled. From this, two contradictory ideas occur: the earth is common ground for all; it is also exclusive, where divisions clarify status and entitlement, as with any kind of border control. As the codified earth becomes demarcated, different types of ground develop, like the gutter and the footpath in Brecht's story. These distinctions in public earth separate the larger society, but can also work to bind groups through their common ground. This essential reading of the earth guided Alexander's comment on the rooted floor, receiving its power by proxy from the earth below. The floor of the individual's home partitions a small space for restricted use, but is still tied into the larger landscape of a people and based on its solidarity and order, showing us that the symbol of the earth looms heavily in how we understand our place in the world.

As it is formed into an idea of belonging, the earth is therefore not a physical surface but a kind of representation, and as a symbolic device it holds great power when used to remind people where they belong. We might consider how the symbol of earth is used in the design of the Platz der Republik – outside the German Reichstag in Berlin – which is part of the Federal Strip plan by landscape architects Axel Schultes and Charlotte Frank. The design is an elegant example of illusion and symbolic meaning. In plan, or from the air, the landscape stretching west of the Reichstag is a series of strips of grass and paving that alternatively reduce and increase in width. To the west it is bounded by a field and to the east by a paved forecourt. From above, these are discrete elements; but from the ground, viewed in perspective, the two types of earth visually blend into each other. The paved earth of the German parliament (and by extension its people) appears to rise out of the natural greenery representing Germany's fundamental earth. The house of parliament concludes this rising, which evocatively seems to come out of the earth, and therefore express the territorialization of nationhood. In the same city, a little to the east, Libeskind's garden at the Jewish Museum defiles the grass with streaks of bitumen. This violent act marks the memory of the Holocaust, and a blight on the rhetoric of common earth and the right to belong.

The Reichstag itself, representing the unified German nation, was described by Norman Foster (2000, 10) in his redesign of the building as a 'museum of memories'. If earth is identity and belonging territorialized, then as it extends beyond the individual it also extends beyond the present time. The public ground of the earth is often attributed with the ability to contain a people's history, thus placing it as an accumulation of time and memory. As Kevin Lynch (1960, 4) wrote, landscapes are the 'skeleton' on which people establish their 'socially important myths'. Edward Casey (1996, 25) furthered the idea when he asserted that memories belong as much to place as to the brain or body. In both comments, earth is presented as physically manifesting the collective memory theorized in the early twentieth century by Maurice Halbwachs (1992, 51). A student of Durkheimian sociology, Halbwachs argued that a process of common remembering is one of the strongest bonds that hold people together; the earth is often treated as collective memory made concrete, retaining the marks of the past and providing people with an ongoing reminder. This has been a recurring theme in urban studies, where the power attributed to the ground is then given cause to be represented in other forms such as monuments or preserved historical façades (Boyer 1994, 4–6). But the idea of historicized and communal earth has also been a device in historiography to understand the experience of history, where earth is made of the mingling *topoi* of distinct historical places (Ethington 2007). In all of these views, the capacity to dwell on common earth links people through the shared struggle of history. Here we begin to risk confusing the earth with other spatial elements that denote historical memory, but it is precisely the way earth is adapted as a synechdochic device to express wider-ranging impressions of time and community that we are looking at. This is about constructed symbolism, and the power invested in the earth when we choose to read our own sociability through this inert mass.

It will be noticed that these discussions of earth range widely in terms of which exact category of ground they describe: they could be the naturalized surfaces of soil and grass, the streets of the city, the public plaza. 'Earth' is here a broad category to capture all of these public grounds and show the similar ideas underpinning them. In this rendition, earth is so abstract it is hardly real at all. There is no unified earth as such, it is a mythic construct whose residue empowers social space. We are dealing with the meaning given to an unattainable surface. It harkens back to an idea of the primitive and unburdened earth on which human beings first gathered and societies first formed, a symbol summarizing a complex combination of location, events, and people. All sub-categories of ground inherently draw from this popular image of earth and one cannot trace its development from the blank state into what it is today.

Although it is impossible to reach this first and pure earth, we may be able to at least identify within recent history an earth that was culturally meaningless – not the 'skeleton' of its people's identity – but which has since developed the same notions of belonging and collective memory. This example is the British colonization of Australia at the turn of the nineteenth century. To indigenous Australians, earth is of the utmost significance, essentially one with society and religion. Their association with earth reflects very similar patterns of thought to those expressed above. However, the first generations of British in Australia had no ties to that earth; it was a material object to be used for other ends and not the site and product of their cultural identity.

The British colonials' attitude toward the Australian earth is reflected in the sentiments of Barron Field, Judge Advocate of the early Sydney settlement. Beyond his official function, Field was also a poet, and author of the first poetry book published in the New South Wales colony. He viewed the Australian landscape as having no significance to the British, and therefore a landscape with no history: a 'prose-dull land' (Field 1823, 15).

This produced a sense of spiritual isolation, or a lack of belonging. If Australian earth had no history to Field then it was because it was a land 'without antiquities' (1823, 11), without historic buildings or remnants of the past that predate the present generation and tie them to history, religion or home. Caught in this sense of isolation and trying to find an alternative to these antiquities, Field (1823, 14–15) transposed the symbolic role of long-standing church architecture onto the ships of Sydney Cove, their 'tall anch'ring masts, a three-spired minster'. In addition to their visual resemblance to the cathedral for the colonial landscape, they also represented the only way for an Englishman to return to British soil.

Here I am again beginning to drift away from the symbolism of earth and into the extensions of its ideas, but Field had some very particular comments to make about soil, history and the claim to earth. He suggested that the implicit qualities that have been identified in earth are not inherent in the land, but only develop over time as the dead are buried and their graves consecrated with Christian rites. Thus, Field remarks, the British did not claim their ownership over the Australian land with a planted flag, but with the burial of the Scottish man Forby Sutherland in 1770, which began the process of their living and dying on Australian earth:

> … and thence a little space
> Lies Sutherland, their shipmate, for the sound
> Of Christian burial better did proclaim
> Possession than the flag, in England's name …
> Fix then th' Ephesian brass. 'Tis classic ground. (1823, 16)

In this portrayal the earth gains its representative power of belonging because it contains our ancestors and thus holds a place in our imagination as retaining our pasts, tying us to particular locations. Over time, physical terrain is shaped as significant places and connections to others. To Field, the only piece of earth to which he could feel connected was Sutherland's burial site – it was the only place in Australia with a story.

Built up slowly over time, the earth accrues notions of stability, operating in a timeframe longer than the individual and providing an enduring point of reference for groups of people. This reading of a mythical earth – a representation of communal belonging in time and space – infuses all of our responses to categories of ground. It shaped Alexander's commentary that the floor's foundations in the earth provide stability in the home. It oriented Leach's comments about the territorialization of identity, and Lynch on the landscape as the skeleton of our social myth-making. It is inherent in Field's poetry and the design of the Platz der Republik. It underpins the realization of ground surfaces in the city streets, and the distinction between the *Bürgersteig* and the gutter. The earth is loaded with symbolic meaning that influences our reading of the social impact of the physical ground plane in spatial design. And hence we return to the well-worn discussion of personality in the nineteenth-century streets, and Simmel's notion that society is a 'mere sum of separate individuals' (1949, 254). In the streets of the expanding modern city, full of strangers, people adopt masks that allow them to blend in, form social bonds and find protection in the group. This is not only because they are left exposed outside of the enclosed walls of the private dwelling; it is also because the public ground they tread connotes this coming together of a larger group character.

FLOOR

Alexander's view of the floor's meaning fits rather neatly with typical renditions of the concept of earth, but there is also another frequent approach to the floor to be considered. This is oppositional to earth, but no less dependent on it. With the floor we are still in an abstracted category of ground plane, one that includes the many instantiations of (usually) interior surfaces.

To begin to look at this conception of the interior's floor, let's consider the story of the fifth-century religious figure St Simeon Stylites. Living in the eastern Roman Empire between modern-day Turkey and Syria, Stylites practised an extreme form of bodily asceticism, aspiring to amplify physical strain as a method of prayer, and attempting to withdraw from his material involvement with people and the world (Lent 2009, iii). However, he found these acts drew people to him, therefore including him in material society. His question was how to distance himself from physical interaction as a means to pursue religious devotion.

Rather than becoming a hermit in unpopulated territories, Stylites' answer was to disentangle himself from the symbol of social unity: the earth. He appeared to create a distance from the physical earth itself, and thus its symbolism of a collective people and the physicality of social interactions and desires. Finding the ruin of a pillar, four metres high, he chose to live on top of it on a small platform. The top of the pillar was a floor with no walls or roof, but which nonetheless established a physical division from the earth below and defined a kind of 'interior'. It was not a complete withdrawal; people climbed ladders up to his retreat, bringing him food and seeking counsel or prayers. And as he attracted more attention, he retreated further and further from the earth, on successively higher pillars. By the end of his life Stylites lived on a pillar 20 metres high, and had spent 37 years separated from the earth. When Buñuel portrayed Stylites in his film *Simon of the Desert* (1965), the image of his open-air platform was dwarfed by the desert around it. Despite his vision being dominated by that from which he sought refuge, the act of removing himself from social life and material concern was symbolized through stepping off communal earth and onto artificial floor. The floor established a disjunction that supported the ascetic's mission.

Stylites' hagiography shows an individual defined against the people of the world not through enclosure, but through the horizontal barrier that took him off the earth. The unity of the people is asserted as masses of pilgrims climbed up from (or out of) the earth below, threatening the quietude and individuality of the floor above. This constructs a clear image of the earth as the collective, and the floor as the individual's retreat away from it. It is not a floor that tries to mimic the earth or draw on its cultural power of time, memory and stability; it is a floor that tries to cut itself off, to break from the communal traditions below and live in a different way. For us, Stylites' pillar may be argued to represent the floor that covers the earth, which forgets it and replaces it with something else. If earth holds on to memory and time, this floor is tabula rasa.

The Japanese architect Arata Isozaki (1986) has presented a similar impression of the floor as distinction, but in a significantly different context. Isozaki traced the development of Japanese architecture from pit dwellings to raised structures. Beginning with earth, he then defines two specific categories of interior ground, 'board' and 'tatami' (Isozaki 1986, 62–4), which successively remove spaces from common earth by rising above it. Isozaki (1986, 65) writes that 'the raised wooden floor is a clean, artificially created surface isolated from the earth, a surface on which people can sit without concern'. This is opposite to Alexander's (1977) view. This floor is not connected to the earth, but stands over and against it, establishing a barrier and therefore a new place that is 'clean'. The concept of 'clean' is particularly important. Literally it means that the dirt of the earth does not permeate this space, and to ensure this, shoes that have direct contact with the earth are not worn on board or tatami. Symbolically it suggests the space is purified of the invested meaning of earth by blanketing and blocking it out; it is a purity that erases the established bonds of the earth and distinguishes the interior floor from the social environment below.

The key difference between Stylites' floor and Isozaki's is not their geographical location, but the move from an individual's floor to that of a small social circle. The Japanese raised floor began as a privileged space: the earth was viewed as 'vulgar' or common, the elevated floor was 'sacred' and aristocratic (Isozaki 1986, 59). While this is rooted in relations of social power, we can also see this demarcation of the floor as creating a space that allowed a small sub-set of society (an aristocracy) to define itself against the commons. It was a place of retreat where only they were entitled to stand, helping to define this group through their distancing from the common earth of the wider society.

Isozaki goes on to distinguish the traditional Japanese concept of floor from its Western counterpart, viewing them as operating in different modes:

> Unlike the raised Japanese wooden floor, the upper stories that have been part of Western homes from early times are not a surface in a comparatively different phase. Although these upper-story rooms are far removed from the surface of the earth, shoes are worn in them; and chairs, tables, shelves, beds, and so on are essential because the floor is 'unclean'. (1986, 65)

He is suggesting that in Western architecture the floor was not as clear an invention as in Japan, and thus did not gather the same symbolic power. Further, Isozaki (1986, 61) writes that in China and the West it is not uncommon to have floors at the same level as earth, and thus the two become an uninterrupted continuation: their 'unclean' status means that the earth's influence is still present because they have not formed a clear disjunction. Even with higher stories, he implies that in these places height may not have the same connotations of retreat and removal as in Japan. As such, these spaces must be read as social interiors, which prompt the creation of a range of additional semiotic barriers that are used to cover and link people, such as objects and furnishings. This is the material culture of sociability, the things we dress ourselves in to construct our identity and project it to others, the things we use to clarify our social position.

Perhaps, though, we need not view the Japanese and Western floors as distinct, but as two aspects of a larger practice. Both are social spaces: the 'unclean' Western floor allows some part of the communal earth onto it; the Japanese floor is a heightening of social exclusivity. By slowly covering over the earth, each place is gradually detached from communal space. The result is the spectrum of gradations of surface that we commonly experience, each providing space for, and defining, increasingly smaller (though not necessarily mutually exclusive) groups of society distinct from the whole. The logical conclusion – the removed floor in its ideal state – may be represented by Stylites' pillar, or the lone person finally extricated from society.

The result breaks the simplistic binary of private and public. It also speaks of a different conception of society and the individual from that which is inherent in common discussions of walls, the public exterior and the private interior. As reflected in Benjamin's (2002, 220) notion of the soft and pliable interior as a manifestation of the person, there is a recurring notion that individuals reveal themselves in the private interior. This implies an understanding of the individual as pre-social, an independent fully formed spirit, and of society as the coming together of these individuals. While Simmel recognized the complex relationships between individual subjectivity and society, he did show preference for the notion that the person is defined before the group, and that the forming of society is a process whereby individuals make concessions and adapt themselves in public gathering (1949, 254; 1950, xxx–xxix). However, the concept of floors as surfaces successively removed from common earth paints the reverse of this picture, suggesting what Sawyer (2002, 244) has labelled as Durkheim's 'theory of emergence', a position that has also been adopted by many who followed in Durkheim's tradition (see Halliday 1978, Halbwachs 1992). This theory looks to the causal power of society, arguing that the group shapes the individual (Sawyer 2002, 235). Through this, we understand the individual not as pre-social, but as emerging out of social relations and context. Out of the wider social organization – which defines roles, status and relationships – smaller groups organize themselves. And from these arise smaller groups again, leading to the construction of personality as a final point, which is created in reference to position in social structure. What this proposal of gradations of ground surface suggests is that differentiation in ground is used to facilitate the organizing of minor social structures, therefore symbolizing either belonging or exclusion. The space created by the ground plane reminds people of their position and what is therefore possible for them, establishing the spatial framework for the distribution of society and the construction of the individual person. It is a process that leads from the mythical primary earth, to the private interior floor. Personality is not something to be revealed in its natural state as one moves behind walls, it is something formed when given the space to separate from the mass through a process of removal, and thus defined through the barrier of the floor.

The Floor as Novel Invention

The floor helps to establish divisions in space, encouraging the re-orientation of smaller groups separate from the traditions of a wider society; but how exactly does the floor operate in this process? To see this we need to again return to the idea of the floor as a covering barrier. In some ways echoing Isozaki's notion of the 'clean' floor, Richard Sennett (1992, 60) wrote that 'up means neutral': the floor manifests as a return of the ground to a blank state, providing an opportunity to begin anew. The raised floor produces an anaesthetic to the effects of the earth, blocking its communal tradition and allowing the invention of new spaces in which groups can define new structures of occupation.

This idea is embedded in our architectural modernity, where the distancing of floor from earth was perhaps one of the key developments that allowed the utopian imagination of the modern movement to reinterpret space. It is particularly evident in the piloti that formed one of Le Corbusier's five principles (2007, 127). These columns were intended to raise the building off the ground, distinguishing the artificial floor from the earth it gently hovers above. When Corbusier proposed the idea of a new city in 1915 – the Pilotis-City – which like his later projects aimed to divorce itself from past conventions, he intended to raise its ground level several metres away from the earth. Practically, the plan is conceived to give access to amenities and show 'all those organs that up to now have been buried in the ground and inaccessible' (Le Corbusier 2007, 127). Symbolically, the piloti uproot the city, distancing its new environment from the enduring earth and allowing the radical transformation of the urban environment. On the smaller scale, in reference to the 1921 Citrohan design, Corbusier (2007, 267) refers to the rooms under the piloti as a 'raised basement' – that is, they are unearthed. And as with the Pilotis-City, this enables revolutionary thinking in the patterns of domestic occupation. No aspect of the new house or new city resides within 'stable' earth, symbolizing the potential to make space anew free of tradition, since, as Sennett (1992, 60) wrote, to go up 'means neutral'.

Sennett's (1992, 60) comment on neutrality was specifically directed toward the American high-rise, whose multiplicity of raised floors exaggerates separation and magnifies the possibilities for constant renewal. In 1909, *Life* magazine published a sectional illustration by A.B. Walker of a steel-framed building (Koolhaas 1994, 83). On each floor stood a different suburban mansion surrounded by trees and lawn, presenting a speculative combination of modern engineering and the values of the City Beautiful movement. Each story is a little piece of the suburbs, vertically stacked. The image gained notoriety in architectural theory through its inclusion in *Delirious New York*, where Rem Koolhaas (1994, 83) gave it a name: the '1909 Theorem'. The concept contained in this image – or perhaps it was the concept Koolhaas embedded in it – was pivotal in his examination of the interior of American skyscrapers in the 1920s and 1930s. It is also key to clarifying the representation of the floor as a barrier to earth.

Every floor in this project holds the capacity for an entire system of alternate versions of space, which through the high-rise can be simultaneously realized upon the same plot of earth.

> *On each floor, the Culture of Congestion will arrange new and exhilarating human activities in unprecedented combinations. Through Fantastic Technology it will be possible to reproduce all 'situations' – from the most natural to the most artificial – wherever and whenever desired. (Koolhaas 1994, 125)*

Koolhaas's history of these American buildings describes a fantasy world within New York's hotels and commercial buildings, where every floor is a new beginning and every room's fantastical themes are completely divorced from its location. The idea finds perfect expression through the opening of the lift, where stepping out onto a new floor is to enter a different world. The floor's isolation from the staid tradition of the earth means that alternatives can be imagined, and novel invention is the key characteristic of this interior design. What Koolhaas described as the 'Culture of Congestion' is not just the increasing speed of the modern American city that he emphasized, it is the glut of ideas and places that reside upon and over each other at the same time. His 'fantastic technology' that reproduces these might as well be the symbol of the floor itself. Through the 1909 Theorem, floor is positioned as new ground, resulting not in repeated copies of the earth below but in ground swept clean of memory and tradition.

Importantly, the many rooms Koolhaas describes are not the domestic retreats of home that define interiors for their personal privacy. They are restricted public places of entertainment and social gathering. Their transformation of social codes makes them places for smaller groups to withdraw from the larger and define themselves outside of the continuation of traditional practices. These are the floors that Isozaki calls 'unclean', but which are essential for the construction of smaller social groups or sub-cultures, and the gradual production of personality in the individual. Any interior typology can be viewed as a space of sub-cultural identity, whether defined by club memberships, religion, working roles or family. In its departure from the earth, the floor allows for social modification through the provision of a kind of blank terrain on which to envision new forms of occupation.

Koolhaas's idea is only latent in the original 1909 drawing, but is given clarity in the pavilion that Dutch architects MVRDV designed in imitation of it. The Netherlands Pavilion at the Hanover World Expo 2000 presented a system of floors seemingly out of order. The logically most 'grounded' layer – the forest – is raised to the fourth floor, over the unrelated 'sand dunes' below. It produces a disconnection from what might be expected to reside in the earth and what, when considered from the earth below, should be on the higher artificial floors. When floors are stacked over floors they contain no sense of being closer or further from the earth. Since every one is blank ground, there is quite simply the floor itself and the new space that it has allowed to be created. MVRDV replicated Koolhaas's version of the original 1909 Theorem, but his characterization of the later 1920s New York skyscraper is arguably brought alive in the Hotel Silken Puérta America in Madrid. SGA Studio designed the building, that is, they put the floors in place. However, the project recognizes the interior's capacity for radical invention by leaving the design of different areas to different architects, who each imagine their own interior world (Hoteles Silken n.d.). Isozaki contributed, designing the 10th floor to echo the raised Japanese floor, 'clean', and where the occupant can be 'without concern' (1986, 65). This is a design that fully embraces the potentiality for fantastical variation that the symbol of the floor instils in spaces, because it removes the connection to earth and its implications of continuity.

If the meaning of earth can be summarized as tradition, then the meaning of floor is imagination. To raise up out of the earth opens the potential of modern interior design, and the floor embodies aspirations for change because it is no longer stable, and can thus be imagined as anything at all. Urban design responds to the symbolism of the earth, either through preservation or development based on the social patterns of use in public spaces; these either maintain the continuity of tradition or fabricate images of tradition (Boyer 1994, 309–10). When dealing with the social and the traces of the past, urban design keeps the long duration in sight, fostering the sense of permanency in the earth. The floor of the interior takes on its importance against this image of permanent social tradition. The work of the interior cuts away time. While the architecture and foundations of the shopping mall may remain, its interior is subject to wild and regular re-imagination that may leave no trace of earlier identities. The architectural house may endure but new tenants and their own accumulations of objects erase previous occupants. The space of the floor lies in flux, where changing definitions are tied to the malleable individuals created through socialization on the earth. To encode changing individuals, the physical form of a space must also change. Personalities are subject to change faster than societies, and thus time runs at different speeds between the earth and floor.

In Benjamin's (2002) view, the interior was soft, bearing the imprint of the individual and taking on traces. But perhaps this well-worn line is misleading. It is the earth that we invest with our memory, absorbing and retaining traces and therefore becoming bound to our concepts of historicity. The floor – that is, the invested symbol of the floor, which has the potential to shape our occupation of spaces – is subject to constant change, a blank slate that cannot retain beyond its life the fixed markings of social identity. The floor in this understanding is therefore most definitely a hard surface, an idea that wipes memory clean and allows imagination and change. This makes the interior floor unstable, a thing more open to experimentation and difference than the earth, since it can always be wiped back to its neutral state.

CONCLUSION

Earth and floor are two fundamental categories of ground plane, each with different effects on our conception of spaces, but they are not to be misinterpreted solely as real and tangible surfaces. In addition, they are ideas, or symbols, which we invest with social meanings that then return to us through specific instantiations of ground surface. They are abstract synechdochic devices, created to represent the qualities of more complex, real human spaces. That ground planes can become such primary symbols shows the spectrum of complex psychological resonances contained in the image of the ground beneath our feet.

In discourses of design and social space, the concept of earth has been laden with themes of social identity, belonging, exclusion and collective memory, all of which refer back to the mythical image of a first ground on which societies were formed. Earth is ground that retains the markings of time, where the bodies of ancestors are buried, and therefore a common element that binds a people to tradition. It is often treated as collective memory given material form. As smaller social groups define themselves, they do so through the demarcation of new grounds. The *Bürgersteig* or the Japanese wooden floor accepts only the few; the gutter and the earth take the rest. The symbol of the floor has been both rooted in the earth, and presented as a means for separation from it. In this dual nature, floor becomes a central device in allowing what can unfold upon it to re-imagine groups and spaces. It is connected to the social sphere, but creates a distinction; it is a destabilizing force that encourages radical transformation because it produces a new terrain wiped clean of old protocols. Floor is what Sennett (1992, 60) calls 'neutral', and what Isozaki (1986, 65) calls 'clean'. Nearly every society is shaped through the notion of earth, and the socialized individual develops through group interaction and 'habitus' in successions of semi-public and private spaces established in part through the barrier of floors, which allow for the recreation of our patterns of occupation. Not only does this suggest the significance of architectural form for the construction of individuals, it has liberating implications for interior design as an activity that uniquely takes place on floors. It suggests that interior design, as both a professional activity and a product of material culture, maintains this capacity for invention as its central project: to build again on unstable ground.

Returning one last time to the *Stories of Mr Keuner*, Brecht (2001, 37) tells us that when entering a new house, Mr K's only concern was to identify its exits. The reason, Mr K sardonically states, is that 'I am for justice; so it's good if the place in which I'm staying has more than one exit': in the interior he becomes particularly aware of his radical leanings and the threat this imposes. To Mr K, the public earth unknowingly confirmed his belonging, and the interior floor heightened a sense of change, inadvertently becoming a space for departure.

REFERENCES

Alexander, Christopher. 1977. *A Pattern Language: Towns, Buildings, Construction.* New York: Oxford University Press.

Bachelard, Gaston. 1994. *The Poetics of Space*. Translated by Maria Jolas. Boston: Beacon.

Benjamin, Walter. 2002. *The Arcades Project*. Translated by Howard Eiland & Kevin McLaughlin. Cambridge, MA: Harvard University Press.

Benzel, Katherine. 1998. *The Room in Context: Design Beyond Boundaries.* New York: McGraw-Hill.

Boyer, M. Christine. 1994. *The City of Collective Memory: Its Historical Imagery and Architectural Entertainments.* Cambridge, MA: MIT Press.

Brecht, Bertolt. 2001. *Stories of Mr Keuner*. Translated by Martin Chalmers. San Francisco: City Lights.

Ching, Francis D.K. 1996. *Architecture: Form, Space, and Order*. 2nd edn. New York: John Wiley & Sons.

Casey, Edward S. 1996. 'How to get from Space to Place in a Fairly Short Stretch of Time: Phenomenological Prolegomena'. In *Senses of Place*, edited by Steven Feld and Keith H. Basso, 13–52. Santa Fe: School of American Research Press.

Ethington, Philip J. 2007. 'Placing the Past: 'Groundwork' for a Spatial Theory of History'. *Rethinking History* 11 (4): 465–93.

Field, Barron. 1823. *First Fruits of Australian Poetry*. 2nd edn. Sydney: Robert Howe.

Foster, Norman. 2000. Preface to *The Reichstag: The Parliament Building by Norman Foster*, by Bernhard Schultz, 9–14. Munich: Prestel.

Halbwachs, Maurice. 1992. *On Collective Memory*. Translated by Lewis A. Coser. Chicago: University of Chicago Press.

Halliday, M.A.K. 1978. *Language as Social Semiotic: A Social Interpretation of Language and Meaning*. London: Edward Arnold.

Heidegger, Martin. 1971. *Poetry, Language, Thought*. Translated by Albert Hofstadter. New York: Harper Perennial.

Hoteles Silken. n.d. *Hotel Puérta America Madrid*. Accessed 1 March 2014, http://www.hoteles-silken.com/content/pdf/pamerica-dossier-de-prensa-en-ingles.pdf.

Huntington, H.W.H. 1888. *History of Australasia, or, our First Century*. Newcastle: Huntington.

Isozaki, Arata. 1986. 'Floors and Internal Spaces in Japanese Vernacular Architecture: Phenomenology of Floors'. *Res: Anthropology and Aesthetics* 11: 54–77.

Koolhaas, Rem. 1994. *Delirious New York*. New York: Monacelli.

Le Corbusier. 2007. *Toward an Architecture*. Translated by John Goodman. London: Frances Lincoln.

Leach, Neil. 1998. 'Dark Side of the Domus'. *Journal of Architecture* 3 (1): 31–42.

Lent, Frederick, trans. 2009. *The Life of Saint Simeon Stylites: A Translation of the Syriac Text in Bedjan's Acta Martyrum et Santorum*. New Jersey: Evolution.

Lynch, Kevin. 1960. *The Image of the City*. Cambridge, MA: MIT Press.

Rice, Charles. 2007. *The Emergence of the Interior: Architecture, Modernity, Domesticity*. London: Routledge.

Sawyer, R. Keith. 2002. 'Durkheim's Dilemma: Toward a Sociology of Emergence'. *Sociological Theory* 20 (2): 227–47.

Sennett, Richard. 1992. *The Conscience of the Eye: The Design and Social Life of Cities.* New York and London: W.W. Norton.

—— 2012. *Together: The Rituals, Pleasures and Politics of Cooperation.* London: Penguin.

Simmel, Georg. 1949. 'The Sociology of Sociability'. *American Journal of Sociology* 55 (3): 254–61.

—— 1950. *The Sociology of Georg Simmel.* Translated by Kurt H. Wolff. Glencoe, Illinois: The Free Press.

Sparke, Penny. 2008. *The Modern Interior.* London: Reaktion.

11

An Insane Perspective to the Occupation of Interiors

Dianne Smith

AN INSANE PERSPECTIVE OF OCCUPATION AND THE INTERIOR

I stare at the images of photographers and commentators such as Christopher Payne (2009) and Dan Marbaix (2014); depictions of emptiness. Spaciousness is created in this case through the vacating of mental asylums. The peeling paint, rotting timber, disused toilets, browned baths, soiled finishes and stained floors are captured as beautiful patterns of light, shade, colour and shape. Absence – visual or aural – is a potent aspect of life. In music and art, silence and emptiness give meaning to the artefact through the juxtaposition of a pause to a beat, a void to a solid, paleness to intensity, and the fall to the rise of a foot. In these images, we sense the meaning in the absences as part of the context of the interior depicted.

Simultaneously, the interior depicted speaks of occupation, not in terms of capturing life, but rather in terms of what preceded the vacating; and maybe, what we are afraid about deep down. Understandings are rooted in stories and myths of those who were deemed mentally ill and how they behaved and lived, and of those who controlled, harmed and manipulated patients in their care through a desire to help, and in many cases, to control. Such stories are evoked by reports in the news or in history books:

> *Jean Taylor has nightmares about that upstairs room. In flashbacks she sees herself on a hospital bed pushed against a white tiled wall and four people are looking down at her. As one of them moves aside to load a hypodermic needle, she sees for the first time the electric shock equipment. This is the ECT room, or as it is more anonymously signposted in many hospitals, the Treatment Area, and it is an image 64-year-old Jean Taylor has never forgotten. (Dobson 1995, 25)*

Places such as that the woman recalls above not only reflect an understanding of society at the time of mental illness and the person with the illness, but also how the person with the cognitive impairment experiences that place. Any place reflects the society's, the client's, the financiers', the designer's constructs of those who will occupy the space in question; and how these future occupants are to

11.1 Ward entrance, Taunton State Hospital, Taunton, Massachusetts, from Payne (2009)
Source: From Christopher Payne. 2009. *Asylum. Inside the Closed World of State Mental Hospitals.* Cambridge: MIT Press, 58. © Christopher Payne 2009.

occupy the places created. For instance, researchers exhibiting in the Brisbane Museum in 2008 sought to understand how the institutions embody the 'dominant social provision and response to mental illness and intellectual disability' (Finnane 2009, 7).

Embedded within the construct are rituals of occupation and power relations between those who are occupying the space, as potently captured in Dobson's example. The physical qualities of a space (such as rooms, finishes, lighting, furniture) reflect and support these embedded understandings and rules. They also impact on how a person perceives him/herself, and how they live in and occupy their environments. An asylum is one setting that enables us to consider such relationships. The insights emerging help us to reflect on other environmental genres and the ways in which they are occupied conceptually, psychologically, emotionally and physically.

Asylums for the mentally ill across the Western world do not exist now in the same way as they did; so we can only experience them by looking back through photographs and other records. What we experience by looking at the image is filtered through myths and stories. These stories involve acts we have read about or those we imagine; stories involving the space that was occupied before it was photographed as empty. The absence yields a space for the imagination to bring the physical attribute together with the stories we have been exposed to, so that we can reconstruct the vacated interior. We occupy it through our imaginings. In contrast, in our everyday lives, when we physically occupy rooms such as a kitchen, TV room, office or gymnasium, we are commonly overloaded or consumed by the intensity of the sensorial stimuli, functional demands, and so on.

However, with absence, there is space and time not only *to be* but also *to create*. We can potentially marry an object, a trace, a surface, a volume, and/or a space with a memory, a story, or an imagining. Depending on which of these three sources is involved, the outcomes do not have the same qualities. Memories may allude to images such as your mad grandmother, times when you personally may have felt unstable, visiting places of disquiet – the direct connection with your past yielding deeper experiences. The emptiness or absence in the image or the vacated building acts as a trigger to story-making that personally resonates. A story can also be created without drawing directly on personal past experiences. Stories of occupation are built upon things remaining from others' pasts – they act as props in a new dialogue, become a new scenario emerging within the present circumstance. Stories that are drawn from news articles or from gossip, for example, do not draw on personal experiences but on others' interpretations. These messages are drawn into the experience of the empty space or absence.

The qualities of place depicted in the images of the vacated asylum act as triggers (as captured in the above examples), but they may also be part of the immediate situation for the viewer of the images or visitor to the premises. The person understands it through the lens of the here and now or that of the future. Each scenario is unique, involving impressions of space and time. Where did the stories or myths associated with or brought to asylums originate? What impression is triggered for the contemporary viewer? To understand, it is useful to consider what the nature of the inhabited asylum was.

The asylum as an institution was created in Europe in the eighteenth century in response to the philosophical directions of government and medical practices of the time. Asylums were constructed responses to the human condition of people who were described as mad, or later as mentally ill. For example:

> *Johann Christian Heinroth [Leipzig, 1773–1843], one of the founders of modern psychiatry … conceived of madness as the complete loss of internal freedom, or reason, depriving individuals of any ability to control their lives and justifying external control by those who 'know best' what is good for patients. Heinroth asserted that the medical scientist was the member of society who knew what was best for patients. He justified this by analogizing the loss of reason to physical illness, thus adopting a medical model for mental illness. In this manner the growing psychology of the day asserted its dominion over people whose unacceptable behavior made them subject to confinement by the state. The state transferred the responsibility for the confined deviant person to the mental health profession … . (Mindell 1993, 236)*

When I deconstruct this quote spatially to gain insight into the philosophy of the time, the following phrases emerge. Each phrase can be visualized in terms of locations, whether relating to a person or society: *internal* freedom (within the mind or body); *external* control (outside the mind or body); *patients* (outside the dominant group, confined to waiting rooms, hospitals, asylums); dominion *over* people (power relationship between groups); *confinement* by the state (removal from and by the dominant group); *confined* deviant person (bonded subgroup). For me, an image of interlocking *matryoshka* or nesting dolls arises. The internal occupation of oneself involves a sense-of-space; a spatiality of inner experience in the same way as we externally occupy a built space – albeit the experience is different. The self is a deep internal domain, inside a more external domain – the body. The body in turn is located in another external place such as a room or building (that may be occupied by others) – and so on.

When one's internal freedom is lost, as implied in the quote above, an individual's fluidity of occupation of space across time and circumstance is controlled. The freedom to occupy as one wishes or chooses is at risk. Psychologically, in normal life we control our boundaries. The degree of rigidity and permeability enables us to cope, and knowing when to put a rigid boundary in place and when to be porous is a craft we all attempt to master. Piedmont et al. (2009) explain that experiential permeability:

> *relates to the ability of an individual to regulate interactions between the inner world of experiences and the outer reality of activities and relationships … a psychological boundary or membrane that delineates the person from his or her environment … . Problems in this boundary develop when a person responds in a disproportional manner to a stressor, either in terms of exhibiting highly unique, autistic-like behaviors that conflict with social norms or by overly conforming to environmental expectations to the detriment of his or her inner needs. This quality would become a personality disorder when the type of response becomes pervasive, characteristic, and socially isolating. (1247)*

There are personal stories illustrating spatial morphing, or the shifting boundary between an individual's inner experience and outer reality, such as when a person loses touch with the reality of their occupation of space. For example, Deegan wrote: 'My world sometimes felt like a distorted house of mirrors *reflecting infinitely inward upon itself*' (quoted in Lysaker and Lysaker 2010, 331, emphasis added). In relation to such scenarios, Minkowski suggests that

> *the disharmony of person and world, so characteristic of many who suffer from schizophrenia, is present long before formal symptoms arise … . Life evolved in fits and starts … not [as]* a continuous line, supple and elastic *but [as]* one broken in several places. *(Quoted in Lysaker and Lysaker 2010, 337, emphasis added)*

I recall words of others from various sources recounting what it is like to be in one's body when the mind moves beyond its norm to a state of occupation that is no longer familiar.

> *She finds that instead of having her thoughts running around in endless circles in her mind, she is now having a discussion with her head, which has somehow, miraculously she thinks, started to appear in the* top corner *of the bedroom, looking down at her … . (Geekie and Read 2009, 1, emphasis added)*

Others describe a feeling of being conscious of where they are in space, while they are simultaneously occupied by the voices. Voices perhaps acting as a 'guiding spirit' (Geekie and Read 2009, 31), or of the 'black dog', or similar feelings or constructs that can disturb (and in some cases overtake) the inner parts of

11.2 Patient toothbrushes, Hudson River State Hospital, Poughkeepsie, New York, from Payne (2009)
Source: From Christopher Payne. 2009. *Asylum. Inside the Closed World of State Mental Hospitals.* Cambridge: MIT Press, 93. © Christopher Payne 2009.

who the person was and is. Eleanor Longden relates, regarding her voices: 'They used to be more *external*, but now tend to be *internal* or *outside*, but *very close* to my ears. It can also vary depending on which voice is speaking' (TED Blog 2013, emphasis added). In addition, the spatiotemporal aspect of schizophrenic voices is 'impossible' 'mythical' and 'sourceless'; voices simultaneously within a person, next to him/her, beyond the walls or beyond the city (Erb 2006, 55).

It is hard to consider these phenomena without being aware of the spatial dimensions; that is, the thoughts and feelings within the person; the person within the room; the room within the building; the building within its physical context; and the site as part of a social and cultural context. If we return to the asylum and its residents (patients or inmates), the inner experience of the person, the experiences of the spaces of confinement, as well as the nature of the physical spaces and setting would be interwoven.

In *The Lives they Left Behind* by Penny and Stastny (2008), a patient (pseudonym E.D.K) demonstrates his relationship with the voices in terms of his contextual setting: ' … When he is hallucinated, he tells the charge of the ward and asks to be kept in because he is afraid to go out. He is oriented as to time, place and person. Has some insight into his condition' (53).

By reflecting on these aspects of occupation in the light of the images, what can we learn about occupation through the lens of the asylum, places that were purpose built for those with mental illness? The images of asylums or mental hospitals found in books or websites, such as Payne's referred to earlier, capture lone brooms leaning, toothbrushes hung out, rusting metal suspended, structures disintegrating, furniture broken or just waiting, cupboards open and vacated, buzzers silent, clothing hanging limp; the bodies are not present, but a sense of occupation is present. Occupation of these *spatial receptacles* engenders emotional responses; the image acts as both an evocator and a repository of meaning as the viewer gazes and ventures into it. Such responses are created through the nature of each artefact, each surface's character, and what they stand for symbolically.

Occupation is largely conceptualized as being about inhabiting a place regardless of how small or how grand the situation. However, a place is also a vehicle to convey what occupation means; what it can be, is, or has been. The purpose or intent of a design of a building evolves through its construction and inhabitation, to enable particular ways of occupying and the experiences of those who live there (physically and emotionally) and the perceptions of those who visit or work there (about the place and the occupants). Collectively, the place is a site of occupation.

THE SOCIAL REALITY OF ASYLUM ARCHITECTURE AND DESIGN

The asylum as a place is a case in point. The artefact – the building and the design – and its siting reflect this. Asylums are commonly understood as intended to keep mentally ill and therefore vulnerable people safe inside the interior, and (though this may not be explicit) to keep the outside world safe from those deemed insane. How the person with mental illness is defined by others influences the nature of that interior and what occurs within it. Asylums, their external boundaries and their interiors, have evolved over the centuries to reflect changing constructions of madness and what it means to society as a whole.

Before the seventeenth century, people with mental illness were regarded as sources of wisdom or of religious significance, 'revered as divine beings, perceived as harmless jesters or fools' (Crowley-Cryer 2005, 41). In medieval times, court jesters are said to have conveyed realistic information about the monarch and about society, because they spoke their minds on controversial topics, while others often only told the monarch what they wanted to hear. Although lowly in status with few belongings, the jesters were retained by the court (Otto 2001, quoted in Issa, Isaias and Kommers 2013, 91–2). In the seventeenth century, most mentally ill people in England were in the care of family or parish communities (Crowley-Cryer 2005, 40). Issa et al. discuss the role of fools, including 'minstrels, players, jugglers, and jesters' in early modern European society (2013, 92). In the seventeenth century, there were two classifications – natural fools and licensed fools – that originated in the twelfth century (Janik 1998, quoted in de Jesus 2012, 22). Natural fools were institutionalized because of their mental limitations, while artificial fools imitated the natural to gain free speech.

However, this earlier understanding of the jester or fool as useful evolved, so that by the 1800s, they were socially constructed to be deficient or dangerous, not mainstream community members. As Foucault describes (1988), the great era of confinement and the birth of the asylum preceded the design of restorative places for people with mental illness. During the seventeenth century, the great houses of confinement were created in France, and very quickly, 1 in 100 Parisians were sent there (Foucault 1988, 38); for example, the Hospital General of Paris housed 6,000 people (1 per cent of the population) (45). Those who were deemed mad were kept from being idle and a 'community of labor' was required; there existed 'an ethical power of segregation, which permitted [society] to eject, as into another world, all forms of social uselessness' (58).

Perron, Rudge and Holmes (2010) point out that this segregation of the mentally ill not only defines their illness and treatment, but it also reflects their exclusion from citizenship. A new system of operating emerged. Perron et al. quote Foucault's description of the emergence of a society 'to manage, govern, and care for those who were deemed to be abnormal: the insane, the poor, the criminal, the feeble minded, and so on' (2010, 102). They interpret his observations of

> *transformations in the ways the insane are first exiled from society (embarked on ships and abandoned at sea), then excluded through what he [Foucault] termed the Great Confinement, which refers to the systematic institutionalization of those considered to be devoid of reason … . One can certainly infer the implications of such classification in relation to the sound practice of citizenship and the resulting denial of a citizen experience as described by contemporary thinkers and activists. (102)*

Mental hospitals during the sixteenth to eighteenth centuries were seen as appalling by many and were constructed to be constraining; small cell-like rooms and corridor layouts conjure up associations with holding pens. Asylums, where occupants were once defined as animals or beasts, focused on safety for the inhabitants, in a 'security system against the violence of the insane and the explosion of their fury' (Foucault 1988, 73). Similarly, even where inmates were deemed non-dangerous but bestial, residents were still not seen as being people with illness, nor as needing protection, cover, or warmth (Foucault 1988, 72). In the extreme, during the eighteenth century, people would visit asylums to see mad people – they became a spectacle for amusement or one of the sights of London (Scull 2004, 420). Designs of occupation were characterized by 'long corridors, separation of keepers and residents, cell doors with bars or small openings, multiple locks and bolts, chains, grated floors, straw to sleep on, and/or food delivered via slots or through barred divisions' (Foucault 1988, 72). Examples given by Foucault include La Salpetrière and the Hospital of Nantes.

However, newer philosophies in Britain, Germany and the USA during the 1800s saw a shift to the asylums being 'therapeutic' (Malcolm 2009, 51) and the 'balance of institutional control with domestic tranquility' (O'Boyle 2010, 3) became the imperative. Asylums evolved to become retreats during the 1800s; that is, they were located in rural settings, and attention was given to 'fresh air, adequate drainage, and suitable surface finishes, as well as zoning to differentiate between degrees of curability' (Porter 2002, 116). The retreat philosophy contrasted with previous models, and reflected a belief that people had curable conditions:

> *When he entered the Retreat he was loaded with chains; he wore handcuffs; his clothes were attached by ropes. He had no sooner arrived than all his shackles were removed, and he was permitted to dine with the keepers; his agitation immediately ceased; 'his attention appeared to be arrested by his new situation'. He was taken to his room; the keeper explained that the whole house was organized in terms of great liberty and the greatest comfort for all, and he would not be subject to any constraint so long as he did nothing against the rules of the house or general principles of human morality. For his part, the keeper declared he had no desire to use the means of coercion at his disposal.*
> *(Foucault 1988, 246)*

Carla Yanni, the architectural historian, points out that we should be cognizant that at the time of each phase of asylum design the intentions may have been meaningful and aligned with that societal context. Architecturally, in the eighteenth century, an era of environmental determinism, when designers believed that built environments could control behaviours, it was believed that 'architecture shapes behaviour' in ways that include the re-education of 'unhealthy minds through asylum design' (Yanni 2007, 8), and that architecture can be an 'instrument of reform' (Middleton, quoted in Fontana-Ginsti 2013, 71). In the nineteenth century, therapeutic design, as an approach to designing as well as a belief system, was intended to re-educate unhealthy minds. Yanni is quoted as stating:

> ... *'traitement' moral[e] encouraged benevolent care that treated the mind rather than the body with activities, a structured environment, strict schedule, and rejection of physical restraints. Nineteenth-century reformers and advocates of moral treatment believed that the environment – including architecture – influenced behavior, and that proper conditions could cure disease.*
> *(Quoted in Garnett, Gray, and Halberg 2014, 2)*

An example of the shift from the earlier corrective/coercive model of care to a more 'productive' or 'enlightened' one is the Kew Asylum, designed during the nineteenth century to replace the asylum Yarra Bend in Victoria, Australia. It was modelled on current English and European approaches to the environmental genre. However, since Australia was a colony with a differing economy and workforce, the visions could not be transferred in their entirety (Finnane 2009). As the architect Kawerau noted, the new design aimed to re-socialize the residents, accommodating gender distinctions in relation to their mental illness, as well as desired activities to assist the patients in undertaking some form of work (quoted in Malcolm 2009, 53). Physicians' treatments were informed by the new social context, and were intended to cure the patients through a 'moral treatment regime', where 'careless habits that simultaneously were the cause and outcome of madness' were to be removed. This approach typically involved transforming people into 'productive citizens' (de Young 2010, 86–7). Kew Asylum was 'intended to display both the progress of enlightened medical science and the benevolence of the newly established and newly wealthy colony' (Malcolm 2009, 51). The historian Tomes relates that asylums became more humane in the nineteenth century (quoted in de Young 2010, 85); for example, in the United States, the Pennsylvania Hospital for the Insane (1840), where the physician Kirkbride was superintendent, is a case in point. Although some heroic treatments (such as bleeding, blistering, purging and vomiting) were used, the regime was opposed to restraint, violence, or self-injury (de Young 2010, 85–6). De Young also comments that design embedded in Romanticism emphasized the restorative qualities of nature and the uplifting effects that beauty and order can create in the mind. Romanticism in the arts refers to the eighteenth-century interest in and expression of nature, emotion and imagination, and is marked by its shift away from classicism as well as from social rules and conventions (*Oxford Dictionary* 2014).

Payne points out that 'The building of asylums required enormous state expenditures and an army of workers who lived on-site during construction. Towns competed fiercely for the asylums, as they insured economic prosperity, especially in rural areas reliant on agriculture' (2009, 9). He adds 'The Kirkbride hospitals were technological marvels of their time, offering modern amenities such as fireproof construction, central heating, plumbing, and gaslight. But they were not hospitals in the modern sense of the word' (10).

The reforms made at this time aimed to be humane; an aim reinforced by Kirkbride's comments that 'a prerequisite for treating diseases of the mind' is an environment that removes any instigating stressors such as family and home (quoted in de Young 2010, 86–7). Consequently, the design of these new places was driven by strong order, and a logic in the layouts intended to foster calmness in the occupants and to assist their recovery of rational thinking (Kirkbride, quoted in Malcolm 2009, 86–7). The Kirkbride design, which was endorsed by the American Psychiatric Association, was a linear plan with a central administration area and accompanying residential pavilions. Yanni (2007) highlights that there were many architects who applied the Kirkbride principles to places for people with mental illness. The aim was to create 'one big surrogate family' (Malcolm 2009, 51) that provided control in a non-institutional setting; a balance between intention and appearance.

More recently, in the post-Second World War period, people again challenged the nature of madness, in ways that contrasted with the Classical period (1650–1800); and as a result, a movement toward deinstitutionalization evolved. This occurred as images of the inner worlds of asylums (such as Bedlam) became available in the 1940s through magazines such as *Life* as well as radio and film (Erb 2006, 48). Comparisons were made to the war camps; Deutsch stated ' … We do not kill them deliberately. We do it by neglect' (quoted in Erb, 49). It is noted by Cynthia Erb that the exposés of the day brought home what 'the enforced isolation of the mentally ill said about a culture as a whole … [that it] created sensation by imagining confinement' (49).

PEOPLE WITH MENTAL ILLNESSES: ACCEPTANCE OR NEGATION?

In our contemporary world, it is recognized that environmental conditions arising from circumstances such as poverty can impact on mental health conditions (such as schizophrenia) (Snyder, Gur and Andrews 2007). Mental health issues can be envisaged as a medical issue, but an alternative view is that 'recovery is holistic', and consequently, where people live is important (Browne and Courtney 2007, 74).

However, despite many shifts towards a more humane approach, asylums remain symbolic of confinement. Confinement is a mode of occupation. So when is an interior confining and when is it protecting? Is the occupant's confinement just physical; or is it an emotional or imaginary response? Consider, for example if someone knocks on your door; what is your response? Is the person a sales person, a religious pilgrim, an invited visitor or an intruder at the door? The relationship of the person with the interior changes with each scenario – the door can be used to welcome, to filter, to restrict or to barricade. The experience of occupying an interior is influenced by the role of the physical boundary – what is kept in, what is external, what we wish to accept and what we need to keep out.

Physical environments are embodiments of social and moral beliefs and understandings (Smith 2012); an 'expression of a particular imagination' of a 'desirable framework' (Finnane 2009, 7). Interior architecture reflects our understanding of people and their right to live a full life (or not) within (or removed) from society. The relationship is symbiotic. The ability to indirectly construct people negatively also needs to be recognized. Goffman, in 1967, noted that settings can facilitate behaviours that demonstrate situational improprieties (quoted in Shalin 2013, 126); that is, the nature of the context facilitates or induces bad behaviour.

Core models of care influence broader patterns of occupation. On an individual level they influence how a person is able to express him/herself, as they have prior to entry. Madness, once it became a unique discourse, with its focus on the naming of the condition, the accommodation, and the treatment, ran the risk of negating the subjective experiences that are involved; thereby reflecting 'an understandable tendency to want to distance oneself from the confusing and painful experience of others' (Geekie and Read 2009, 27). It has also isolated those who are mentally ill, as Foucault and others have highlighted, by dividing those who lack reason from those who can reason; and by the 'subjugation of non-reason to reason' (Fontana-Giusti 2013, 55). For example, the person who is mentally unwell was (and often still is) marginalized within everyday life to become socially erased (although they are often spoken about and depicted visually and graphically) (Erb 2006, 54). Earlier in the twentieth century, artists such as surrealist André Breton and the German Expressionists drew on the unstable, and in the 1930s, 'championed l'art des fous, art produced by institutionalized persons' (Erb 2006, 54). Erb critiques film makers such as Hitchcock, who represent madness as part of a 'value/waste' system; for example, 'the psychotic, will never have a relation to money … . Madness is that which must be expelled, sent down the drain, into the swamp, into oblivion … There will be no arrival at the final conclusive term "humanity", only passage into absence' (Erb 2006, 60). The cultural outcome is to negate madness in order to preserve a particular social order (Fontana-Giusti 2013, 69).

Some would consider the physical places of occupation also reinforce this removal, negation, or erasure. Occupation through the lens of *ruin*, *repudiation* and *revolution* highlights such strategies as part of the overwriting of place and its impact on occupational experiences. The *ruining* of the original intention through the meanings or actions that we bring to the situation (or to our understandings of an occupant) can also result in damage, destruction or the bringing down of place or person (with somewhat distorted traces remaining). Similarly, *repudiation* is evident through the denial, negation, or refutation of occupant or place. Probably *revolution* is the most implicated through the naming of madness. The transformation of the human condition, through the historical trajectory captured above, shows the person with mental illness from being a free agent, to a beast, to a productive citizen, to a societal norm; a progression that involves both subtle and aggressive upheavals of a foundational situation or idea of person. Each of these lenses or viewpoints disrupts the taken-for-granted situation to show the evolving influences upon the base conditions of place and occupant, and thereby, to affect the experiences of site, materials and surfaces. Asylums draw us into this conversation not only through absence and emptiness but also through negation and erasure.

CONSTRUCTING OCCUPATION

Reading first-hand accounts or viewing images brings design aspirations alive in ways that resonate with the occupation of place. Dr Urquart, a late nineteenth-century practitioner, describes his impressions of a visit to Kew Asylum near Melbourne, Australia (1880, 486):

> *At the time of my visit one man in camisole and gloves, was tied to his chair. Many wore gloves alone, and many strong dresses ... .*
>
> *The bedding and beds are clean and tidy, but throughout there is a want of home-like comfort that strikes one harshly ... .*
>
> *The dining hall is spacious and cheerful, and here there are frequent amusements ... .*

The physicality of the built form (as well as the therapeutic intent) of settings – such as those mentioned by Urquart above – are rendered less significant because they are overtaken by what arises for the viewer. They are subsumed both emotionally and imaginatively.

In summary, a society creates places of occupation in which individuals are located according to that society's understanding of them and their place in the world at a micro and macro level. Individuals live within these places and this inhabitation involves rituals – personal and collective. Each situation reflects a particular power relationship that enables varying degrees of freedom and control. The layout, the surfaces, the finishes, and the furniture and furnishings, as well as more ephemeral qualities such as odours, light, breezes, and moisture, reflect the mode of occupation – real and potential – as well as the differences between the understandings and experiences of residents/patients/inmates, staff and management.

Each resident experiences him/herself as part of a social setting, and their identity and sense of self is developed and/or impacted upon. Simultaneously, each person lives within the experience, moulded by individual personal thoughts, dreams, memories of where they exist in space and time. Places of occupation are built by sectors of the society, and therefore, the experience for each individual occupant is also constructed collectively through this constructed context.

When the built form is vacated, the dimensions of occupation are simultaneously suspended and transformed. The viewer is left not knowing – wondering, seeking clues as to what was, but also to what this place is, and in some cases, could be. The interior architect lives in this dimension, as we navigate the complexities of adapting emptiness toward renewed genres and modes of occupation. Adaptive re-use – whether formally by practitioners or informally by occupants – is inherent in what we do. In such activities, transforming and ruining of the past (and its physicality) is evident – and in extreme cases, revolution may be involved.

It is provoking to reflect on what must be similar processes that squatters or homeless people in our towns and cities engage in, as they appropriate society's abandoned spaces, and envisage them as places that contribute to their lives for an instant in time, or if possible, for extended times. Their occupation reflects their means as well as their imagination and creativity, combined with intuition and resilience. They gather around themselves the attributes of the abandoned or empty space to occupy it. The physical place, though steeped in history or stories of others, is simultaneously laden with potential within the mind or the body of the newcomer – intruder or invited.

Occupation is the lived, innate experience of our daily activities; mostly things *just are* and we give them little thought or attention. However, the asylum, inhabited, empty, or represented through images, also stimulates and challenges us to engage with awareness. The empty space and its attributes offer opportunities for transformation or revolution while simultaneously denying or negating the asylum's past. These tangible aspects provide the potential for further traces, which are representations as well as understandings, ideas, or comprehensions. These various outcomes have implications for interior occupation and the evolving experiences of designers and those they design for.

Absence or emptiness still provides a palette from which to draw the richness of our contemporary stories and future speculations. As humans we strive to create order, and by focusing on various aspects over others we create the world we inhabit (Schreyach 2013, 65). So too when viewing images of or visiting asylums, we filter the information before us. When topics are emotive and cloaked in myths (and at times fear) such as these are, we do not approach them analytically; rather the experience is phenomenological. This process is indirectly explained by Schreyach in the way he discusses Jackson Pollock's artwork to highlight how the object emerges from the work rather than being identified through pre-thought by the viewer (2013, 56). Similarly, Merleau Ponty acknowledges the 'spontaneous organization of things we perceive' in relation to experiencing Cezanne's paintings (2013, 56); a 'lived perspective' that contrasts with a 'geometric or photographic one' of the objectified world (57). The work of Kasuma, the Japanese artist and a mental hospital resident, challenges the conception of madness (by some) as a way of being that does not involve having knowledge (Fontana-Giusti 2013, 57). Kasuma's work opens up questions regarding the nature of the occupant with mental limitations compared to the dominant population (Fontana-Giusti 2013, 57). Urban design and built forms in the public domain have also been linked to how we interpret places or representation of place. The architect and theorist, Tschumi, claims that his design of the Parisian park at la Villette (1982–98) was informed by madness – a representation of the disjunctions within society's values, form, and use (quoted in Fontana-Giusti 2013, 69). He states that all societies need 'lunatics, deviants, and criminals to mark their own negativity' – and similarly within architecture to express the 'fragile cultural and social world' (69). In regard to asylum images, Curt Miner makes explicit that we draw meaning from our surroundings and its representation because of what the context is: 'These places can produce some very strong images precisely because there were asylums, whereas if the subject were a paediatric hospital, the message of the photographs would be different' (Miner 2010, 105).

When I return again to the images of the asylum, the juxtaposition of beauty and risk is evident. Risk in the tension of what I know such spaces to have been; risk in that mental illness is often disturbing, due to the unpredictability of where it will arise and how it is performed; risk in that it reflects the worst in how we may treat others even if we believe we never would; and risk in that the cycle may repeat itself once more over history. Can we erase the past behaviours and intentions from the physicality of the place? I do not know the answer, but it is evident that many feel that we cannot. The ephemeral and intangible dimensions are conceived as having ill-defined form and longevity; a sense of past occupants, ghosts and spirits, and feelings such as heaviness, being watched, movement still haunt the place. Such abstract or ethereal phenomena of occupation are yet to be captured in academic literature and scholarly journals and given legitimacy. There is also a risk associated with wandering outside the dominant paradigm of what can be explained and understandable.

The asylum image depicted in Figure 11.3 from Christopher Payne's book *Asylum: Inside the Closed World of State Mental Hospitals* is chosen to illustrate my occupation of such images; a personal occupation triggered by the constituent attributes. A deconstruction of the image charts the underlying basis to my unfolding experience; and therefore, may reflect the foundations for other observers of the image or visitors to the empty asylum today. All these attributes are part of the place's embodied narrative.

Decaying surfaces of acid teal and lemon paint reflect the peeling of time, and in association, care, pride, order and the medical model. It reads as a hospital – repetition, schedules, corridors, uniformity and anonymity are represented by the past grandeur of the space. The rusting ceiling and masonry walls reflect the solidity of grandeur, yet the faces of both surfaces peel away, erasing the identity that was. Industrial fixtures hang from the ceiling and traverse the walls, reflecting the pragmatic edge to that past identity. The metal grilles along the top of the right-hand wall hint of small cell-like rooms. But is my assumption reasonable or part of the asylum myth passed down from others' stories and research? The dirt on the floor, dado rails and other surfaces reinforces the forgotten building's life; the physical box remains but the residents, cleaners, maintenance men and other carers are long gone.

The graffiti raises queries of transient occupants – visitors, voyeurs or squatters? For me, the symbol reflects someone, but not of somewhere. The chair as artefact is poignant through form, colour, placement and scale. In human scale within the large volume of the corridor, it implies it could be used today yet it reeks of a time when someone sat in the light from the door looking out. Were they left alone? Happy? Ill? Depressed? It is hard not to load the object with memories and speculation, yet it is just an image. The absence of people or signs of inhabitation reinforces the tension between the composition and the experiences that are embedded within it, purely because we know it is an asylum.

11.3 Patient ward, Buffalo State Hospital, Buffalo, New York, from Payne (2009)
Source: From Christopher Payne. 2009. *Asylum. Inside the Closed World of State Mental Hospitals*. Cambridge: MIT Press, 61.
© Christopher Payne 2009.

The intention of asylums was and is clear. An asylum is about marking people as 'other' and then caring for this sub-group in such a way as to remove them, and later, bring them closer to the norms of the society. As discussed above, the 'other' can be beast-like, demonic, irreparably ill, or able to be like mainstream people, given enough time.

Within the ruins, traces can assist my ability to enter into the image or work – to occupy it in various modes, while not being physically there at all. For me, there is a *presence* created through the decaying spaces or volumes, their sequence into the distance and the chair at the door. The spatial dynamic has a sense of place – albeit decaying and abandoned, ruined.

Life's marks have been removed – not in the sense of pristine surfaces – but rather in the lack of human activity. The marks of time and absence of attention are present but not what was evolving through activity and engagement with the environment. Likewise, my knowledge of mental health design and the informal myths that have impregnated my consciousness indicate that in this image there are many stories not told or even hinted at. As a result, the unsaid can induce further speculation and story making. Other images may capture sleeping dorms, bathing rooms, personal items, as well as facilities such as the hairdressers (the photographer's notes reflect that the patients never went out); images that reinforce these inner stories of disempowerment, constraint and hardship.

The grandeur of the building's scale hints at the ability to conceal or de-emphasize the micro-activities, the inmates' concerns in daily life, through the imagery of the buildings, grounds and public decor. The place can stand out, but other aspects of occupation are hidden. The balance of elements within the design enables clues to be found or suppressed, and therefore, allows the stories that are emerging for the viewer to be manipulated. Interestingly, who we are and what we embrace and/or fear acts as a potent filter. Do we think we could end up in this place if it still operated? Does it relate to family and friends in the past, or those with cognitive difficulties now? Does it act as a metaphor for issues of empowerment and/or the role of collective care versus individual responsibility? What emotions are evoked? Which are authentic to our philosophy and which resonate only through the collective norms or hegemonies?

CONCLUSION

Asylums' past lives are often tainted by the rituals and regimes imposed during caring for or confining people with varying degrees of mental illness. The person who has a mental illness or cognitive impairment experiences where they live in their own way because of who they are; this may differ from what others know or expect of them. The way each occupies the world occurs within themselves, and also, within settings – interiors, buildings, sites, suburbs and regions. The asylum is one such setting that is almost erased; and although there are other places where people with a range of cognitive impairments live, the images of an asylum potently raise the necessary questions regarding how one should live, how one wishes to live, the differences between would-should-could modes of living, who sets the agenda, and importantly, how the physical space symbolically, emotionally and functionally enables or inhibits modes of occupation. The building, as the context for the lives of these people, reflects social and cultural understandings of people and their conditions.

These beliefs construct the assumptions of how a person should occupy the world, and in particular, in relation to the dominant group. We need to take care of such assumptions, as Oliver Sack's essay implies:

> *We tend to think of mental hospitals as snake pits, hells of chaos and misery, squalor and brutality. Most of them are now shuttered and abandoned – and we think with a shiver of terror of those who once found themselves confined in such places ... However, the old term for asylum was 'refuge, protection, sanctuary' ... 'affording shelter to ... the afflicted, the unfortunate, or destitute'. (2009, 1)*

This concept of refuge is supported by Sack's story of Anna who 'felt profound relief when the institute closed protectively around her, and most especially having her madness recognized' (2009, 1). Finnane similarly warns that amongst the negative stories and images of the abandoned model, it is important to not miss the positive aspects that may have been played out in people's lives (Finnane 2009).

The empty interior images are evocative – abandoned asylums stir strong emotions. The images or the actual empty buildings provide opportunities to occupy them with our own stories and/or those built from others' tales. The emptiness of abandoned spaces stimulates questions about the physical, the human, and ideas or thoughts that construct how we occupy our world. Historical examples of asylums narrate physically and symbolically how those deemed mentally ill were conceptualized and accommodated, and how these constructions have evolved over time until today.

My aim through this discussion was for you, the reader, to imagine the beauty of this genre's photographs – constructions of light, shape, colour, texture – while simultaneously engaging in story-making. And by doing so, to reflect on the potent role of the physical world for occupation. Occupation implies ownership, a freedom to choose – to occupy, to live, to inhabit. However, if we take an insane view of occupation it is about confinement. Is the emptiness captured in the image or ruin symbolic of the person within the asylum? Or rather, does it symbolize how these individuals with cognitive impairments were conceived at a particular time in history?

An insane view challenges contemporary theorists and practitioners of occupation to rethink the occupant in terms of interlocking spatial domains, as in the nesting dolls described above. The physical world is seamlessly interdependent with the inner voices, and therefore, needs to be understood and catered for through our work.

REFERENCES

Browne, Graeme, and Mary D. Courtney. 2007. 'Schizophrenia housing and supportive relationships'. *International Journal of Mental Health Nursing* 16 (2): 73–80.

Campbell, Andy. 2014. 'These Photos of Abandoned Asylums Will Keep You Awake Tonight', *HuffPost. Weird News*, Accessed 18 August, http://www.huffingtonpost.com/2013/09/04/abandoned-asylums-photos_n_3866248.html.

Crowley-Cyr, Linda. 2005. 'The Incarceration Archipelago of Lunacy "Reform" Enterprises: An Epochal Overview'. *James Cook University Law Review* 12: 33–64.

de Jesus, Leila Vieira. 2012. 'A Study of Fools: Lear's Fool in Shakespeare's *King Lear* and Vladimir and Estragon in Beckett's *Waiting for Godot*'. Master's diss., Universidade Federal do Rio Grande do Sul. www.lume.ufrgs.br/bitstream/handle/10183/54076/000837693.pdf. Accessed July 2014.

de Young, Mary. 2010. *Madness. An American History of Mental Illness and its Treatment*. Jefferson, NC: McFarland.

Dobson, Roger. 1995. 'Patients Join the Fight to Curtail Shock Treatment (Growing Opposition to Electric Shock Treatment)'. *The Independent*, 14 February: 25.

Erb, Cynthia. 2006. '"Have You Ever Seen the Inside of One of Those Places?": Psycho, Foucault, and Post-War Context of Madness'. *Cinema Journal* 45 (4): 45–63.

Finnane, Mark. 2009. 'Australian Asylums and Their Histories: Introduction'. *Health and History* 11 (1): 6–8.

Fontana-Giusti, Gordana. 2013. *Foucault for Architects*. Hoboken: Taylor and Francis.

Foucault, Michel. 1988. *Madness and Civilization: A History of Insanity in the Age of Reason*. New York: Vintage Books.

Garnett, Diana, Stephanie Gray and Kayla Halberg, 'The Story: An Historical Narrative of the South Carolina State Hospital at Bull Street', *Digitizing Bull Street* (blog), July 2014. http://www.digitizingbullstreet.com/story. Accessed July 2014.

Geekie, Jim and John Read. 2009. *Making Sense of Madness: Contesting the Meaning of Schizophrenia*. New York: Routledge.

Issa, Tomayess, Pedro Isaias and Piet A.M. Kommers, eds. 2013. *Information Systems and Technology for Organizations in a Networked Society*. Hershey, PA: Business Science Reference.

Jandrić, Petar. 2013. 'Academic Community in Transition: Critical Liberatory Praxis in the Network Society'. In *Information Systems and Technology for Organizations in a Networked Society*, edited by Tomayess Issa, Pedro Isaias and Piet A.M. Kommers, 88–106. Hershey, PA: Business Science Reference.

Longden, Eleanor. 2013. 'Everything You Ever Wanted to Know About Voice Hearing (But Were Too Afraid to Ask)', *TED Blog*, 8August, http://blog.ted.com/2013/08/08/everything-you-ever-wanted-to-know-about-voice-hearing-but-were-too-afraid-to-ask/. Accessed July 2014.

Lysaker, Paul H. and John T. Lysaker. 2010. 'Schizophrenia and Alterations in Self-Experience: A Comparison of 6 Perspectives'. *Schizophrenia Bulletin* 36 (2): 331–40.

Malcolm, E. 2009. 'Australian Asylum Architecture through German Eyes: Kew, Melbourne, 1867'. *Health and History* 11 (1): 46–64.

Mindell, Jodi A. 1993. *Issues in Clinical Psychology*. Madison, WI: Brown & Benchmark.

Miner, Curt. 2010. 'Institutions'. In *Modern Ruins: Portraits of Place in Mid-Atlantic Region*, edited by Shaun O'Boyle, 2–37. University Park: Pennsylvania State University Press.

Payne, Christopher. 2009. *Asylum: Inside the Closed World of State Mental Hospitals*. Cambridge: MIT Press.

Penney, Darby and Peter Stastny. 2008. *The Lives They Left Behind: Suitcases from a State Hospital Attic*. New York: Bellevue Literary Press.

Perron, Amelie, Trudy Rudge and Dave Holmes. 2010. 'Citizen Minds, Citizen Bodies: The Citizenship Experience and the Government of Mentally Ill Persons'. *Nursing Philosophy* 11 (2): 100–111.

Piedmont, Ralph L., Martin F. Sherman, Nancy C. Sherman, Gabriel S. Dy-Liacco and Joseph E.G. Williams. 2009. 'Using the Five-Factor Model to Identify a New Personality Disorder Domain: The Case for Experiential Permeability'. *Journal of Personality and Social Psychology* 96 (6): 1245–58.

Porter, Roy. 2002. *Madness: A Brief History*. Oxford: Oxford University Press.

Sacks, Oliver. 2009. 'Asylum'. In *Asylum: Inside the Closed World of State Mental Hospitals*, edited by Christopher Payne, 1–5. Cambridge: MIT Press.

Schreyach, Michael. 2013. 'Pre-Objective Depth in Merleau-Ponty and Jackson Pollock'. *Research in Phenomenology* 43 (1): 49–70.

Scull, Andrew. 2004. 'The Insanity of Place'. *History of Psychiatry* 15 (4): 417–36.

Shalin, Dmitri N. 2014. 'Goffman on Mental Illness: Asylums and "The Insanity of Place" Revisited'. *Symbolic Interaction* 37 (1): 122–44.

Smith, Dianne. 2012. 'Pandora's Box: Creative Practice in the Becoming of "Cognitive Impairment"'. In *Interior: A State of Becoming: 2012 IDEA Symposium, Perth, 6–9 September 2012*, edited by Lynn Churchill and Dianne Smith.

Snyder, Kurt, Raquel E. Gur and Linda Wasmer Andrews. 2007. *Me, Myself, and Them: A Firsthand Account of One Young Person's Experience of Schizophrenia*. Cary, NC: Oxford University Press. http://www.copecaredeal.org/Files/Teens/MeMyselfandThem_EN.pdf. Accessed July 2014.

Urquart, A.R. 1880. 'Three Australian Asylums'. *British Journal of Psychiatry* 25: 480–89.

Yanni, Carla. 2007. *The Architecture of Madness: Insane Asylums in the United States*. Minneapolis: University of Minnesota Press.

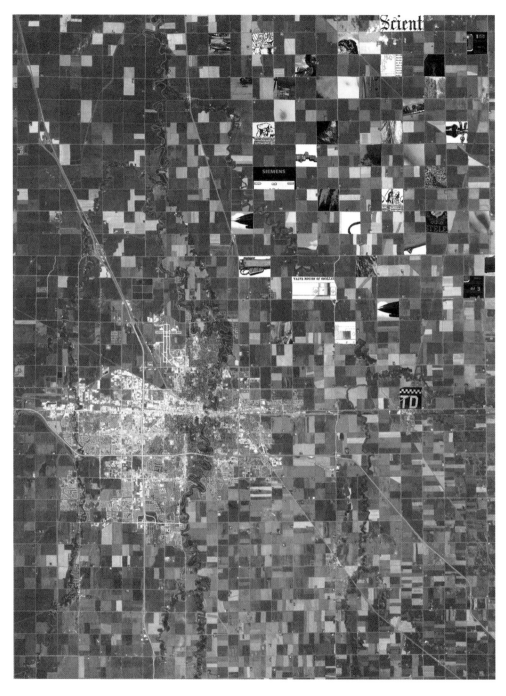

Plate 5   'What is that … driving away … they recede … pixels? But we lean forward … '
(adapted from Kerouac 1970, 156). 2014

Index

Illustrations are indicated by page numbers in **bold**.

abandoned spaces 9, 35, 171–3, 175–6, 181–6
Abercrombie, Stanley 101, 102–3
Aboriginal peoples 56–9, 161
absence 18, 21, 24, 77, 91, 101, 102, 108, 109, 171–3, 181–6; *see also* emptiness
Acconci, Vito 6, 7
advertising 9, 122, 127, 137, 140, **143**, 143–5, 146, 147, 152, 153
Advertising Standards Bureau 144, 146
agency 138, 140, 141, 142, 153
Akulova, Olga 110
alchemy 50, 59–62
Alexander, Christopher 158, 159, 162
Allen, Smout 44
alteration 8, 119, 123, 128–30
American National Exhibition, Moscow 119, 124–7, 133
American Psychiatric Association 179
Anatta 133
ancestral knowledge 5
Anderson, Pamela 138, **139**
Armfield, Neil 68, 76
arms race 119, 127
Armstrong, Gillian 74
asylums 9, 171–86, **172**, **175**, **184**
Attiwill, Susie 23, 24
Augustus 18, 21
Australia 7, 55–9, 61, 62, 67, 74, 138, 140, 142–9, 161–2, 178, 181

Bachelard, Gaston 158
Bakst, Leon 72
Ball, Edward 123
Ballet Russes 72
Bangkok 67, 71–3

Barthes, Roland 105, 109
Barton Fink (Coen brothers) 77, 78
Bataille, Georges 49
Baudrillard, Jean 33, 119, 120, 133
Ben Hur (Wyler) 71
Benjamin, Andrew 42
Benjamin, Walter 89, 158, 164, 167
Benzel, Katherine 157
Berleant, Arnold 1, 3
Berlin 8, 31–5, 41–5, 159–60, 162
Bewitched (TV series) 127
Biesenbach, Klaus 69–70
blind writing 37, 38
Bloch, Ernst 92
Bobrova, Yekatherina 38
body, *see* female body; human body; male body
body art 68, 71, 78
'Bonsai Tree and a Watering Hose, A' (Yasumura) 87
boundaries 6, 38, 40–41, 46, 174, 180
Brecht, Bertolt 157, 168
Bredlau, Susan M. 4
Breitbach, Julia 90
Breton, André 180
bricolage 16–17
Broadbeach Cats Football Club 142
Broadhurst, Florence 67–8, 70, 71, 73–6, 78, 79
Brott, Simone 77, 78
Brown, Bill 83, 89, 91–2, 95
Bryson, Norman 85, 91, 92, 95
Buddhism 133
Buffalo State Hospital, New York 183, **184**
built environment 84, 120, 178
Buñuel, Luis 163
Butler, Judith 140, 149

Campi Phlegraei (Hamilton) 52
Candy (Armfield) 68, 76–8, 79
'Candy Bar, A' (Yasumura) 92
capitalism 119, 121, 122, 124–7, 128, 133
car washes 145–9
Carax, Leos 70
Casebere, James 84
Casey, Edward 160
Ceci n'est pas une Pipe (Magritte) 106–7, 111
Cezanne, Paul 182
Chambers, Sir William 50–51, 52
Charles I 21–3, 26, 27
Ching, Francis 157
Cicero 18
Ciprut, Jose V. 37, 38
City Beautiful movement 166
'Coat Hook, A' (Yasumura) 87–9
Cockroach Diary (Fox) 84
Cold War 119, 124–7, 133
Colomina, Beatriz 103, 109, 126, 139
colonization 161–2
confinement 173, 175, 176–7, 180, 185–6
consumerism 121–2, 124–7
Corletts, David 144–5
Corning Incorporated
   A Day Made of Glass 119, 130–31, 133
   A Day Made of Glass 2: Same Day 119, 130–31, 133
   A Day Made of Glass 2: Unpacked 131, 133
Crabbe, Maree 144–5
Craig, James 41
'Cranes (26)' (Broadhurst) **75**, 76
Crewdson, Gregory 87
Cronin, Anne 140
Crowley, David 125
'Crude Hints Towards an History of My House' (Soane) 52–3

da Udine, Giovanni 19, 21, 27
Dagerman, Stig 44
damnatio memoriae 17–27
Dance, George 52
Davey, Moyra 84
Day Made of Glass (Corning) 119, 130–31, 133
Day Made of Glass 2: Same Day (Corning) 119, 130–31, 133
Day Made of Glass 2: Unpacked (Corning) 131, 133
de Beauvoir, Simone 99
de Young, Mary 178–9
Debord, Guy 119, 121, 122–3, 133

Deleuze, Gilles 77
Delirious New York (Koolhaas) 166–7
Derrida, Jacques 7–8, 33, 35, 36–8
DeSilvey, Caitlin 17
Dobson, Roger 171–2
Domestic Landscapes (Teunissen) 84
Domestic Scandals (Yasumura) 83, 84–96, **85**, **86**, **88**, **90**, **93**
domestic, the 9, 24, 70, 83–96, 103–4, 122, 124–5, 130, 166
Domus Aurea, see Golden House
Donaghue, Ngaire 151
Dorey, Helen 53
Dovey, Kim 138
Durkheim, Émile 160, 164–5
dystopia 117–19

Eames, Charles 124, 126–7
Eames, Ray 124, 126–7
earth 9, 158–63, 167–8
Edensor, Tim 17
Eisenman, Peter 32–3
Election, An (Hogarth) 51
empowerment 68, 124, 128, 129, 137, 140, 141, 149, 150, 151, 153, 185
emptiness 9, 171–3, 175–6, 181–6; *see also* absence
enclosure 23, 26, 162, 163
envy 126–8
ephemerality 49, 51, 120, 133, 181, 183
Epigrams (Martial) 19–20, 21, 26
Erb, Cynthia 179, 180
everyday life 3, 7, 70, 83–96, 99, 101, 104, 112, 120, 123, 126–8, 141
exclusion 100, 109, 111
Exeter poet 15–16, 17, 27
experience
   and abandoned spaces 171–6, 180–83, 185
   and architecture 49, 69–70, 118, 128–9
   of the external world, *see* external world
   and floors 158, 164
   and hypersexuality 142, 145, 149
   internal, *see* internal world
   of the interior 104, 171–6, 180–83, 185
   and museums 8, 55, 56, 58, 61
   of occupation 1–2, 3–4, 7, 104, 171–6, 180–83, 185
   of the urban 122, 123, 139, 142, 145, 149
   and vagrancy 31–46
   see also phenomenology
external world 3, 5, 7, 50, 59–60, 173–5

Fahey, Cassandra 138, 152
faire tapisserie 68–71
'Fan Heater, A' (Yasumura) 89–90, **90**, 93–5
'Father, A' (Yasumura) 84, 85, **86**, 87–9, 91
female body 67, 68–9, 71, 77, 78, 137–53
feminism 137, 141, 144, 147, 152–3
Field, Barron 161–2
Finnane, Mark 185
floors 9, 157, 158–9, 162–8
Florence Broadhurst (O'Neill) 74
Flower, Harriet 18, 21, 24
fools 176
forgetting 17–27, 44
Foster, Norman 160
Foucault, Michel 99–101, 103, 106–9, 111, 149, 176–8, 180
Fox, Anna 84
fragmentation 16, 17
Frank, Charlotte 160
French Revolution 121
Freud, Sigmund 5, 7, 118
Friedan, Betty 127
Fuller, Buckminster 126
Futurism 16, 17

Gaddafi, Muammar 25
Garden City model 121
gender stereotypes 138, 140, 142, 145, 148, 152, 153
George III 52
German Expressionism 180
Gill, Rosalind 144
Gilman, Charlotte Perkins 70, 78
glass 119–20, 130–31
Glimpses of the USA (Eames & Eames) 126–7
Goethe, Johann Wolfgang von 60
Goffman, Erving 180
Golden House 19–21, 26, 27
Goldstein-Gidoni, Ofra 87
Gotye 78, 79, **79**
Graves, Michael 129
Grotteschi 19, 27
ground planes 9, 157–68
Guedes, Tiago 35
Guy, John 73
Gwathmey, Charles 129

Hack, Emma 68, 71, 78
Halbwachs, Maurice 160
Hamilton, Sir William 52
Hanover World Expo 167

Harkness, James 106–7
Hartzell, Freyja 68–9
Heidegger, Martin 89, 158
Heinroth, Johann Christian 173
heterotopias 107–10, 111
high-rise buildings 121, 127, 166
Hill, Christopher 22
Hitchcock, Alfred 180
Hitler, Adolf 42
Hogarth, William 51
Holmes, Dave 177
Holocaust 31, 33, 160
Holy Motors (Carax) 70
Hooters 142
Hortensius 18
Hospital General, Paris 177
Hotel Silken Puérta America, Madrid 167
House Beautiful magazine 127
housewives 124, 125–6, 127
Howard, Ebenezer 121
Hudson River State Hospital, New York **175**
human body 3, 5–7, 67, 68–71, 77, 78, 130
Hussein, Saddam 25
hypermedia 131–2, 133
hypersexuality 9, 137–53

'I took bread and cheese and slipped out the door' (Dyer) **ii**
IDEA Symposium 7
idealized interior images 9, 99–112, **100**, **110**
identity 4, 9, 50, 53, 70, 74, 138, 141, 149, 159–62, 168, 181
imagination 2, 5, 7, 9, 87, 118, 161–2, 165, 167–8, 172, 179, 182
'Imagine Peace' (Ono) 119
immersion 32, 33, 70
indeterminacy of site 37, 38
Institute of Architecture and Urban Studies, New York 129
institutions 104–6, 109, 111–12
internal world 3, 5, 7, 50, 59–60, 173–5
interior, the 9, 23–7, 68–70, 73, 76–8, 83–96, 99–112, 159, 162–8, 171, 176, 180
Issa, Tomayess 176
Isogowa, Akira 71
Isozaki, Arata 163–4, 165, 167, 168

Jackson, Stevi 147
Jaeggi, Martin 87
'Japanese Oranges' (Yasumura) 92, **93**, 95
Jay, Martin 37–8
Jeffreys, Sheila 141

jesters 176
Jewish Museum, Berlin 31–2, 33–5, 45, 160
Jim Thompson: The Unsolved Mystery (Warren) 71–2
Jim Thompson Foundation 73
Jubilee Gardens, London 39
Jung, Carl 8, 50, 53, 59–61, 62

Kawano, Yoh 2
Kawerau, Frederick 178
Keillor, Patrick 17
KENZO apartment design (Akulova) **110**, 110
Kerouac, Jack 1
Kew Asylum, Victoria 178, 181
Khrushchev, Nikita 124
Kimbra 78, **79**
King and I, The (Lang) 71
King's Bench 21–3, 27
Kirkbride, Thomas 178–9
Kitten's Car Wash 145–9, **146**, **148**, 152
Knight, Richard Payne 16
knowledge 100, 103, 106, 109, 182
Kodja Place Visitor and Interpretive Centre 8, 49, 55–9, 61, 62
Koetter, Fred 16–17
Kojonup 49, 55–9, 61, 62
Koolhaas, Rem 166–7
Krull, Germaine 72
Ksubi **143**, 143–4, 148, 152
Kuraishi, Shino 84, 92, 93–5
Kurz, Tim 151
Kusama, Yayoi 182
Kwon, Miwon 39

labyrinths 58
Landscape: a Didactic Poem (Knight) 16
languages 40
Lavin, Sylvia 69, 77
Le Corbusier 121, 165
Leach, Neil 159, 162
Léger, Fernand 68, 69, 79
Lennie, David 78
Levittown 121
Levy, Ariel 141
Libeskind, Daniel 31, 32, 160
Life magazine 126, 166, 179
Life by Design, A (O'Brien) 74
lived experience 4, 7, 104, 123; *see also* experience
London 17, 39, 74
Long Life Cool White (Davey) 84
Longden, Eleanor 175

Loos, Adolf 101–2, 109
Lukács, Georg 89
Lynch, Kevin 160, 162
Lyotard, Jean-François 36, 37

McLuhan, Marshall 131–2, 133
McNair, Brian 147–8, 150
McQuire, Scott 139
McRobbie, Angela 137
McVee, Craig 57
Magritte, René 106–7, 111
Maguire, Emily 141
male body 68, 70–71, 78
'Man, A' (Yasumura) 84, 91
Marbaix, Dan 171
Marie Antoinette 25–7
Marinetti, Filippo T. 16
Martial 19–20, 21, 26
Marxism 121
Matta-Clark, Gordon 119, 120, 128–30, 133
mazes 58
Meat, Metal and Code (Stelarc) 6–7
media cities 138–40
Meier, Richard 128, 129
Melbourne 138, 140, 143–4, 145–9
Melchionne, Kevin 101
Memorial for Marcel Duchamp (Matta-Clark) 129
memory 9, 17–27, 160–61, 167, 168, 173
mental illness 171–86
Merleau-Ponty, Maurice 3–4, 7, 182
Mezei, Kathy 87
Minde 35–8
Mindell, Jodi 173
Miner, Curt 183
mirrors 108
mobility 119, 120–21
modernism 16, 17, 49, 68, 128
More, Sir Thomas 9, 117–18, 123–4, 133
Museum of Modern Art (MoMA), New York 69–70, 150
museums 8, 49–59, 61–2
myth 50, 53, 54–5, 57–8, 59–62, 171–3, 182–4

Nabokov, Vladimir 95
Naples 52
narratives 171–3, 183–6
national anthems 38–41
national identity 38–41, 157, 159–62, 168
National Memorial to the Murdered Jews of Europe, Berlin 32–5, **34**, 45

nationhood 41, 160
Nature Tracing (Yasumura) 84
Nero 19–21, 26, 27
Netherlands Pavilion, Hanover World Expo 167
New Babylon project 119, 123–4
New York 69–70, 129, 150, 166
Newman, Sam 138, 152
   house in Melbourne 138–9, **139**, 140, 152
Nietzsche, Friedrich 60
Nieuwenhuys, Constant 123–4
Nixon, Richard 124–5
Nolli, Giambattista 158
Noongar people 56–9
Numa 18

objects 83, 89–90, 91–2, 95–6
O'Brien, Siobhan 74
On the Road (Kerouac) 1
O'Neill, Helen 74
Ono, Yoko 119
ordinary life, *see* everyday life
ordinary objects 54, 59, 83–96, 104
ordinary people 121, 123, 124, 127, 128
Orlan 6, 7
Ozga-Lawn, Matt 41

Paestum 51, 52
Painter, Colin 84
'Pair of Slippers, A' (Yasumura) 84, 85, **85**, 92
'Palimpsest' (Dyer) **116**
Patrwn (Anderson) 35–8, 41, 45–6
patterned surfaces 9, 67–80
Pavitt, Jane 125
Payne, Christopher 171, 175, 179, 183
Penney, Darby 175
Pennsylvania Hospital for the Insane 178–9
performance 32–3, 35–8, 41, 44–6, 74
performance archaeology 45
Perron, Amelie 177
phenomenology 3–4, 61, 182; *see also* experience
'Phone, A' (Yasumura) 87–9
Photo-fry (Matta-Clark) 129
photography 83–96, 105–6, 108, 109
Pianta Grande di Roma (Nolli) 158
Piedmont, Ralph L. 174
Pilotis-City (Le Corbusier) 165
Piranesi, Giovanni Battista 50–51, 55, 128
Platz der Republik, Berlin 159–60, 162

Playtime (Tati) 119, 121–2, 130, 133
Plaza of Nations (Anderson/Bobrova) 38–41, **39**, **40**, 45–6
Pole Dance project 150–52, **151**, **152**
pole dancing 138, 146, 150–52
Pollock, Jackson 182
Pompeii 52
Poor Little Rich Man (Loos) 101–2
porno chic 137, 138, 141, 144–5, 147, 148
pornography 141, 144, 147–8, 149–50, 153
post-feminism 137, 141, 151–2, 153
postmodernism 16–17
'Pour Your Body Out' (Rist) 69–70
power 141, 143, 148, 149, 153, 172, 181; *see also* empowerment
Praz, Mario 23–4
Presner, Todd 2
Pringle, Patricia 69
Prior, Lindsay 106
Publius Valerius Poplicola 18

Radiant City, The (Le Corbusier) 121
Raphael 19, 21, 27
raunch culture 138, 141, 151
Rees, Marc 36
Reichstag, Berlin 159–60
Reid, Susan 124–5, 127
relation
   with the external world 3, 4, 7, 49
   with images 83, 84, 100, 103–4, 106, 111
   with the interior 26, 27, 61, 87, 100, 103–4, 106, 111, 180
   with location 158, 159
   with objects 61, 87, 89–90, 96, 107
   with surfaces 9, 69–70, 76, 78–9
remnants 42
repudiation 6, 7, 8, 122, 180–81
Repulsion (Polanski) 77
revolution 6, 8, 117, 119, 121–4, 128–30, 133, 181
Rice, Charles 24, 103–4
Ring Cycle (Wagner) 32
Rist, Pipilotti 69–70
'Rolls of Toilet Paper and a Plastic Flower' (Yasumura) 92–3, **94**
Romanticism 24, 179
Rome 5, 16–21, 158
Roman Baths 8, 15–16, 27
Rose, Gillian 105, 109
Rosewarne, Lauren 140, 144
Rossi, Aldo 16
Rowe, Colin 16–17
Royal Academy 51, 53

Rudge, Trudy 177
ruin 7–8, 33, 35, 36–7, 180
'Ruin, The' (Exeter poet) 15–16, 17, 27
ruins 15–17, 19–21, 23–4, 35–8, 41–6, 51, 52
Rybczynski, Witold 101

Sack, Oliver 185
Saks, Sol 127
Sawyer, R. Keith 164
Schmidt, Christine 74
Schreyach, Michael 182
Schultes, Axel 160
Scott, Sue 147
Sebald, W.G. 44, 45
Second World War 41–5
Seedbed (Acconci) 6
self-anaesthesia 44, 45
'Self Portrait' (Dyer) **14**
self-portraits 7, 33, 35, 36–7, 44–5
self-ruining 8, 33, 35–46
Sennett, Richard 165–6, 168
Seti I, King, sarcophagus of 52
sexuality 6, 9, 72, 137–53
sexualization 9, 137–53
Shaginian, Marietta 125
Shepard, David 2
Sherlock Holmes: A Game of Shadows (Ritchie) 70–71
shoah, see Holocaust
'Shortcake, A' (Yasumura) 92
Simeon Stylites, St 162–3
Simmel, Georg 158, 162, 164
Simmons, Laurie 84
Simon of the Desert (Buñuel) 163
simulacra 33, 45
Sinclair, Iain 17
Sir John Soane's house 8, 49–55, 61–2
site-specific performance 32, 35, 38, 45
situated vagrancy 31–46
Situationists International 119, 120–21, 122–4, 128, 133
Smith, Edward 56–7
Soane, George 54
Soane, Sir John 8, 49–55, 61–2
Soane, John 54
'Somebody That I Used to Know' (Gotye) 78, 79, **79**
Sontag, Susan 105
sovereignty 40, 41, 56, 59, 123, 129
Soviet Union 124–7
space race 119, 124, 127, 133
spectatorship 6–7, 35, 37, 41, 45

Speer, Albert 42–3
Splitting (Matta-Clark) 129
Stark, Christine 147
Stastny, Peter 175
Stelarc 6–7
Stenglin, Marie 158–9
still life 83, 91–5
Stories of Mr Keuner (Brecht) 157, 168
strip clubs 145–9, 151
'Stuffed Pheasant, A' (Yasumura) 92
sublime, the 36, 37
Suetonius 20, 21, 26
Summerson, John 16
Surfaces, *see* patterned surfaces
Survarnabhumi Airport 67
Sutherland, Forby 161
Sydney 67, 74
'Symbiosis' (Dyer) **66**

Tacitus 20, 21, 26
Tafuri, Manfredo 128
Tagg, John 105–6
'Tape Recorder, A' (Yasumura) 87, **88**
Tati, Jacques 119, 121–2, 130, 133
Taunton State Hospital, Massachusetts **172**
technology 2, 6–7, 119, 121, 123, 124–5, 128, 130–32, 133
television 122, 125, 127, 131
Teufelsberg 41–6, **43**
Teunissen, Bert 84
Text as Zero (Eisenman) 33
Thai silks 67, 71–3
Thailand 67, 71–3
Theory of Ruin Value (Speer) 42
thing theory 8, 9, 83, 89–90, 91–2, 95–6
Thompson, Jim 67–8, 70, 71–3, 79, 80
Thornton, Peter 52
Through a Glass Darkly (Bergman) 77
Tomes, Nancy 178
Tomkins, Leah 4
Tomorrow: A Peaceful Path to Real Reform (Howard) 121
topography 32, 33, 40, 41, 42–3, 46
transformation
  and abandoned spaces 181–2
  and floors 165, 168
  of the interior 8, 103, 105, 111, 112
  of the land 56
  of life experience 2, 4, 58–9
  of materials 129
  and media 132, 139
  and mental illness 177, 178, 181

radical 9, 165, 168
and technology 132, 133
Trümmerberge 41–3
Trümmerfrauen 41–3
Tschumi, Bernard 182–3
Turner, J.M.W. 52
Turturro, John 78
Twelve Caesars (Suetonius) 20, 21, 26

unconscious mind 5, 59, 60
Unfolding Florence (Armstrong) 74
urbanism 121, 128
Urquart, A.R. 181
Utopia (More) 9, 117–18, 123–4, 133
utopias 9, 107–8, 117–33

vagrancy 31–46
Vasari, Giorgio 27
Versailles 25–6
Verushka 78
Vestal Virgins 18
viewing, *see* spectatorship; voyeurism
virtual realities 2
Vitruvius 18
voices 174–5
voyeurism 6–7, 35, 78
Vuillard, Edouard 68–9, 70

Wagner, Richard 32
Walker, A.B. 166
wallpaper 67–71, 73–6, 7, 79
Warner, Maria 95–6
Warren, William 71–2
Weller, Richard 118–19
Westminster Hall 21–3, 26, 27
'What is that… driving away… they recede… pixels?' (Dyer) **188**

Whisnant, Rebecca 147
Whitehead, Kally 151
Wightwick, George 54
Wigley, Mark 74–6
Window Blow-Out (Matta-Clark) 129
Wittgenstein, Ludwig 2
Wolman, Gil J. 123
Wren, Christopher 52
Wright, Patrick 17

Yanni, Carla 178
Yarra Bend Asylum, Victoria 178
Yasumi, Akihito 93, 96
Yasumura, Takashi 83–96
  'A Bonsai Tree and a Watering Hose' 87
  'A Candy Bar' 92
  'A Coat Hook' 87–9
  Domestic Scandals 83, 84–96, **85**, **86**, **88**, **90**, **93**
  'A Fan Heater' 89–90, **90**, 93–5
  'A Father' 84, 85, **86**, 87–9, 91
  'Japanese Oranges' 92, **93**, 95
  'A Man' 84, 91
  Nature Tracing 84
  'A Pair of Slippers' 84, 85, **85**, 92
  'A Phone' 87–9
  'Rolls of Toilet Paper and a Plastic Flower' 92–3, **94**
  'A Shortcake' 92
  'A Stuffed Pheasant' 92
  'A Tape Recorder' 87, **88**
Yellow Wallpaper, The (Gilman) 70, 78

Zevi, Bruno 101
Zumthor, Peter 118